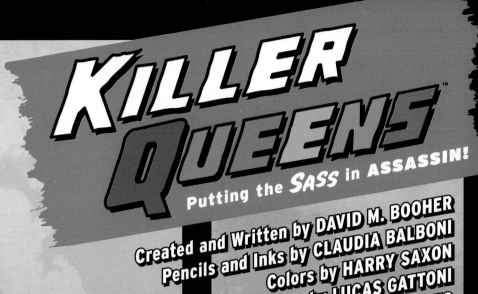

KILLER QUEENS

Putting the *SASS* in ASSASSIN!

Created and Written by DAVID M. BOOHER
Pencils and Inks by CLAUDIA BALBONI
Colors by HARRY SAXON
Letters by LUCAS GATTONI
Cover by CHRIS ABLES

DARK
HORSE
BOOKS

President and Publisher MIKE RICHARDSON
Editor SPENCER CUSHING
Assistant Editor KONNER KNUDSEN
Designer KATHLEEN BARNETT
Digital Art Technician SAMANTHA HUMMER

NEIL HANKERSON Executive Vice President • TOM WEDDLE Chief Financial Officer • DALE LAFOUNTAIN Chief Information Officer • TIM WIESCH Vice President of Licensing • MATT PARKINSON Vice President of Marketing • VANESSA TODD-HOLMES Vice President of Production and Scheduling • MARK BERNARDI Vice President of Book Trade and Digital Sales • RANDY LAHRMAN Vice President of Product Development • KEN LIZZI General Counsel • DAVE MARSHALL Editor in Chief • DAVEY ESTRADA Editorial Director • CHRIS WARNER Senior Books Editor • CARY GRAZZINI Director of Specialty Projects • LIA RIBACCHI Art Director • MATT DRYER Director of Digital Art and Prepress • MICHAEL GOMBOS Senior Director of Licensed Publications • KARI YADRO Director of Custom Programs • KARI TORSON Director of International Licensing

This volume collects issues #1 through #4 of the Dark Horse comic book series *Killer Queens*.

Published by Dark Horse Books
A division of Dark Horse Comics LLC
10956 SE Main Street, Milwaukie, OR 97222

DARKHORSE.COM

To find a comics shop in your area, visit COMICSHOPLOCATOR.COM

Library of Congress Cataloging-in-Publication Data

Names: Booher, David, writer. | Balboni, Claudia, penciller, inker. |
    Saxon, Harry, colourist. | Gottoni, Lucas, letterer.
Title: Killer queens / written by David M. Booher ; pencils and inks by
    Claudia Balboni ; colors by Harry Saxon ; letters by Lucas Gottoni.
Description: First edition. | Milwaukie, OR : Dark Horse Books, 2022. |
    "This volume collects issue #1 through #4 of the Dark Horse comic book
    series Killer Queens." | Summary: "Meet Max & Alex. Reformed
    intergalactic assassins-for-hire. On the run. Also super-duper gay.
    Their former boss-a fluffy monkey with a jetpack-is hot on their tail to
    take back his stolen ship"-- Provided by publisher.
Identifiers: LCCN 2021046423 (print) | LCCN 2021046424 (ebook) | ISBN
    9781506722153 (trade paperback) | ISBN 9781506722160 (ebook)
Subjects: LCGFT: Queer comics. | Science fiction comics. | Humorous comics.
Classification: LCC PN6728.K55 B66 2022 (print) | LCC PN6728.K55 (ebook)
    | DDC 741.5/973--dc23/eng/20211006
LC record available at https://lccn.loc.gov/2021046423
LC ebook record available at https://lccn.loc.gov/2021046424

FIRST EDITION: MARCH 2022

EBOOK ISBN 978-1-50672-216-0
TRADE PAPERBACK ISBN 978-1-50672-215-3

1 3 5 7 9 10 8 6 4 2

PRINTED IN CHINA

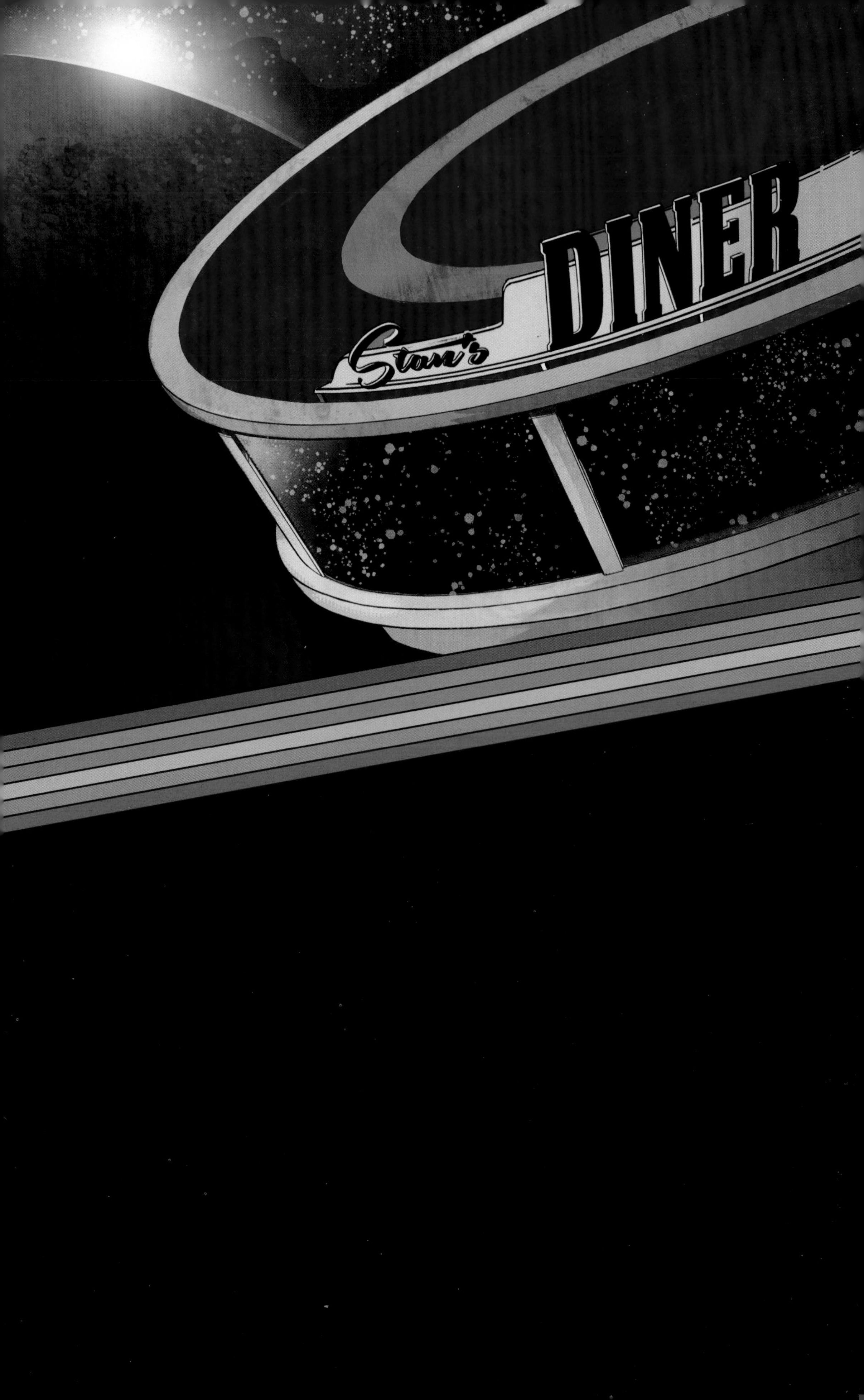
Stan's
DINER

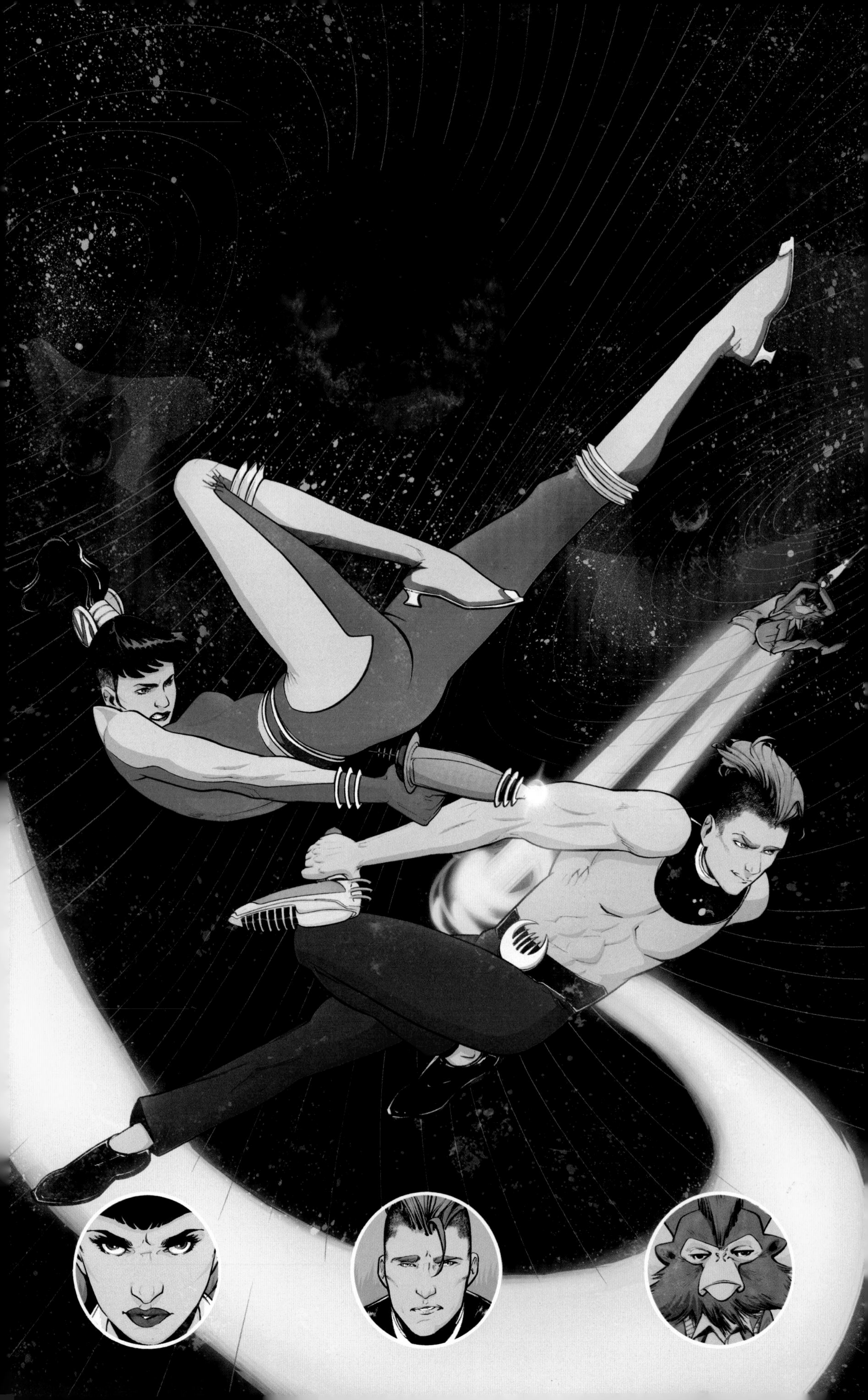

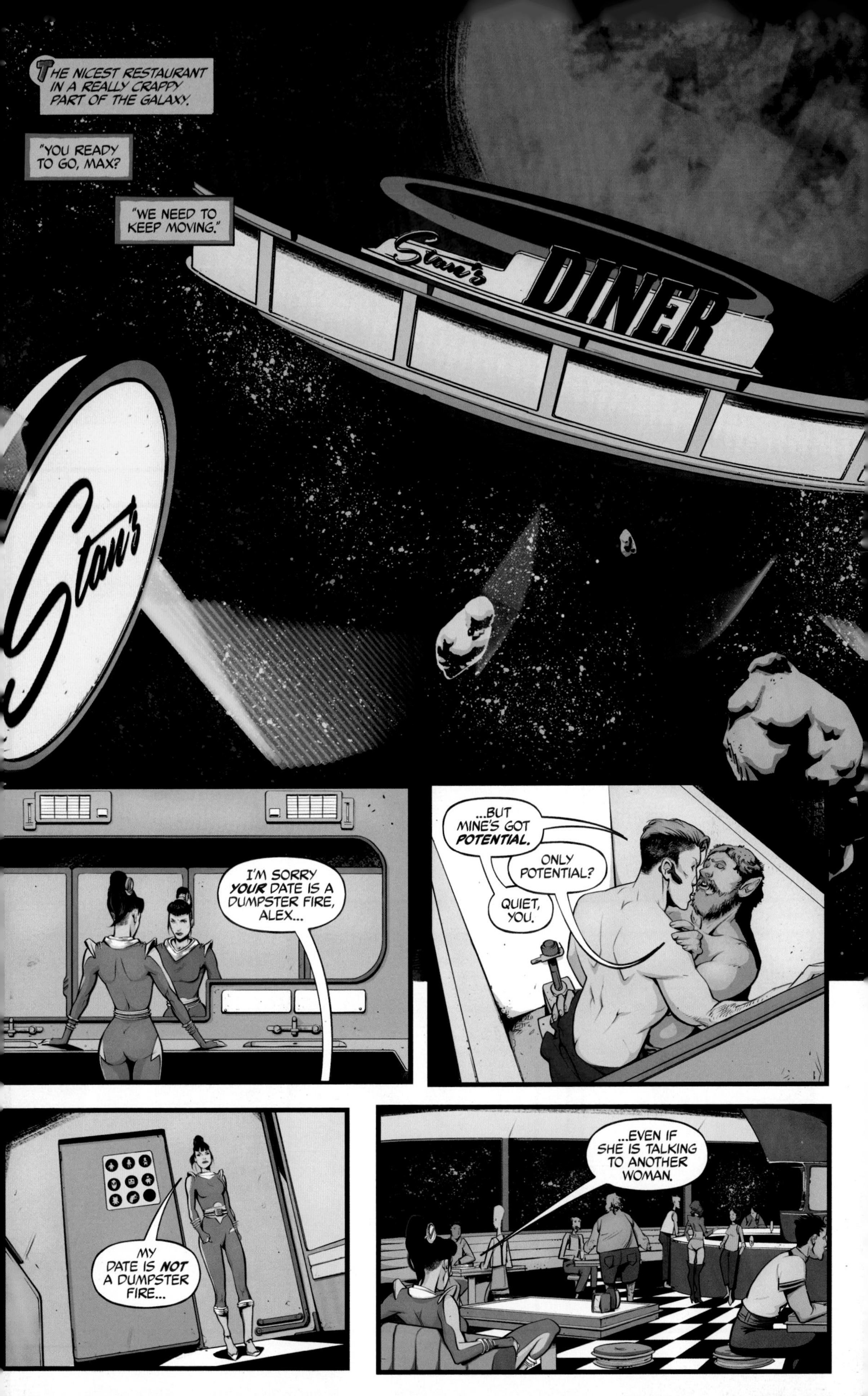
THE NICEST RESTAURANT IN A REALLY CRAPPY PART OF THE GALAXY.
"YOU READY TO GO, MAX?
"WE NEED TO KEEP MOVING."
Stan's DINER
Stan's
I'M SORRY YOUR DATE IS A DUMPSTER FIRE, ALEX...
...BUT MINE'S GOT POTENTIAL.
ONLY POTENTIAL?
QUIET, YOU.
MY DATE IS NOT A DUMPSTER FIRE...
...EVEN IF SHE IS TALKING TO ANOTHER WOMAN.

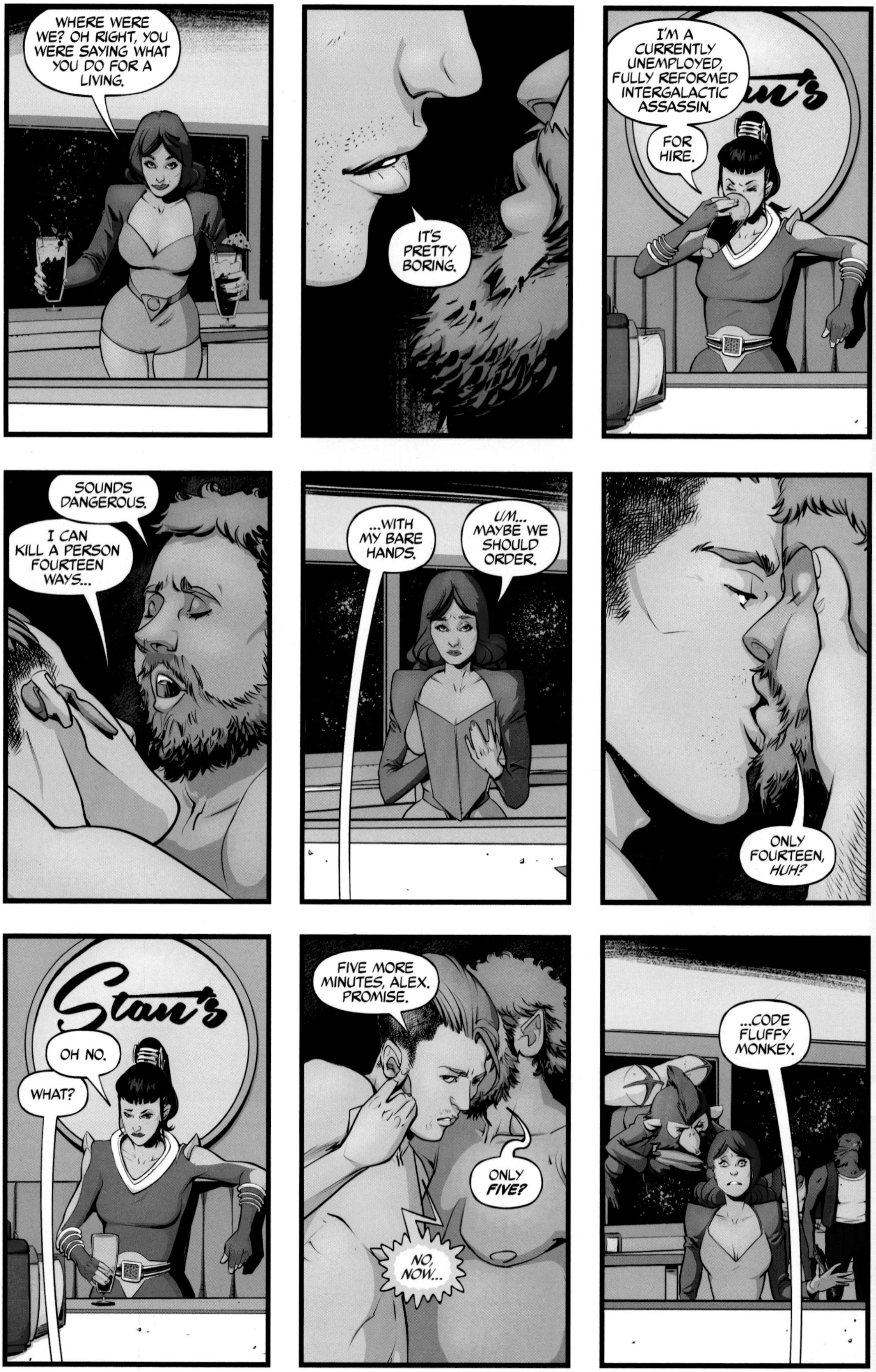
WHERE WERE WE? OH RIGHT, YOU WERE SAYING WHAT YOU DO FOR A LIVING.
IT'S PRETTY BORING.
I'M A CURRENTLY UNEMPLOYED, FULLY REFORMED INTERGALACTIC ASSASSIN.
FOR HIRE.
Stan's
SOUNDS DANGEROUS.
I CAN KILL A PERSON FOURTEEN WAYS...
...WITH MY BARE HANDS.
UM... MAYBE WE SHOULD ORDER.
ONLY FOURTEEN, HUH?
Stan's
OH NO.
WHAT?
FIVE MORE MINUTES, ALEX. PROMISE.
ONLY FIVE?
NO, NOW...
...CODE FLUFFY MONKEY.

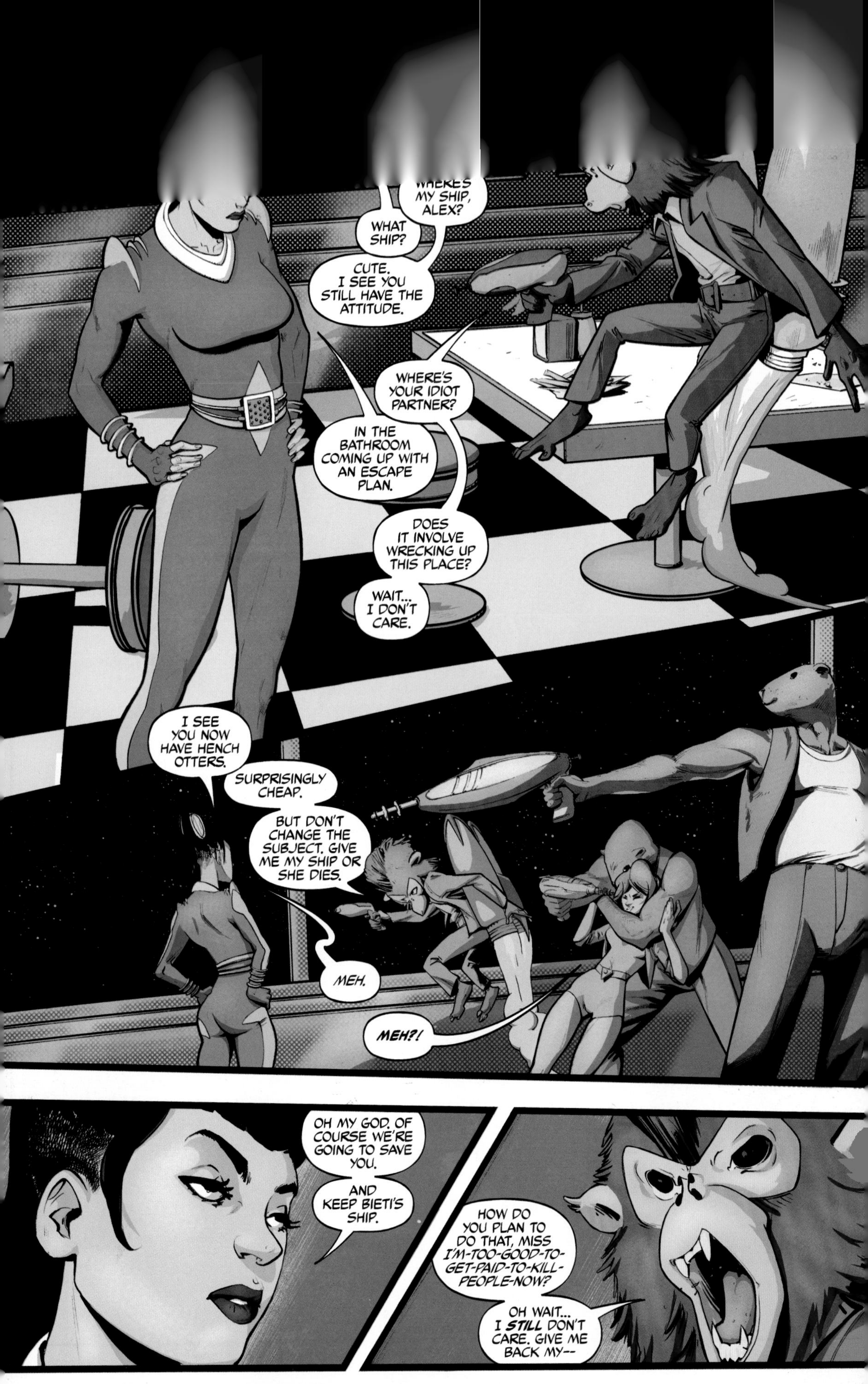

MY SHIP, ALEX?
WHAT SHIP?
CUTE. I SEE YOU STILL HAVE THE ATTITUDE.
WHERE'S YOUR IDIOT PARTNER?
IN THE BATHROOM COMING UP WITH AN ESCAPE PLAN.
DOES IT INVOLVE WRECKING UP THIS PLACE?
WAIT... I DON'T CARE.
I SEE YOU NOW HAVE HENCH OTTERS.
SURPRISINGLY CHEAP.
BUT DON'T CHANGE THE SUBJECT. GIVE ME MY SHIP OR SHE DIES.
MEH.
MEH?!
OH MY GOD, OF COURSE WE'RE GOING TO SAVE YOU.
AND KEEP BIETI'S SHIP.
HOW DO YOU PLAN TO DO THAT, MISS I'M-TOO-GOOD-TO-GET-PAID-TO-KILL-PEOPLE-NOW?
OH WAIT... I STILL DON'T CARE. GIVE ME BACK MY--

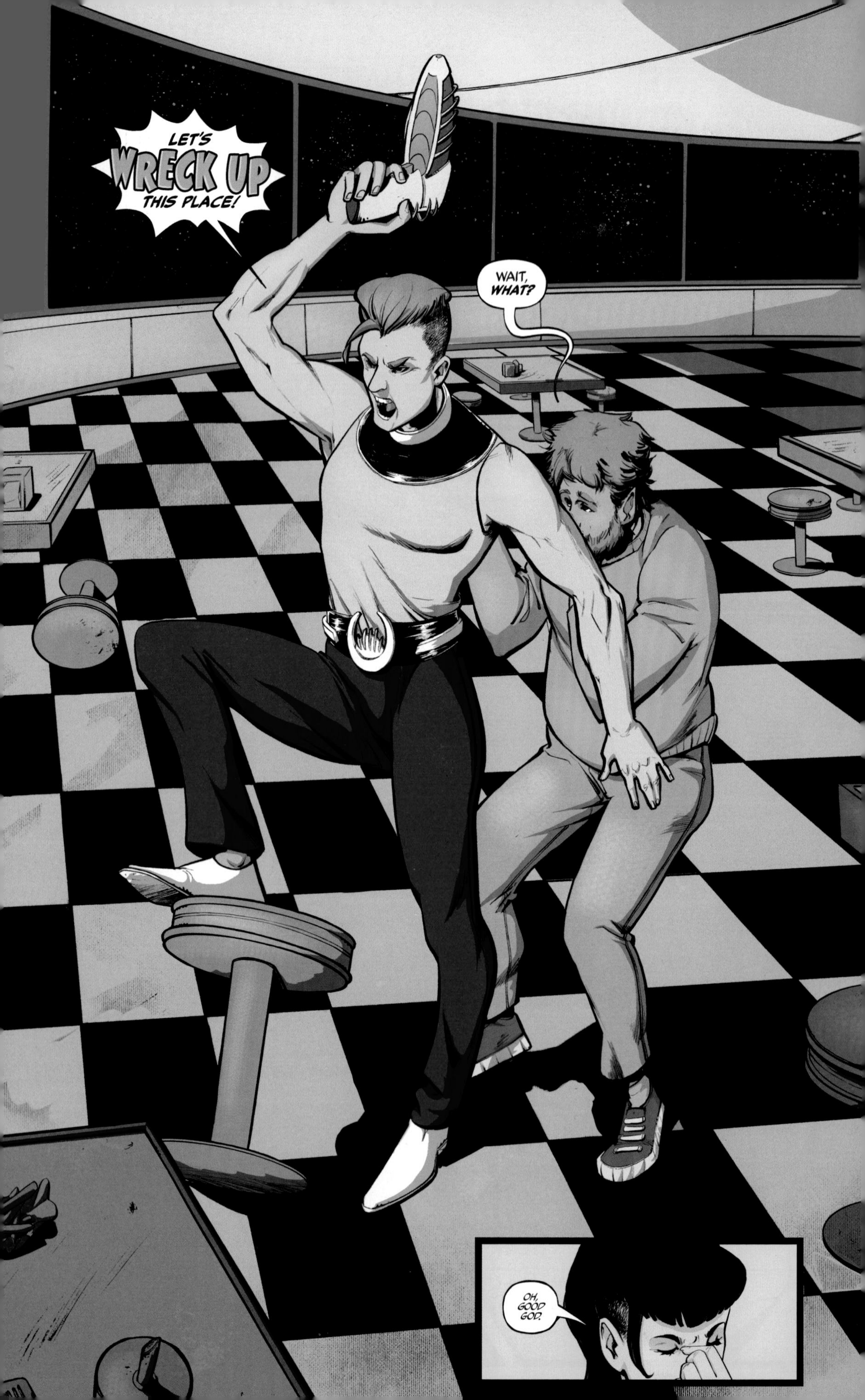
LET'S WRECK UP THIS PLACE!
WAIT, WHAT?
OH, GOOD GOD.

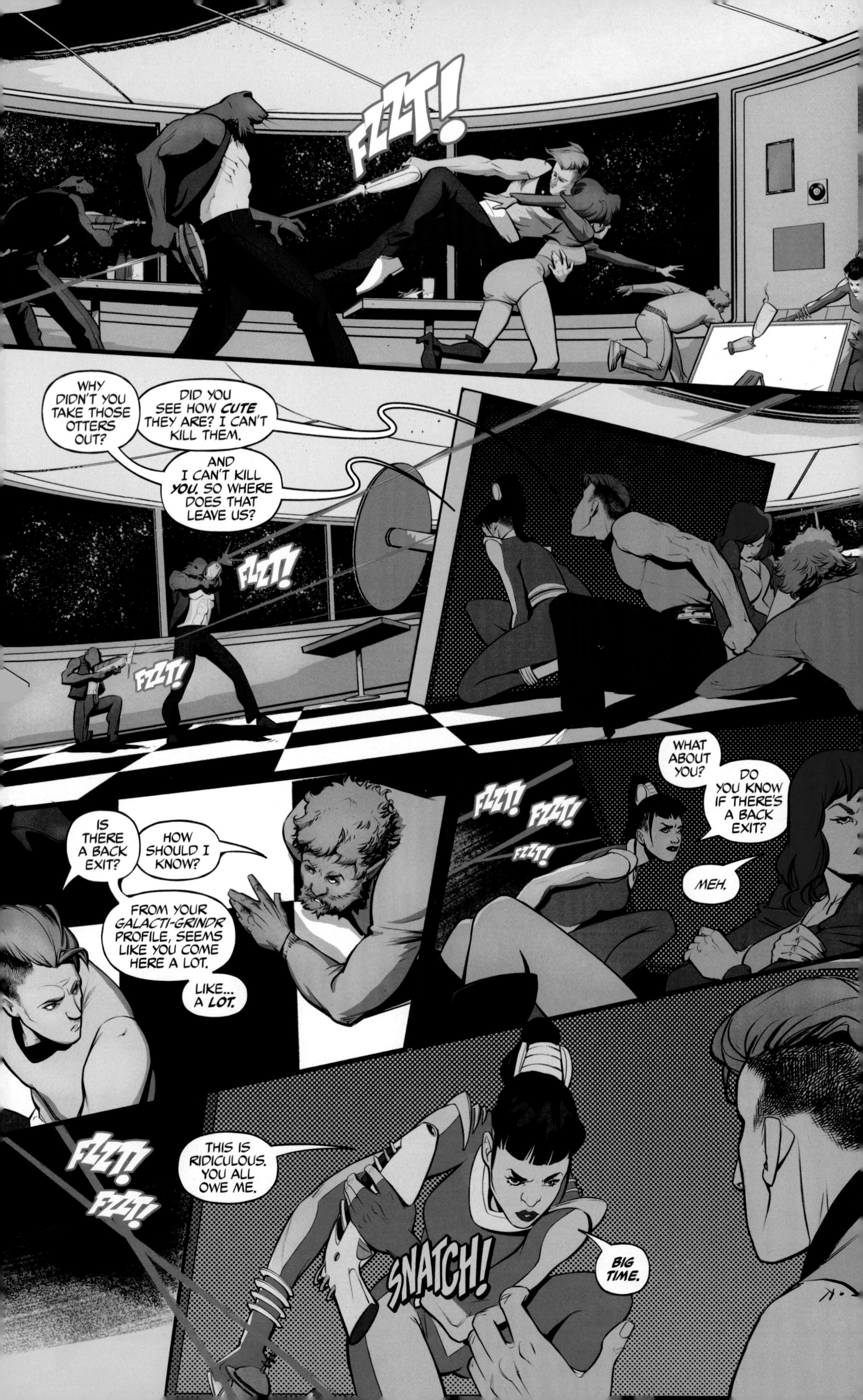
FZZZT!
WHY DIDN'T YOU TAKE THOSE OTTERS OUT?
DID YOU SEE HOW CUTE THEY ARE? I CAN'T KILL THEM.
AND I CAN'T KILL YOU. SO WHERE DOES THAT LEAVE US?
FZZT!
FZZT!
IS THERE A BACK EXIT?
HOW SHOULD I KNOW?
FROM YOUR GALACTI-GRINDR PROFILE, SEEMS LIKE YOU COME HERE A LOT.
LIKE... A LOT.
FZZT! FZZT! FZZT!
WHAT ABOUT YOU?
DO YOU KNOW IF THERE'S A BACK EXIT?
MEH.
FZZT! FZZT!
THIS IS RIDICULOUS. YOU ALL OWE ME.
SNATCH!
BIG TIME.

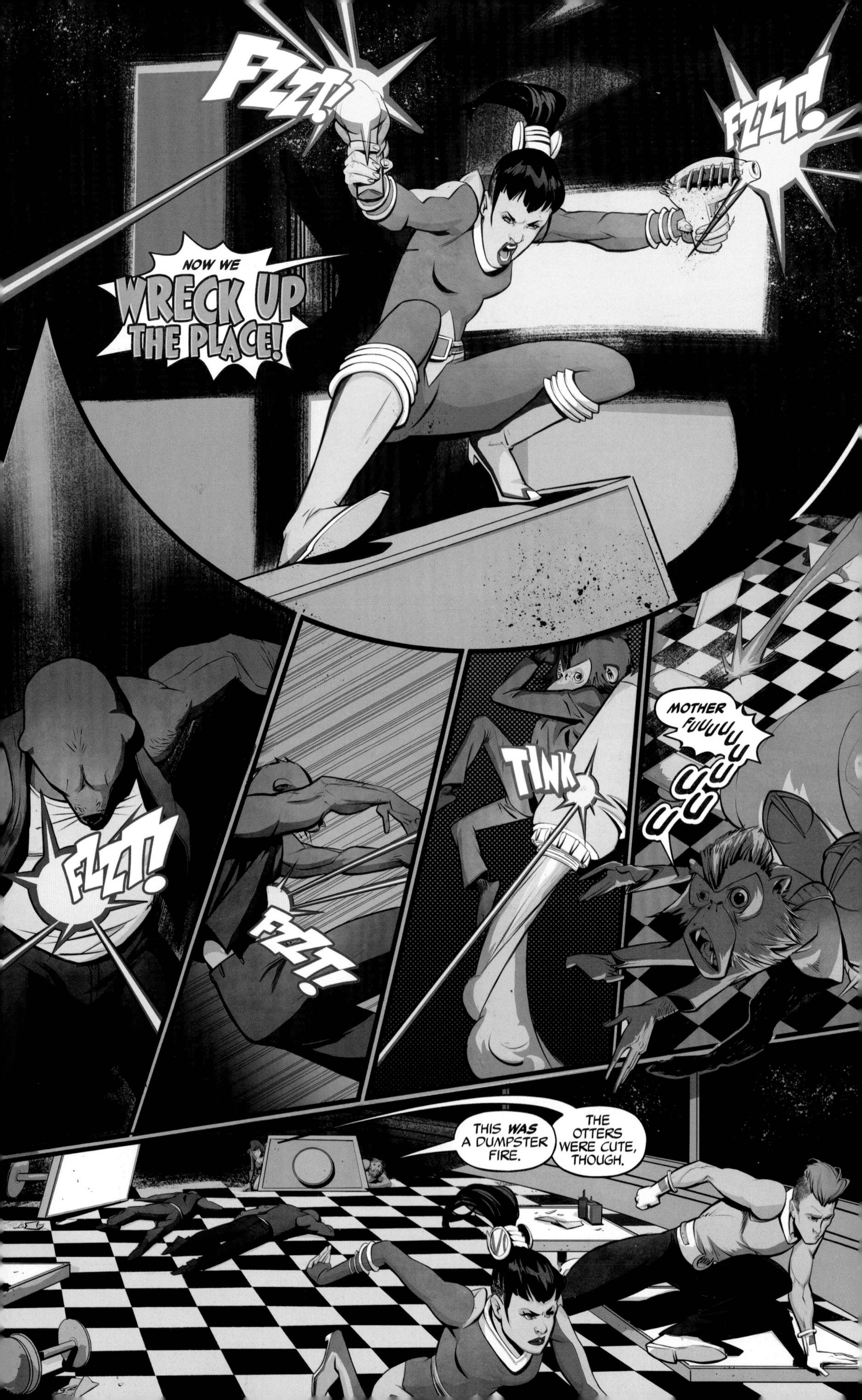
FZZT!
FZZT!
NOW WE WRECK UP THE PLACE!
FZZT!
FZZT!
TINK
MOTHER FUUUUUUUUUU
THIS WAS A DUMPSTER FIRE.
THE OTTERS WERE CUTE, THOUGH.

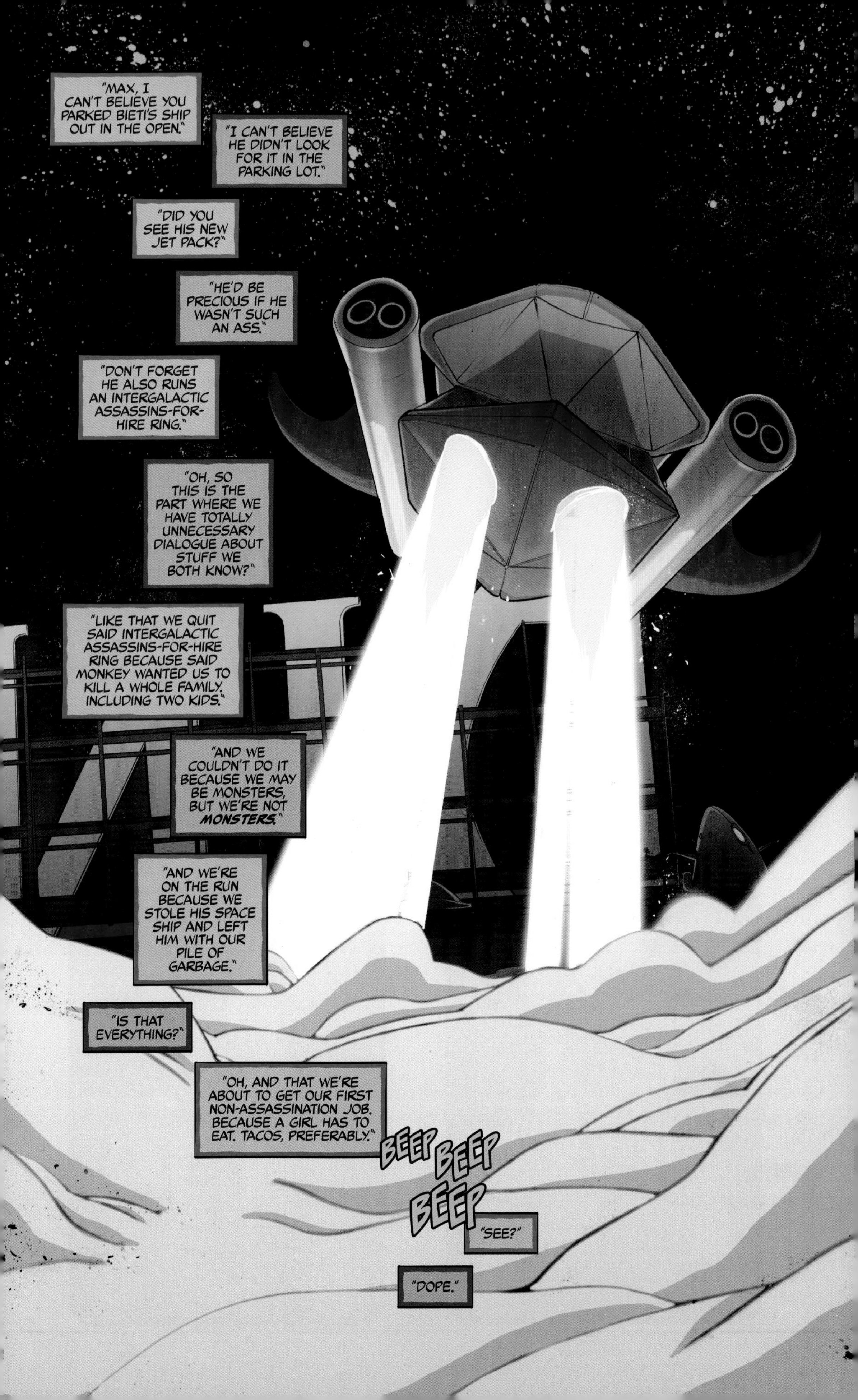
"MAX, I CAN'T BELIEVE YOU PARKED BIETI'S SHIP OUT IN THE OPEN."
"I CAN'T BELIEVE HE DIDN'T LOOK FOR IT IN THE PARKING LOT."
"DID YOU SEE HIS NEW JET PACK?"
"HE'D BE PRECIOUS IF HE WASN'T SUCH AN ASS."
"DON'T FORGET HE ALSO RUNS AN INTERGALACTIC ASSASSINS-FOR-HIRE RING."
"OH, SO THIS IS THE PART WHERE WE HAVE TOTALLY UNNECESSARY DIALOGUE ABOUT STUFF WE BOTH KNOW?"
"LIKE THAT WE QUIT SAID INTERGALACTIC ASSASSINS-FOR-HIRE RING BECAUSE SAID MONKEY WANTED US TO KILL A WHOLE FAMILY. INCLUDING TWO KIDS."
"AND WE COULDN'T DO IT BECAUSE WE MAY BE MONSTERS, BUT WE'RE NOT ***MONSTERS***."
"AND WE'RE ON THE RUN BECAUSE WE STOLE HIS SPACE SHIP AND LEFT HIM WITH OUR PILE OF GARBAGE."
"IS THAT EVERYTHING?"
"OH, AND THAT WE'RE ABOUT TO GET OUR FIRST NON-ASSASSINATION JOB. BECAUSE A GIRL HAS TO EAT. TACOS, PREFERABLY."
BEEP BEEP BEEP
"SEE?"
"DOPE."

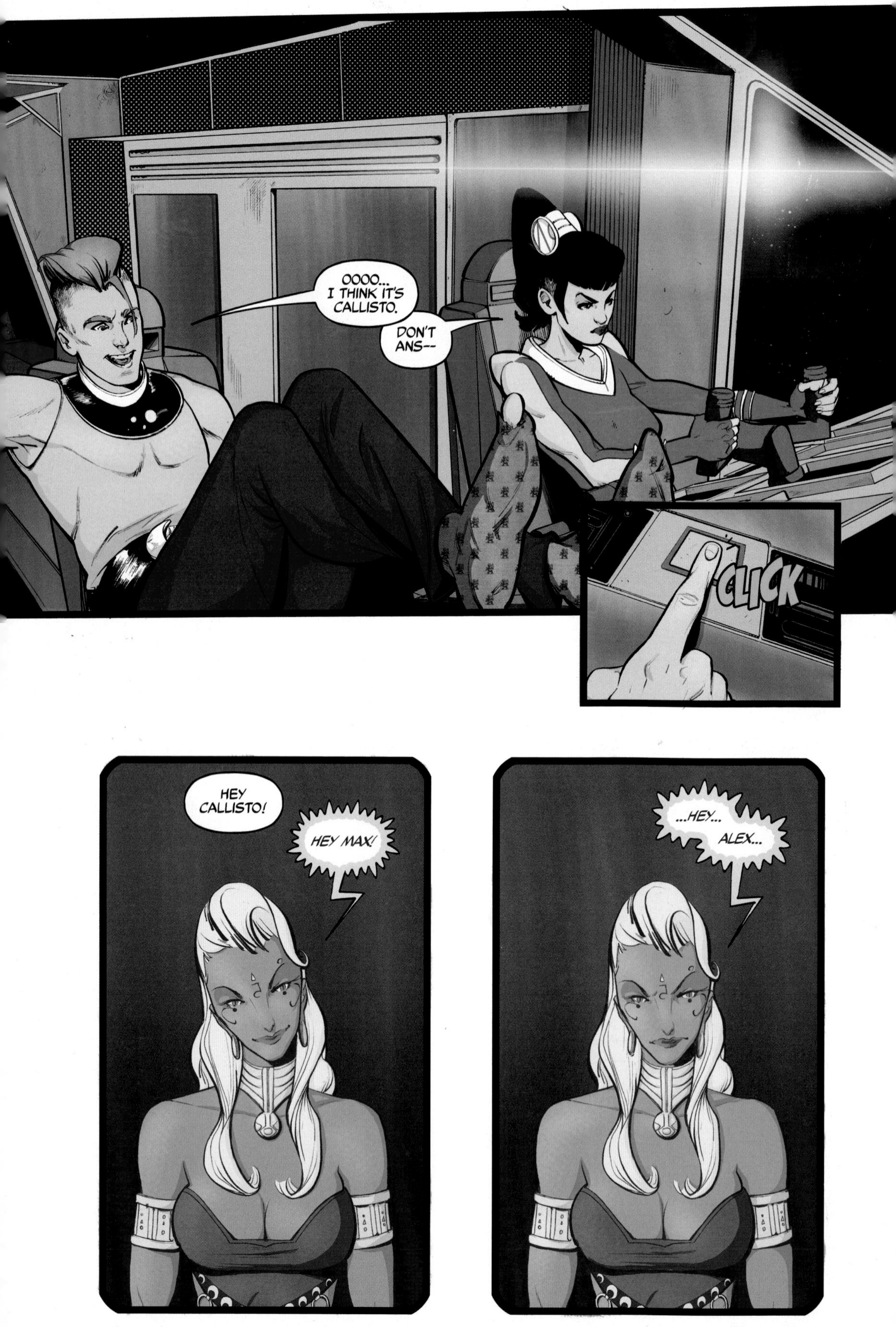
OOOO... I THINK IT'S CALLISTO.
DON'T ANS--
CLICK
HEY CALLISTO!
HEY MAX!
...HEY... ALEX...

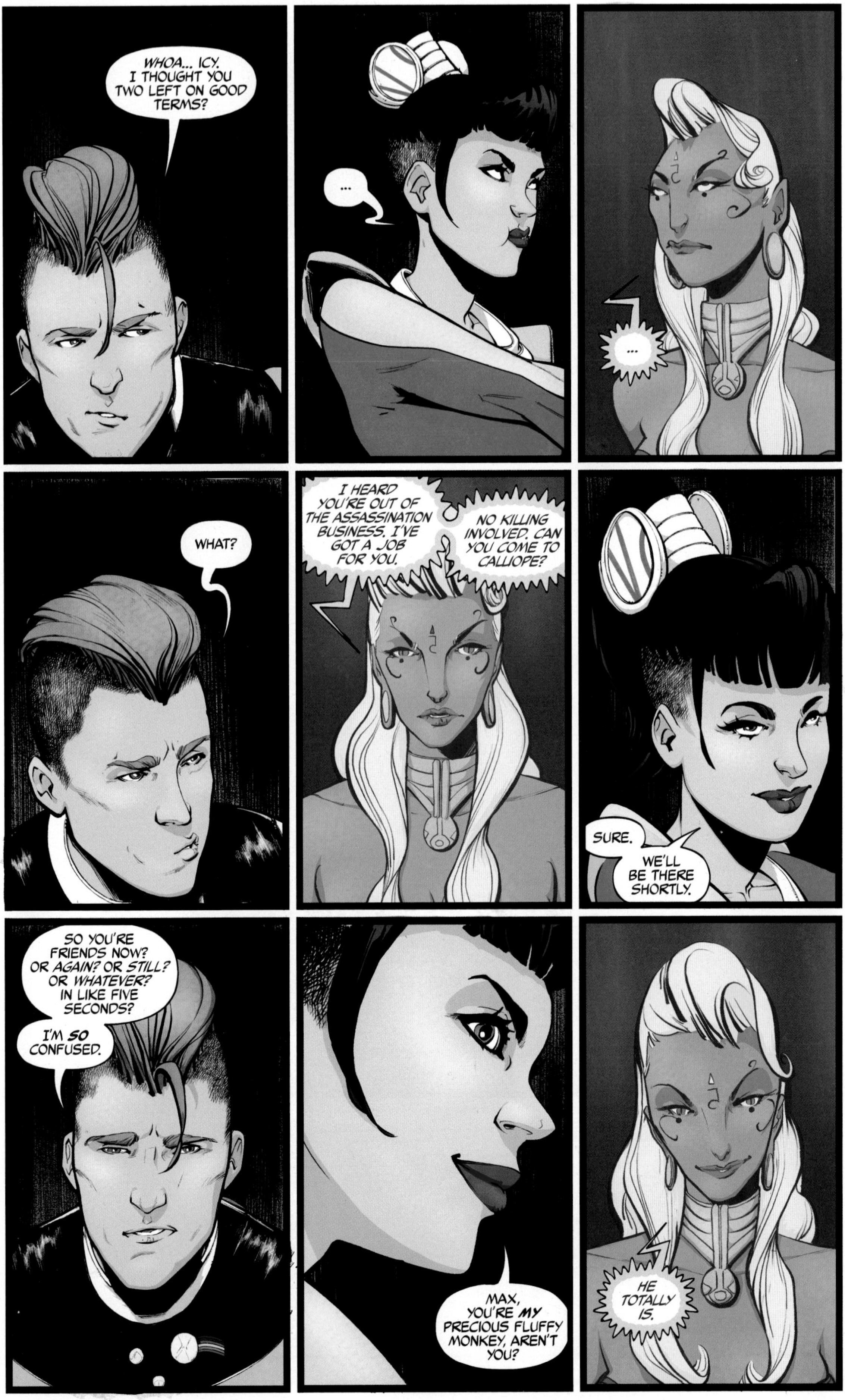
WHOA... ICY. I THOUGHT YOU TWO LEFT ON GOOD TERMS?
...
...
WHAT?
I HEARD YOU'RE OUT OF THE ASSASSINATION BUSINESS. I'VE GOT A JOB FOR YOU.
NO KILLING INVOLVED. CAN YOU COME TO CALLIOPE?
SURE.
WE'LL BE THERE SHORTLY.
SO YOU'RE FRIENDS NOW? OR AGAIN? OR STILL? OR WHATEVER? IN LIKE FIVE SECONDS?
I'M SO CONFUSED.
MAX, YOU'RE MY PRECIOUS FLUFFY MONKEY, AREN'T YOU?
HE TOTALLY IS.

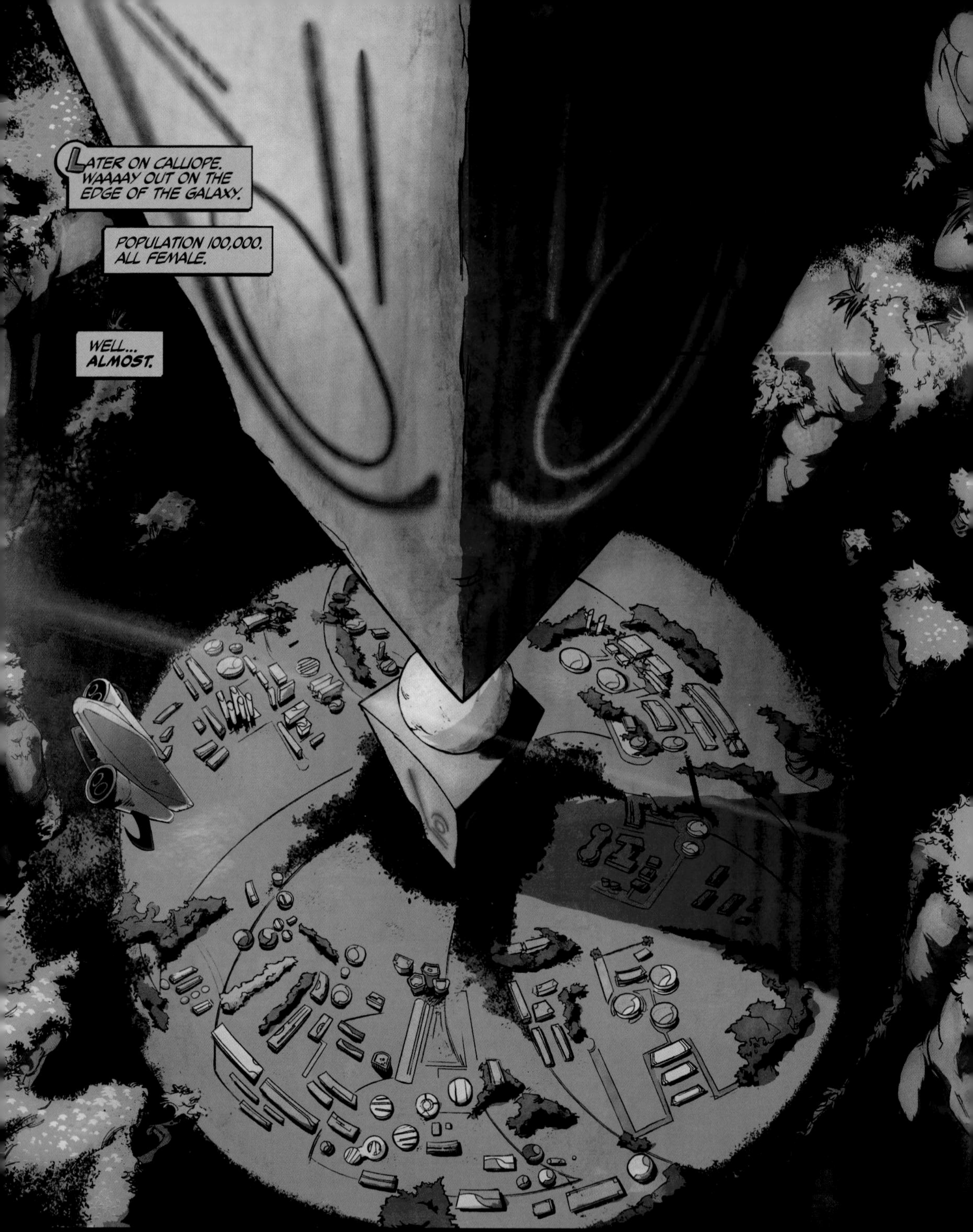
LATER ON CALLIOPE. WAAAAY OUT ON THE EDGE OF THE GALAXY.
POPULATION 100,000. ALL FEMALE.
WELL... ALMOST.

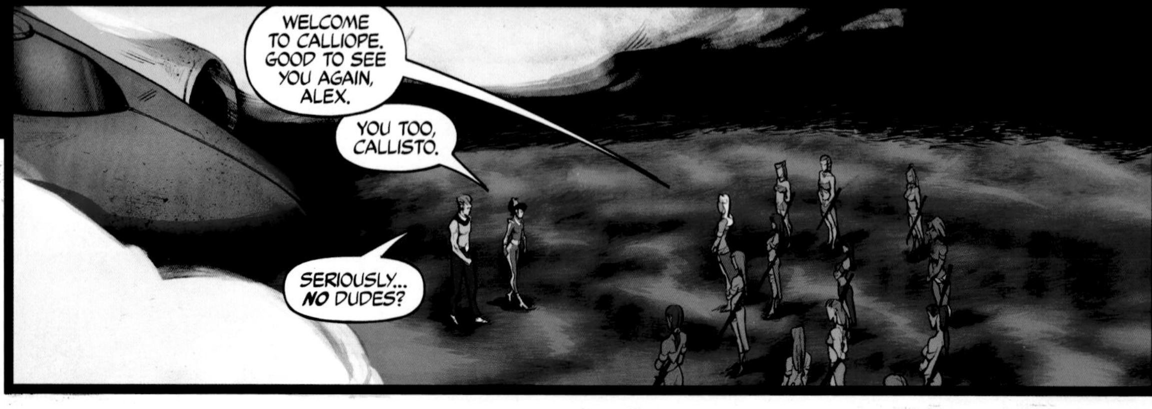
WELCOME TO CALLIOPE. GOOD TO SEE YOU AGAIN, ALEX.
YOU TOO, CALLISTO.
SERIOUSLY... NO DUDES?

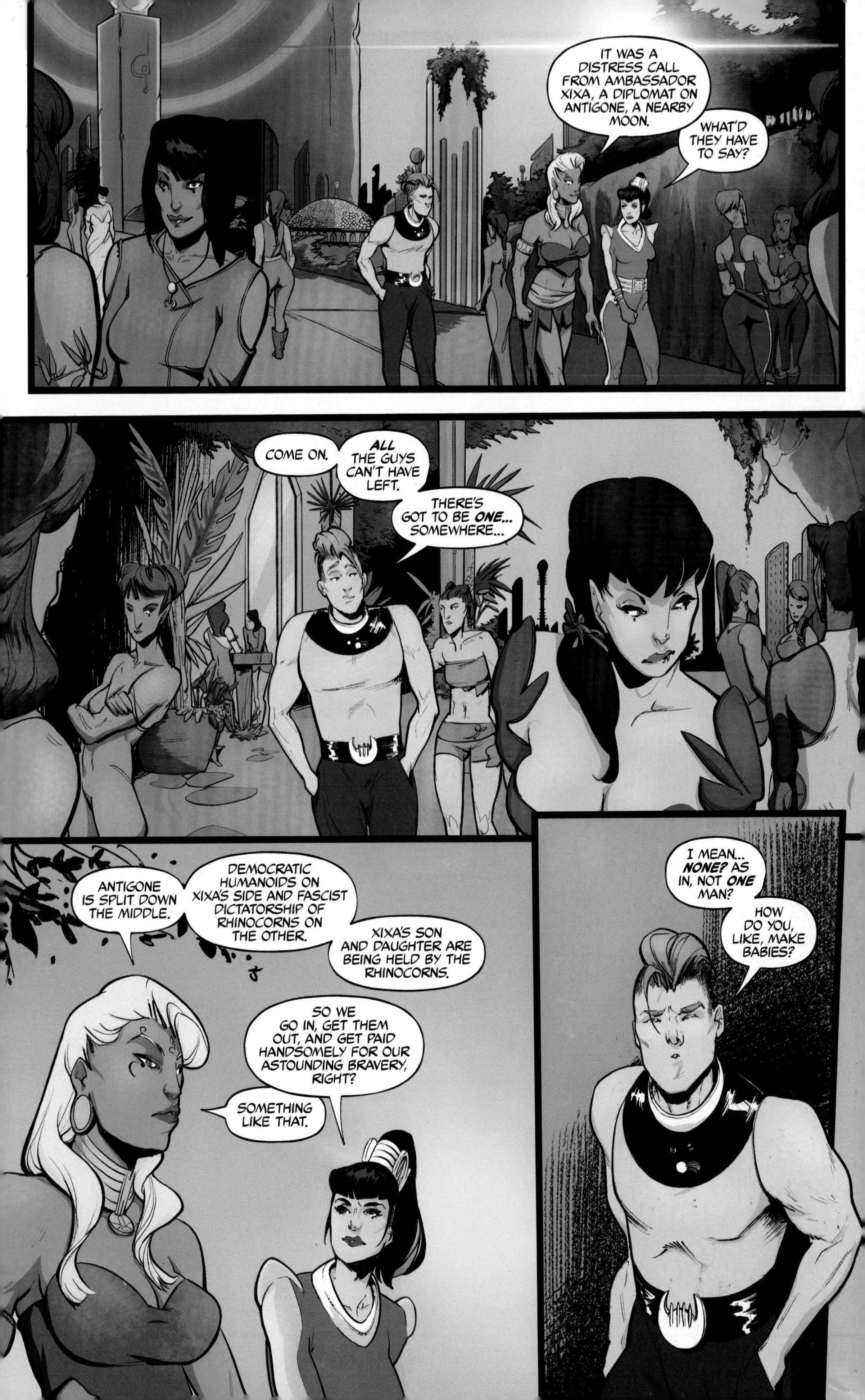
IT WAS A DISTRESS CALL FROM AMBASSADOR XIXA, A DIPLOMAT ON ANTIGONE, A NEARBY MOON.
WHAT'D THEY HAVE TO SAY?
COME ON.
ALL THE GUYS CAN'T HAVE LEFT.
THERE'S GOT TO BE ONE... SOMEWHERE...
ANTIGONE IS SPLIT DOWN THE MIDDLE.
DEMOCRATIC HUMANOIDS ON XIXA'S SIDE AND FASCIST DICTATORSHIP OF RHINOCORNS ON THE OTHER.
XIXA'S SON AND DAUGHTER ARE BEING HELD BY THE RHINOCORNS.
SO WE GO IN, GET THEM OUT, AND GET PAID HANDSOMELY FOR OUR ASTOUNDING BRAVERY, RIGHT?
SOMETHING LIKE THAT.
I MEAN... NONE? AS IN, NOT ONE MAN?
HOW DO YOU, LIKE, MAKE BABIES?

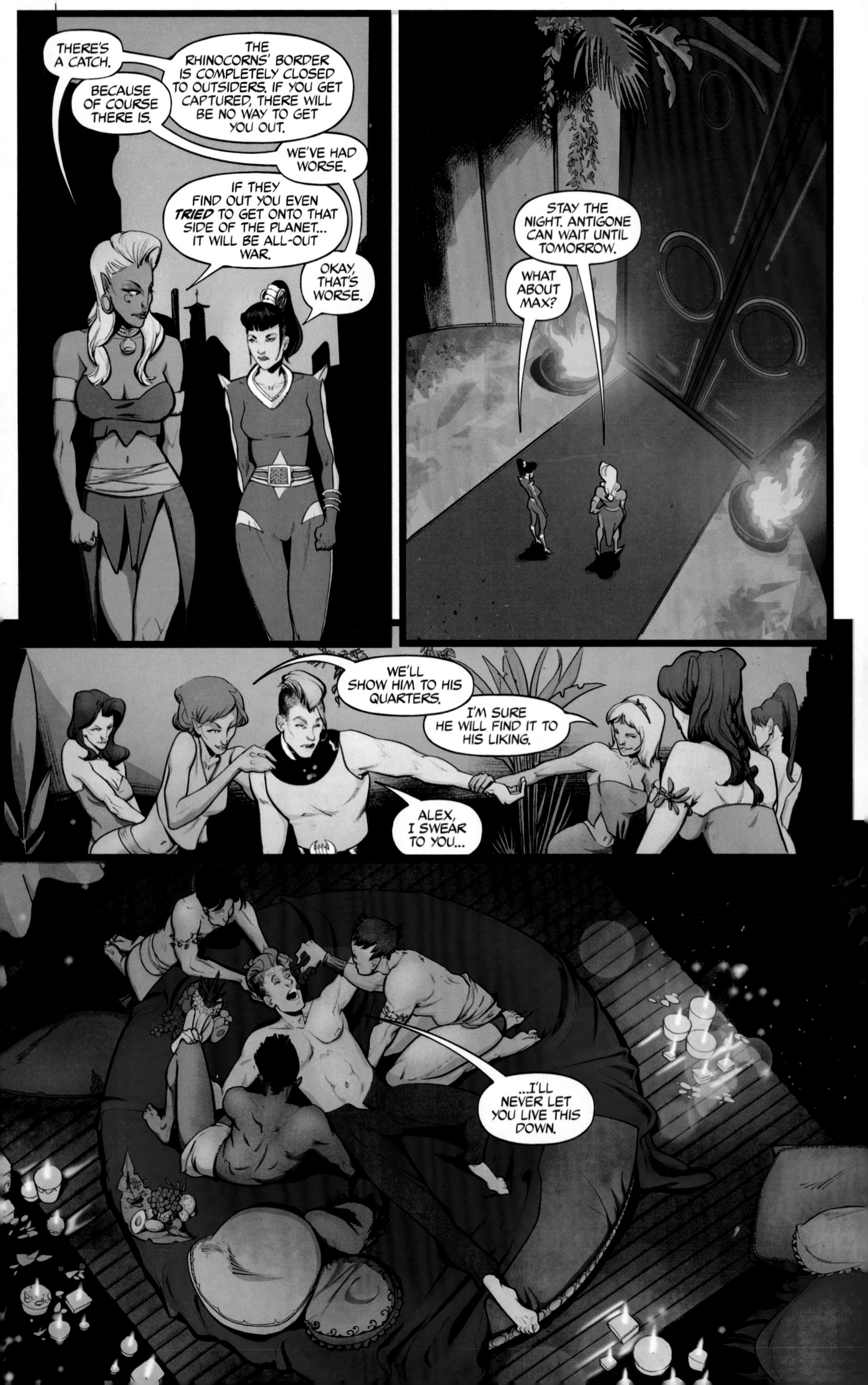
THERE'S A CATCH.
THE RHINOCORNS' BORDER IS COMPLETELY CLOSED TO OUTSIDERS. IF YOU GET CAPTURED, THERE WILL BE NO WAY TO GET YOU OUT.
BECAUSE OF COURSE THERE IS.
WE'VE HAD WORSE.
IF THEY FIND OUT YOU EVEN *TRIED* TO GET ONTO THAT SIDE OF THE PLANET... IT WILL BE ALL-OUT WAR.
OKAY, THAT'S WORSE.
STAY THE NIGHT. ANTIGONE CAN WAIT UNTIL TOMORROW.
WHAT ABOUT MAX?
WE'LL SHOW HIM TO HIS QUARTERS.
I'M SURE HE WILL FIND IT TO HIS LIKING.
ALEX, I SWEAR TO YOU...
...I'LL NEVER LET YOU LIVE THIS DOWN.

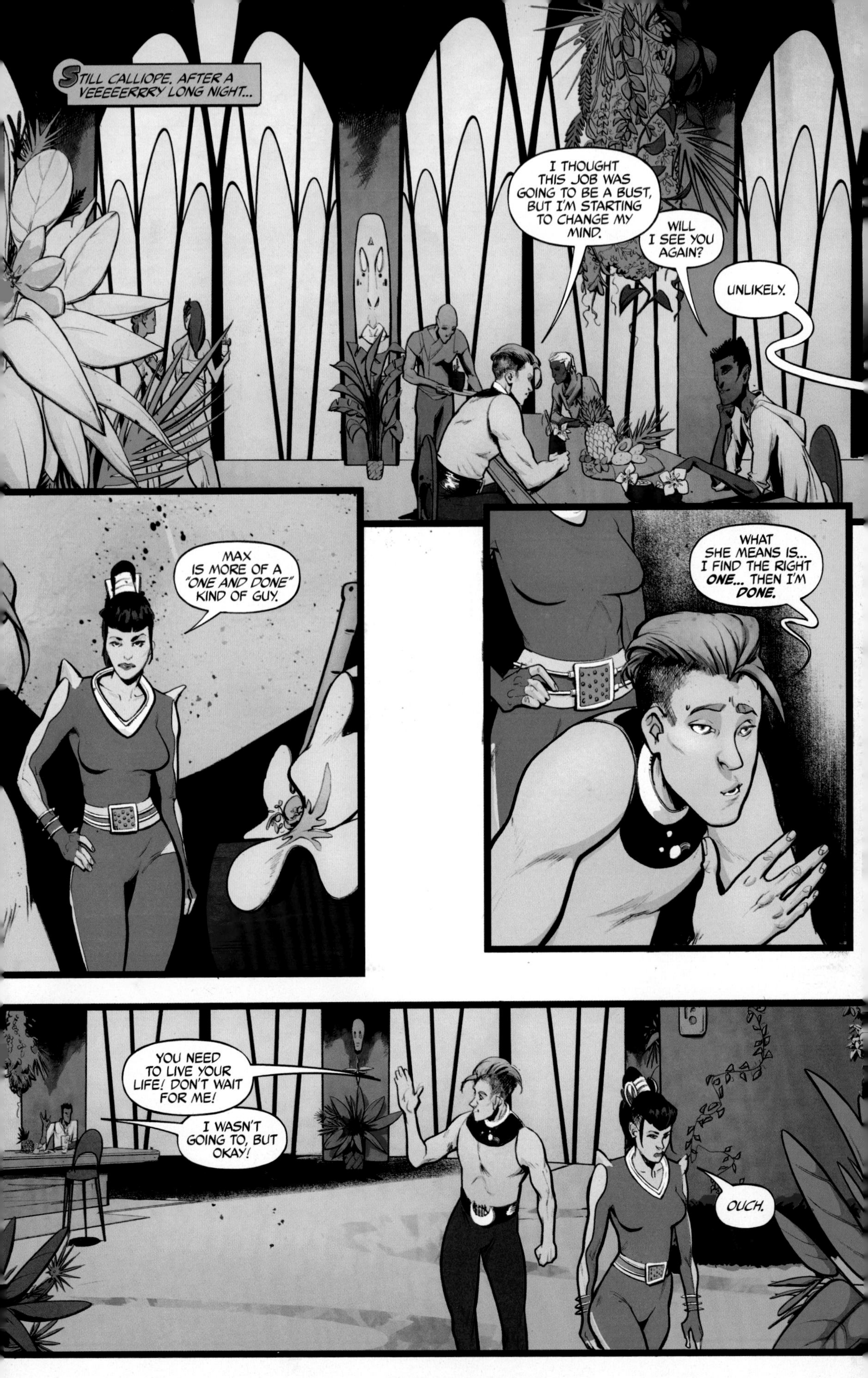
STILL CALLIOPE. AFTER A VEEEEERRRY LONG NIGHT...
I THOUGHT THIS JOB WAS GOING TO BE A BUST, BUT I'M STARTING TO CHANGE MY MIND.
WILL I SEE YOU AGAIN?
UNLIKELY.
MAX IS MORE OF A "ONE AND DONE" KIND OF GUY.
WHAT SHE MEANS IS... I FIND THE RIGHT ONE... THEN I'M DONE.
YOU NEED TO LIVE YOUR LIFE! DON'T WAIT FOR ME!
I WASN'T GOING TO, BUT OKAY!
OUCH.

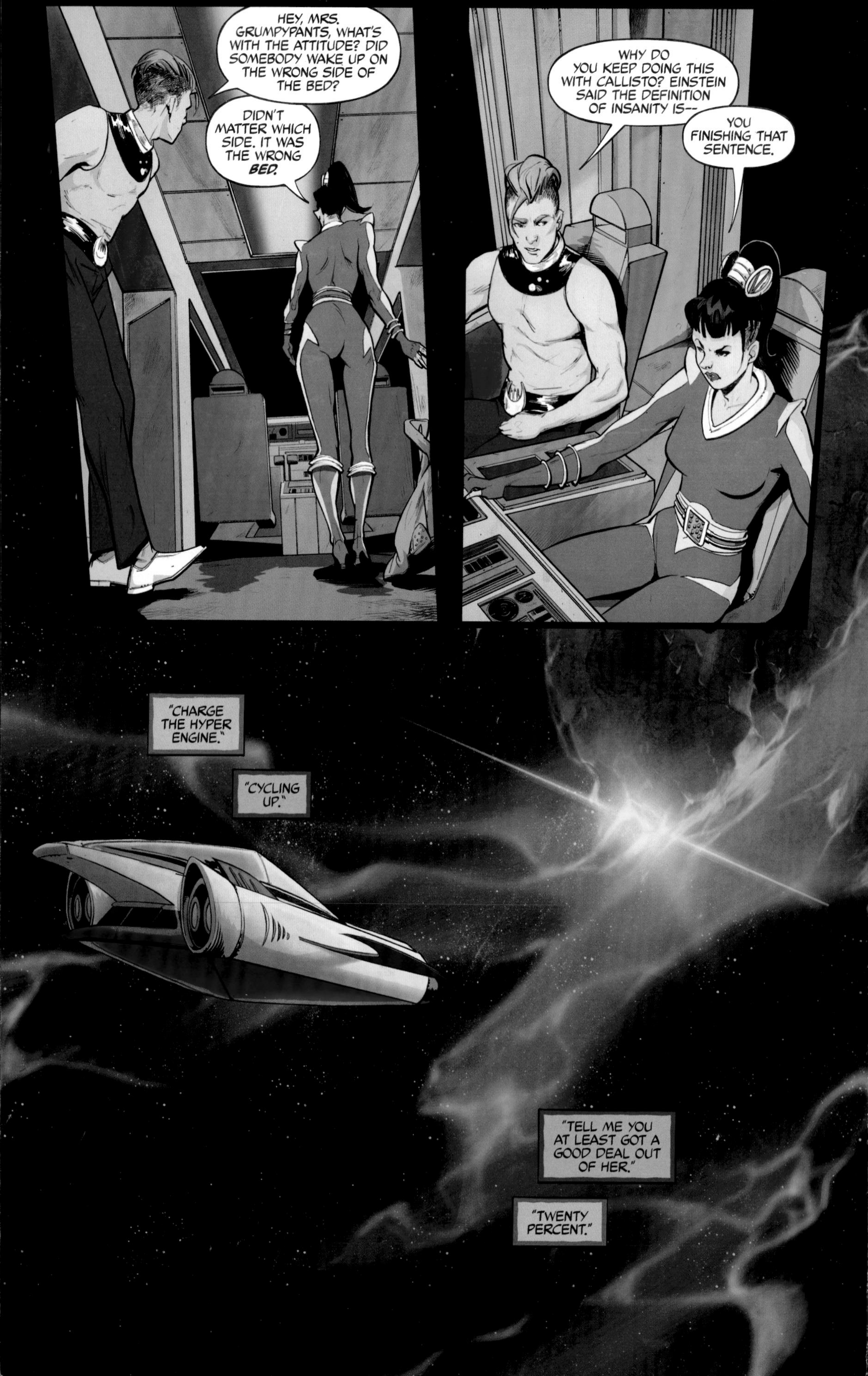
HEY, MRS. GRUMPYPANTS, WHAT'S WITH THE ATTITUDE? DID SOMEBODY WAKE UP ON THE WRONG SIDE OF THE BED?
DIDN'T MATTER WHICH SIDE. IT WAS THE WRONG BED.
WHY DO YOU KEEP DOING THIS WITH CALLISTO? EINSTEIN SAID THE DEFINITION OF INSANITY IS--
YOU FINISHING THAT SENTENCE.
"CHARGE THE HYPER ENGINE."
"CYCLING UP."
"TELL ME YOU AT LEAST GOT A GOOD DEAL OUT OF HER."
"TWENTY PERCENT."

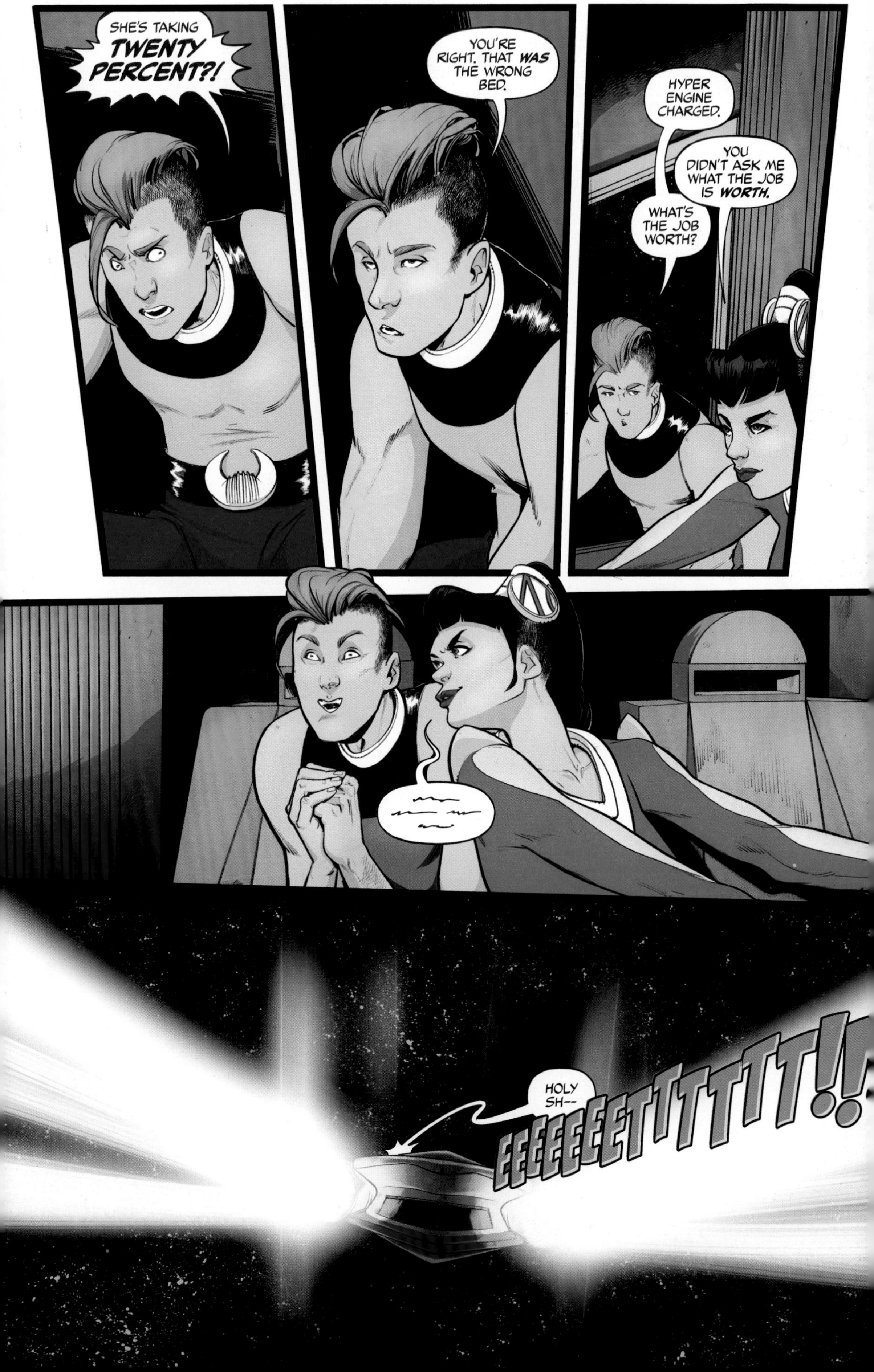

SHE'S TAKING TWENTY PERCENT?!
YOU'RE RIGHT. THAT WAS THE WRONG BED.
HYPER ENGINE CHARGED.
YOU DIDN'T ASK ME WHAT THE JOB IS WORTH.
WHAT'S THE JOB WORTH?
HOLY SH--
EEEEEEETTTTTTT!!

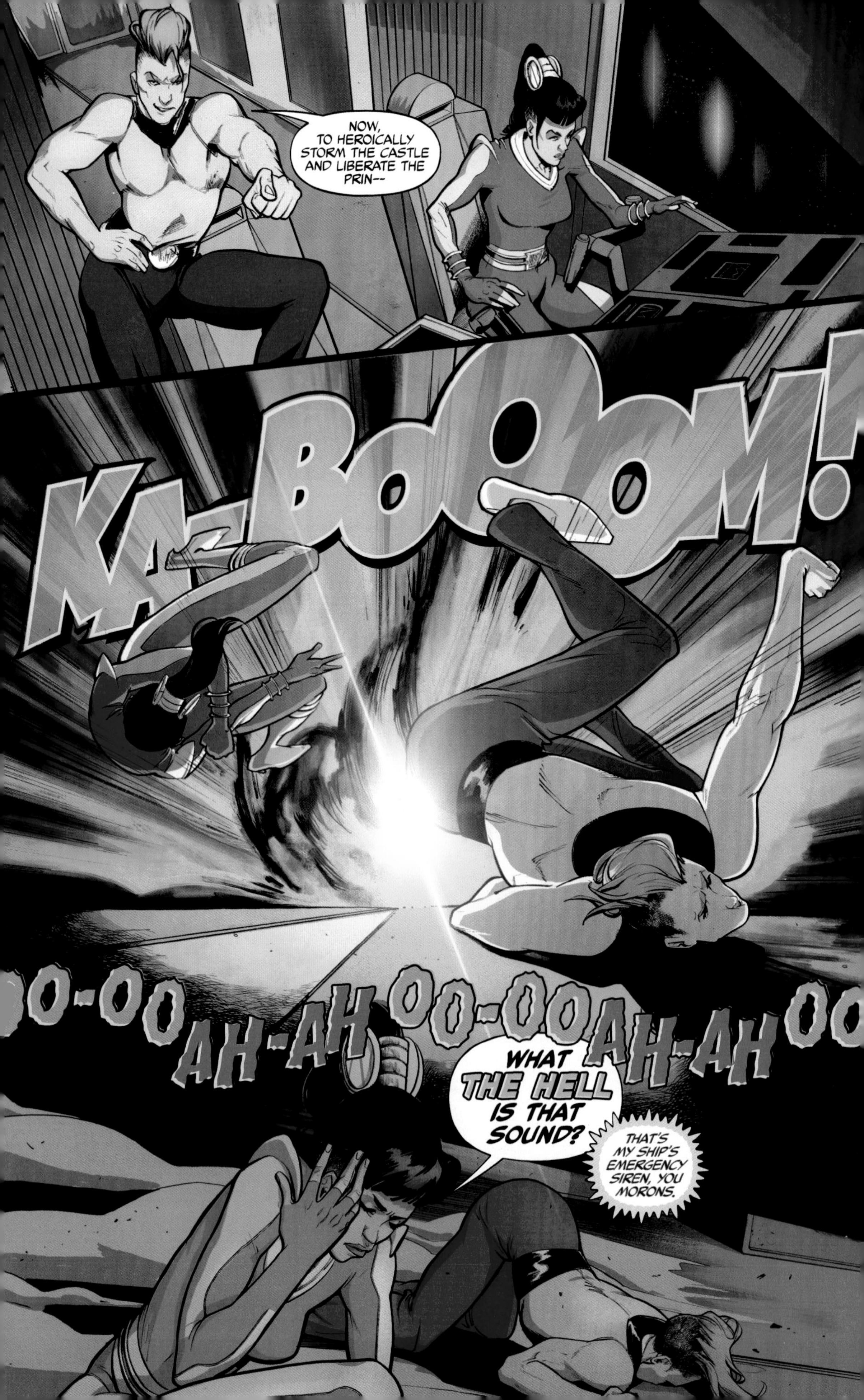
NOW, TO HEROICALLY STORM THE CASTLE AND LIBERATE THE PRIN--
KA-BOOOM!
OO-OO AH-AH OO-OO AH-AH OO
WHAT THE HELL IS THAT SOUND?
THAT'S MY SHIP'S EMERGENCY SIREN, YOU MORONS.

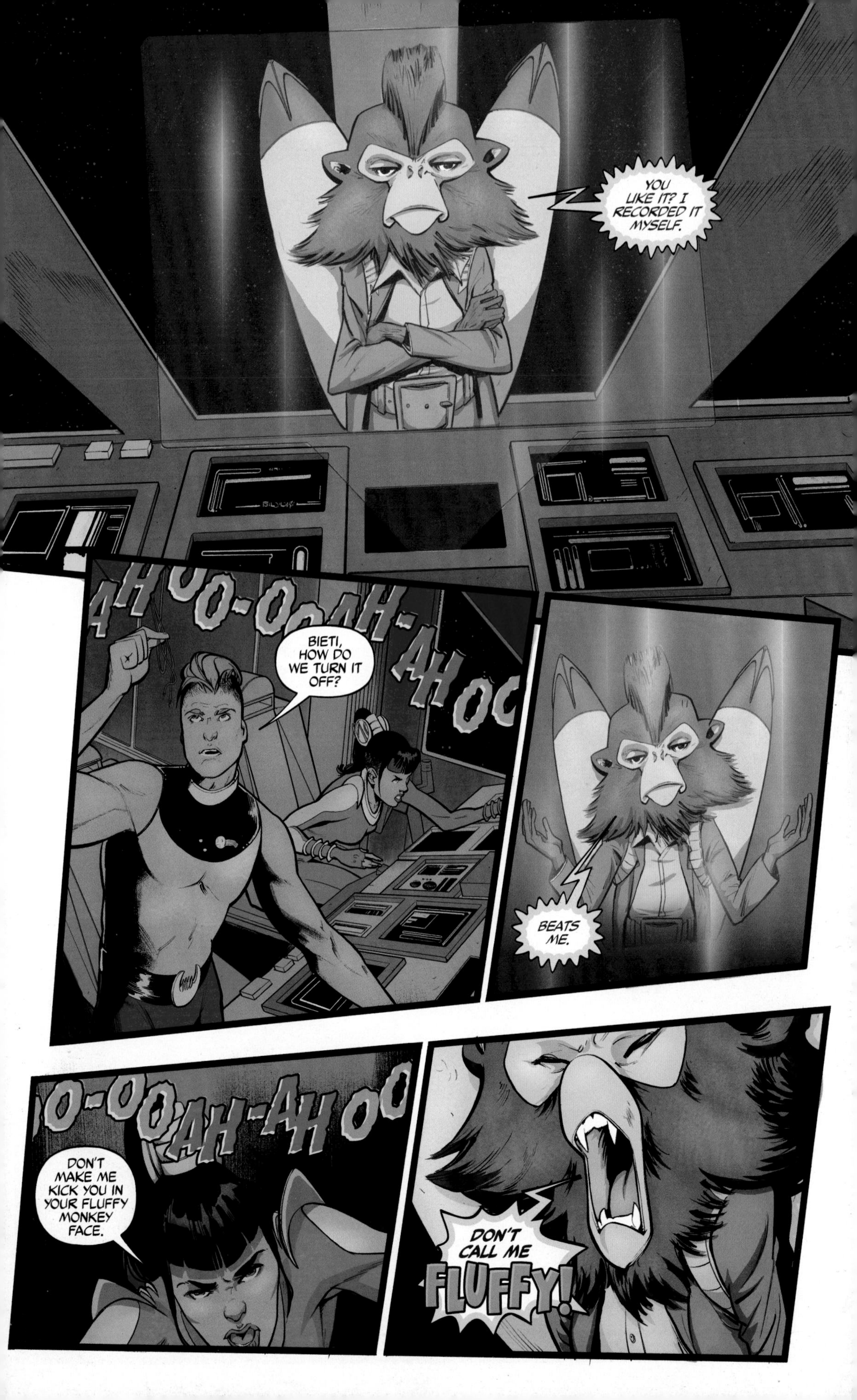
YOU LIKE IT? I RECORDED IT MYSELF.
AHOO-OOAH-AHOO
BIETI, HOW DO WE TURN IT OFF?
BEATS ME.
OO-OOAH-AHOO
DON'T MAKE ME KICK YOU IN YOUR FLUFFY MONKEY FACE.
DON'T CALL ME FLUFFY!

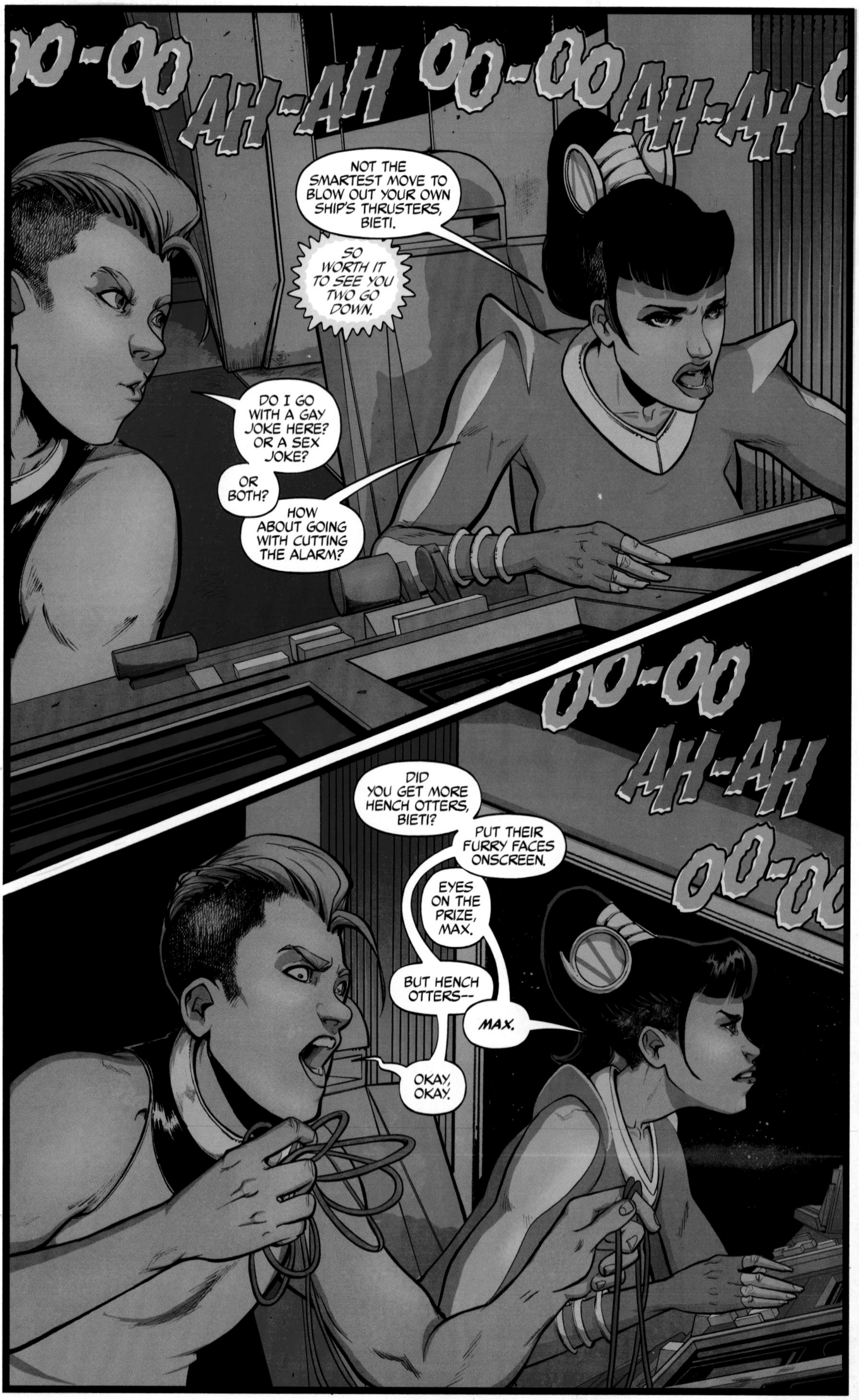
OO-OO AH-AH OO-OO AH-AH
NOT THE SMARTEST MOVE TO BLOW OUT YOUR OWN SHIP'S THRUSTERS, BIETI.
SO WORTH IT TO SEE YOU TWO GO DOWN.
DO I GO WITH A GAY JOKE HERE? OR A SEX JOKE?
OR BOTH?
HOW ABOUT GOING WITH CUTTING THE ALARM?
OO-OO AH-AH OO-OO
DID YOU GET MORE HENCH OTTERS, BIETI?
PUT THEIR FURRY FACES ONSCREEN.
EYES ON THE PRIZE, MAX.
BUT HENCH OTTERS--
MAX.
OKAY, OKAY.

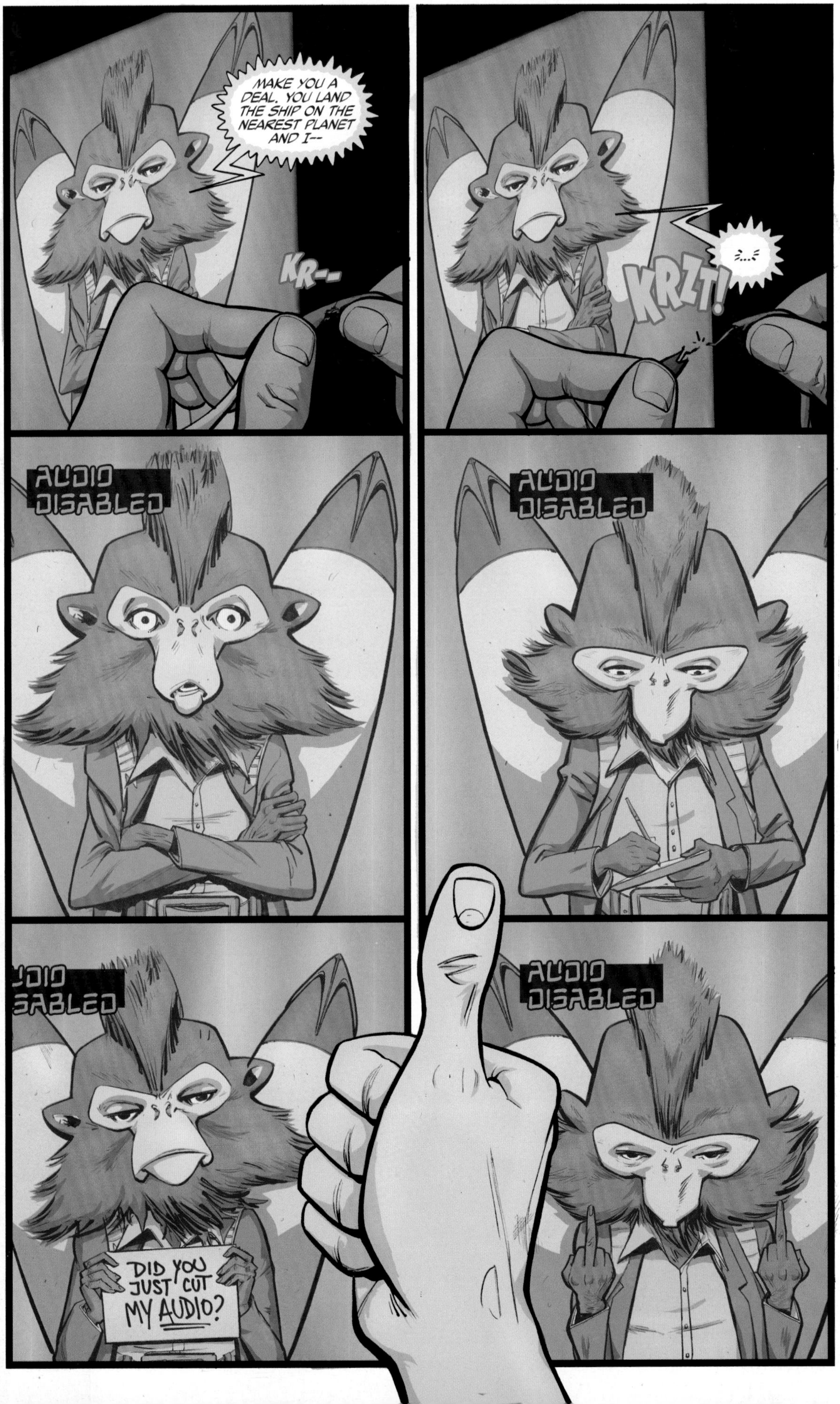
MAKE YOU A DEAL. YOU LAND THE SHIP ON THE NEAREST PLANET AND I--
KR--
...
KRZT!
AUDIO DISABLED
AUDIO DISABLED
UDIO SABLED
DID YOU JUST CUT MY AUDIO?
AUDIO DISABLED

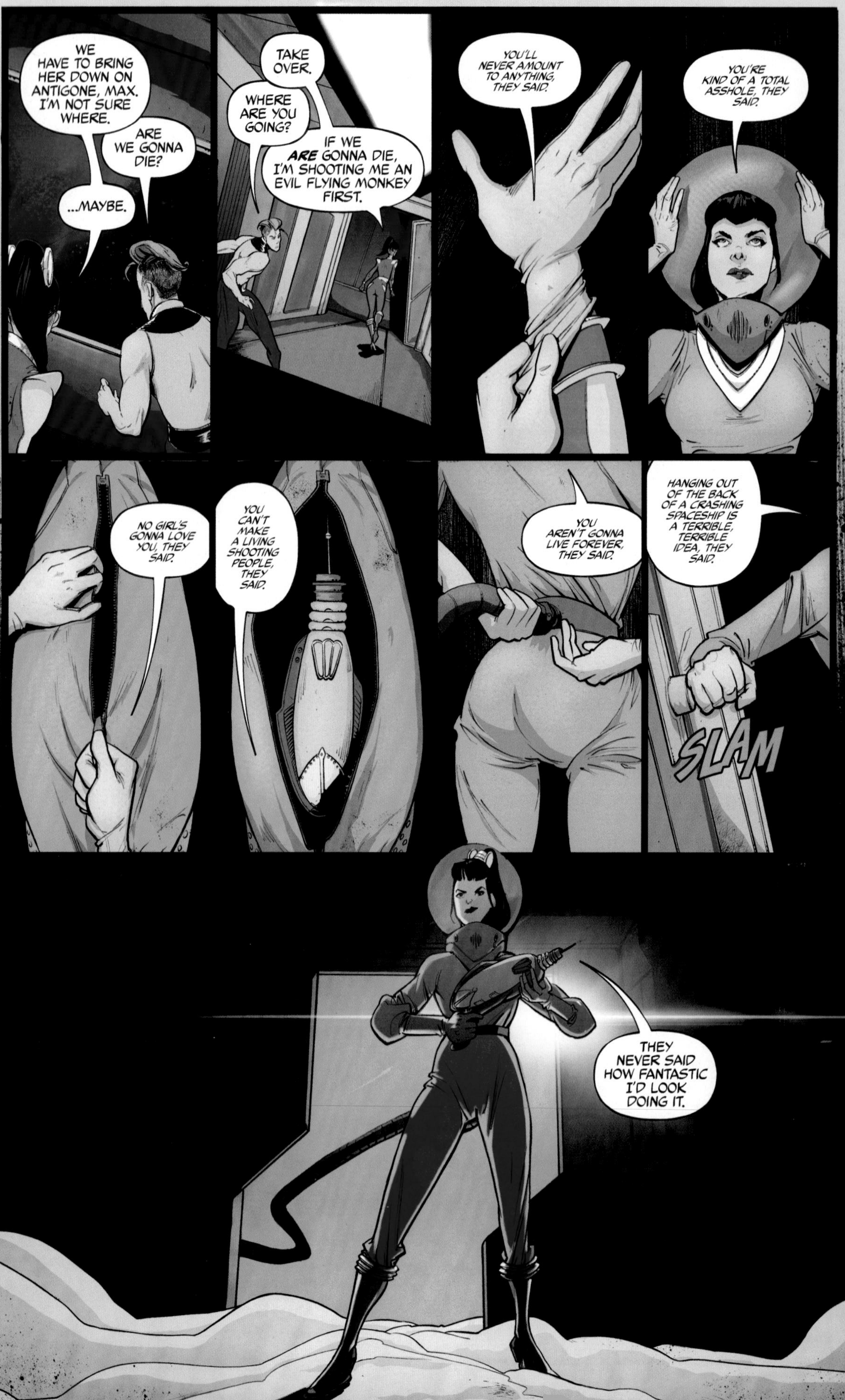
WE HAVE TO BRING HER DOWN ON ANTIGONE, MAX. I'M NOT SURE WHERE.
ARE WE GONNA DIE?
...MAYBE.
TAKE OVER.
WHERE ARE YOU GOING?
IF WE ARE GONNA DIE, I'M SHOOTING ME AN EVIL FLYING MONKEY FIRST.
YOU'LL NEVER AMOUNT TO ANYTHING, THEY SAID.
YOU'RE KIND OF A TOTAL ASSHOLE, THEY SAID.
NO GIRL'S GONNA LOVE YOU, THEY SAID.
YOU CAN'T MAKE A LIVING SHOOTING PEOPLE, THEY SAID.
YOU AREN'T GONNA LIVE FOREVER, THEY SAID.
HANGING OUT OF THE BACK OF A CRASHING SPACESHIP IS A TERRIBLE, TERRIBLE IDEA, THEY SAID.
SLAM
THEY NEVER SAID HOW FANTASTIC I'D LOOK DOING IT.

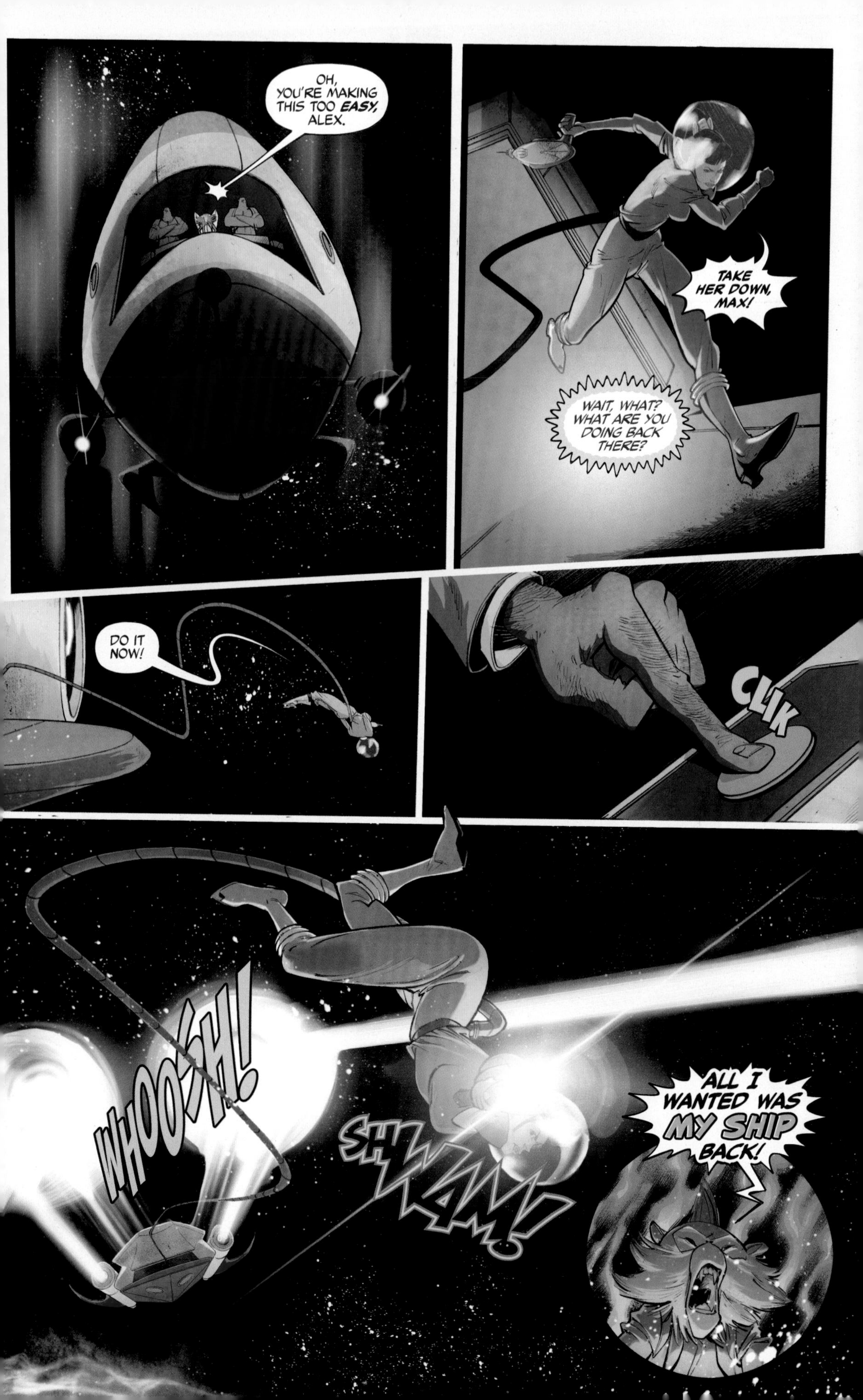
OH, YOU'RE MAKING THIS TOO EASY, ALEX.
TAKE HER DOWN, MAX!
WAIT, WHAT? WHAT ARE YOU DOING BACK THERE?
DO IT NOW!
CLIK
WHOOSH!
SHWAM!
ALL I WANTED WAS MY SHIP BACK!

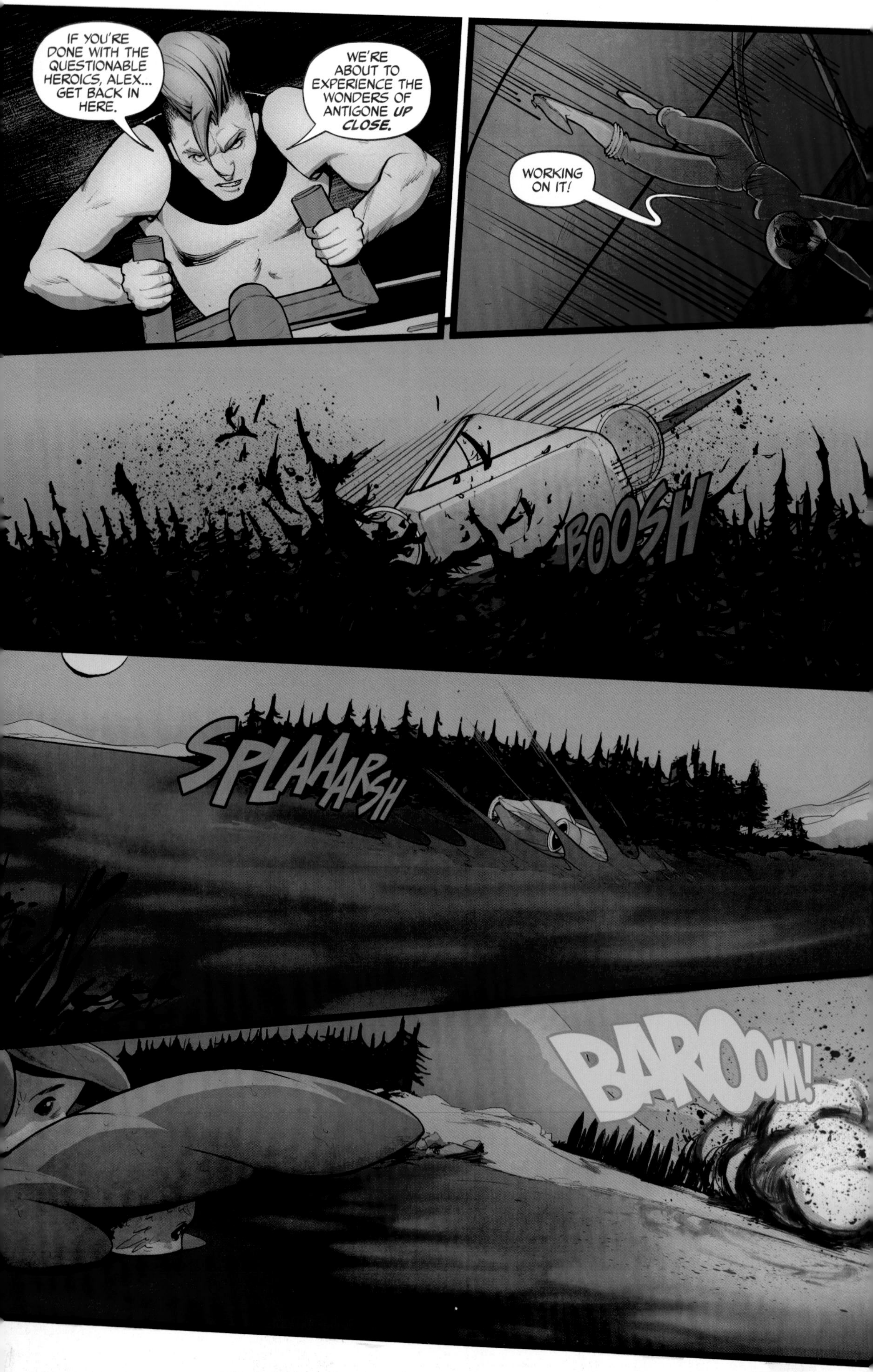
IF YOU'RE DONE WITH THE QUESTIONABLE HEROICS, ALEX... GET BACK IN HERE.
WE'RE ABOUT TO EXPERIENCE THE WONDERS OF ANTIGONE *UP CLOSE.*
WORKING ON IT!
BOOSH
SPLAAAARSH
BAROOM!

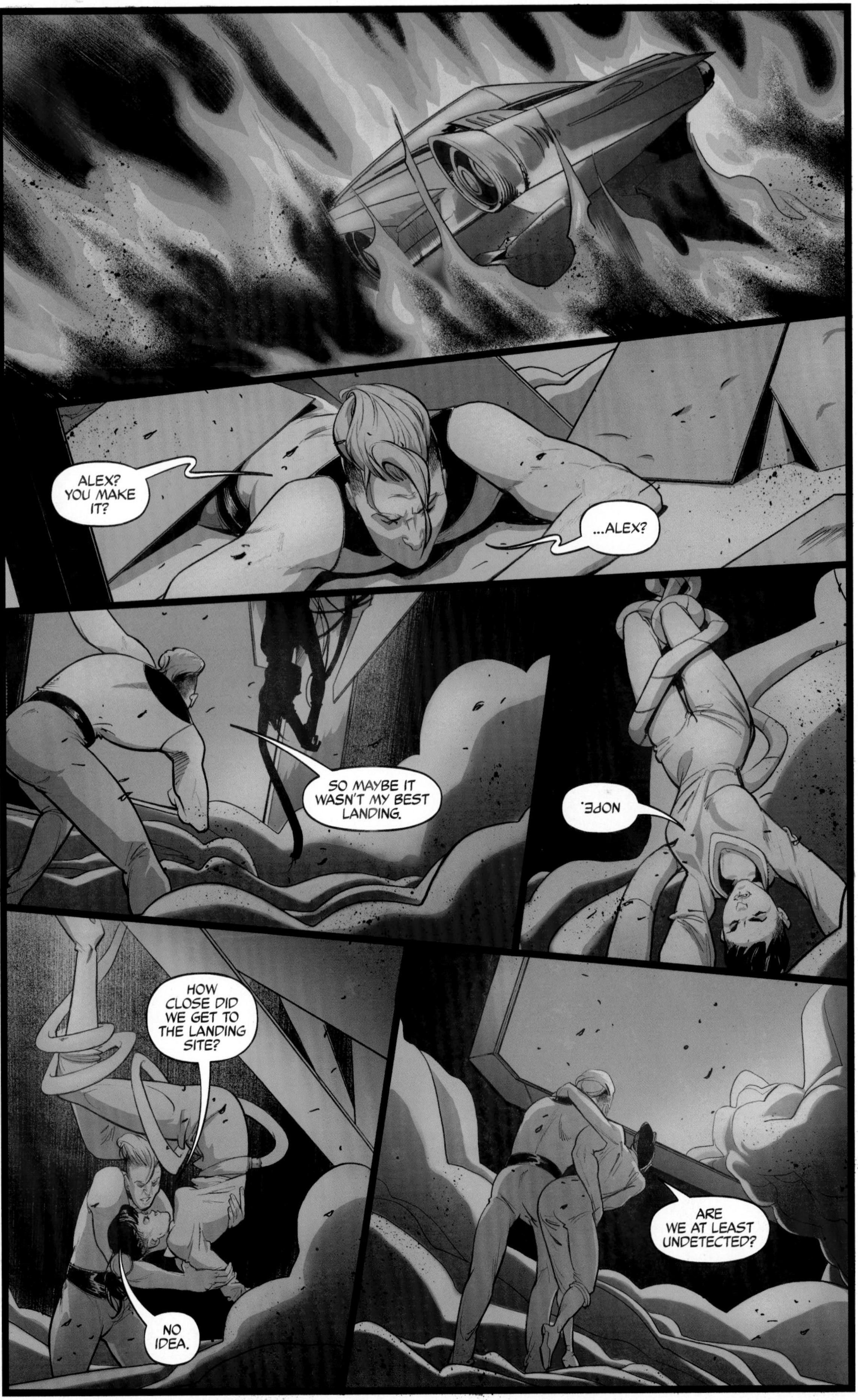
ALEX? YOU MAKE IT?
...ALEX?
SO MAYBE IT WASN'T MY BEST LANDING.
NOPE.
HOW CLOSE DID WE GET TO THE LANDING SITE?
NO IDEA.
ARE WE AT LEAST UNDETECTED?

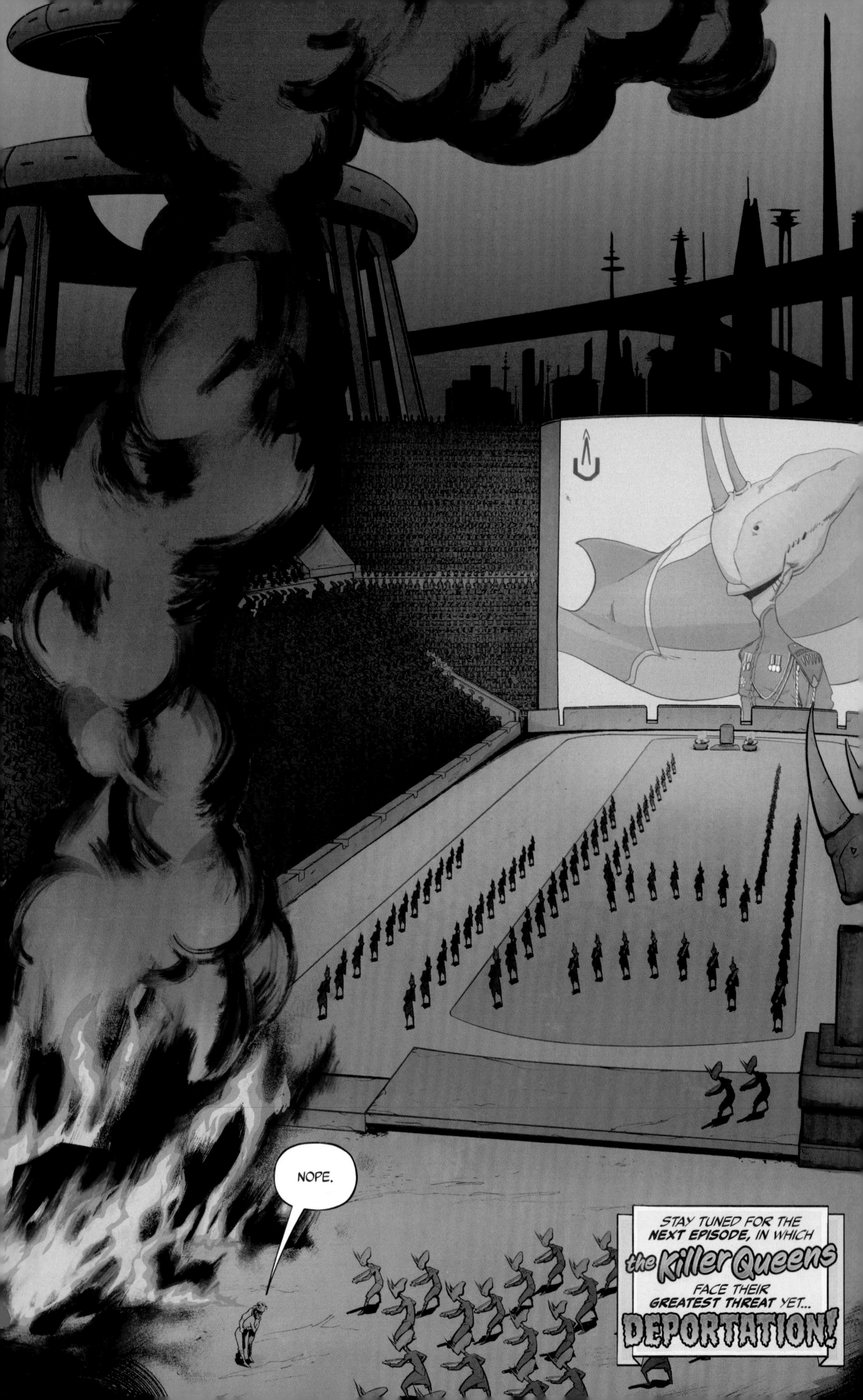
NOPE.
STAY TUNED FOR THE NEXT EPISODE, IN WHICH
the Killer Queens
FACE THEIR GREATEST THREAT YET...
DEPORTATION!

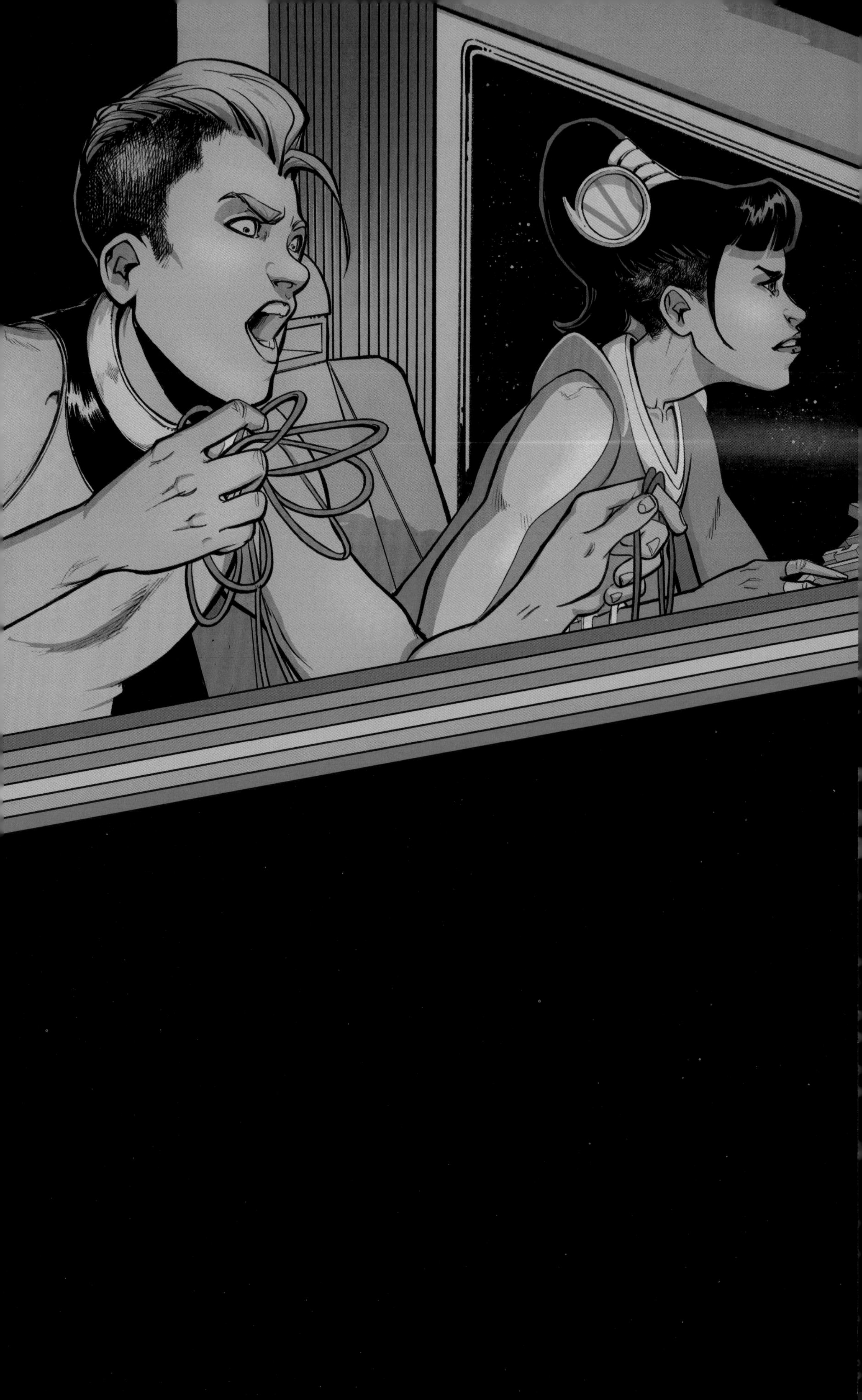

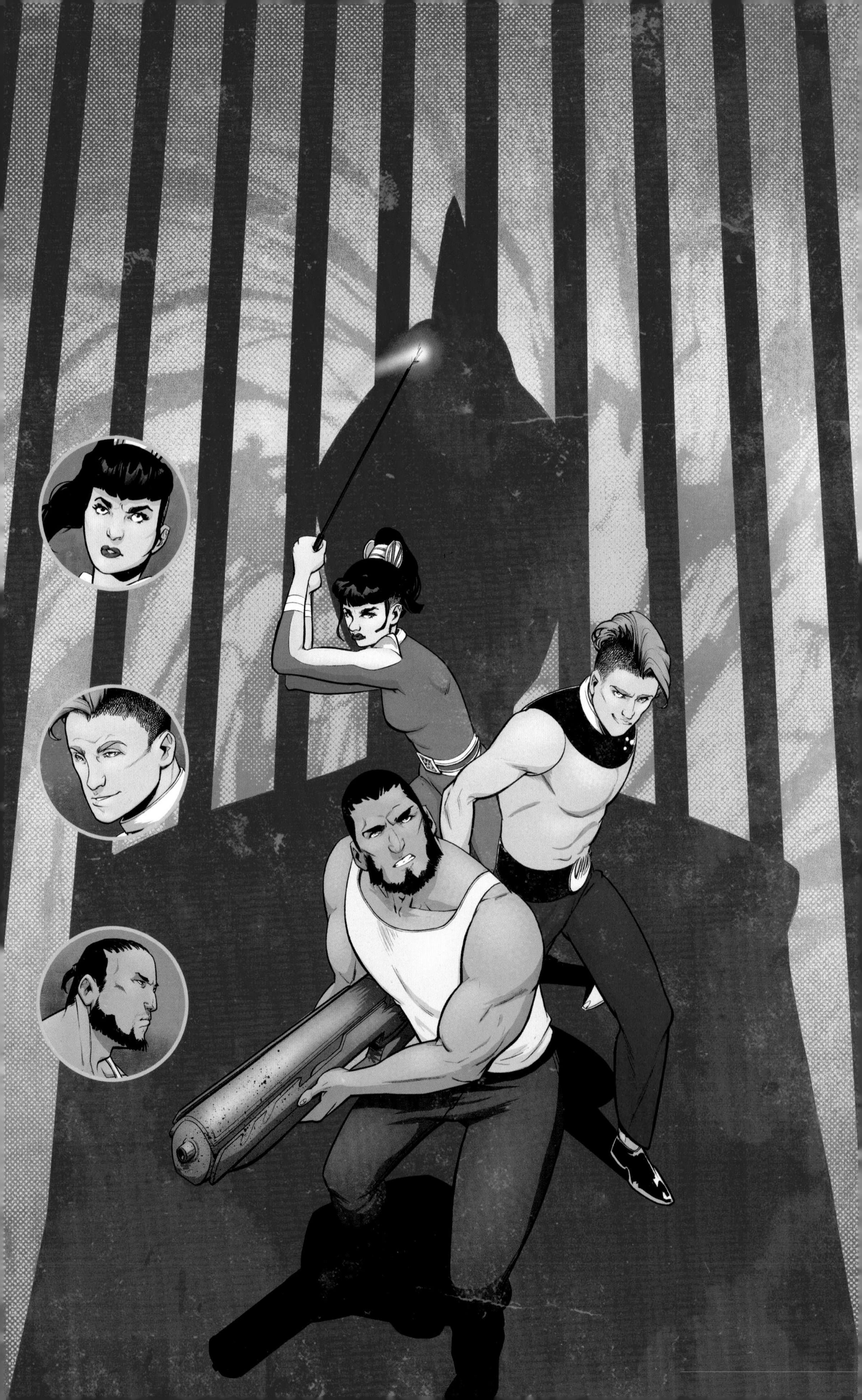

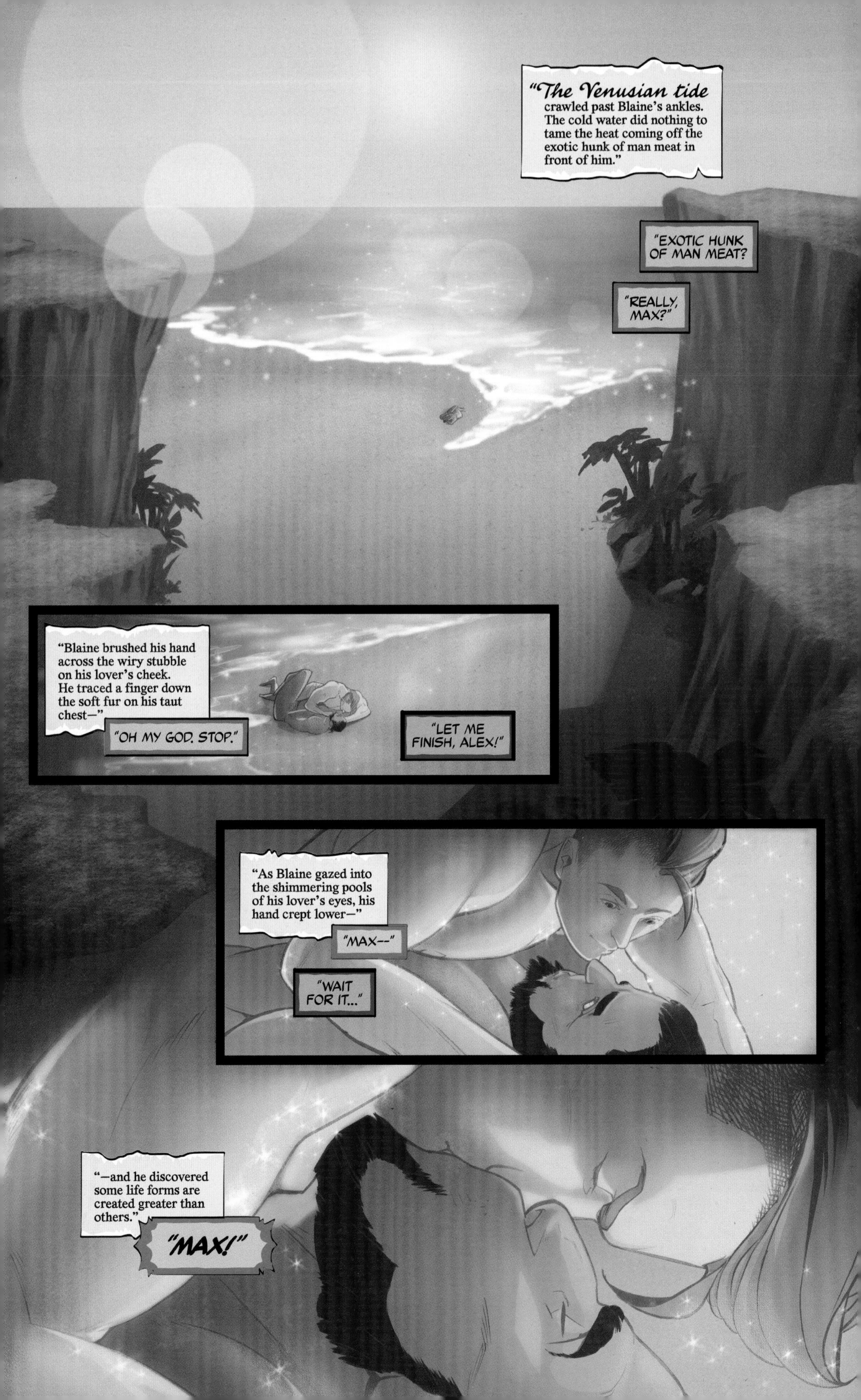
"The Venusian tide crawled past Blaine's ankles. The cold water did nothing to tame the heat coming off the exotic hunk of man meat in front of him."
"EXOTIC HUNK OF MAN MEAT?
"REALLY, MAX?"
"Blaine brushed his hand across the wiry stubble on his lover's cheek. He traced a finger down the soft fur on his taut chest—"
"OH MY GOD. STOP."
"LET ME FINISH, ALEX!"
"As Blaine gazed into the shimmering pools of his lover's eyes, his hand crept lower—"
"MAX--"
"WAIT FOR IT..."
"—and he discovered some life forms are created greater than others."
"MAX!"

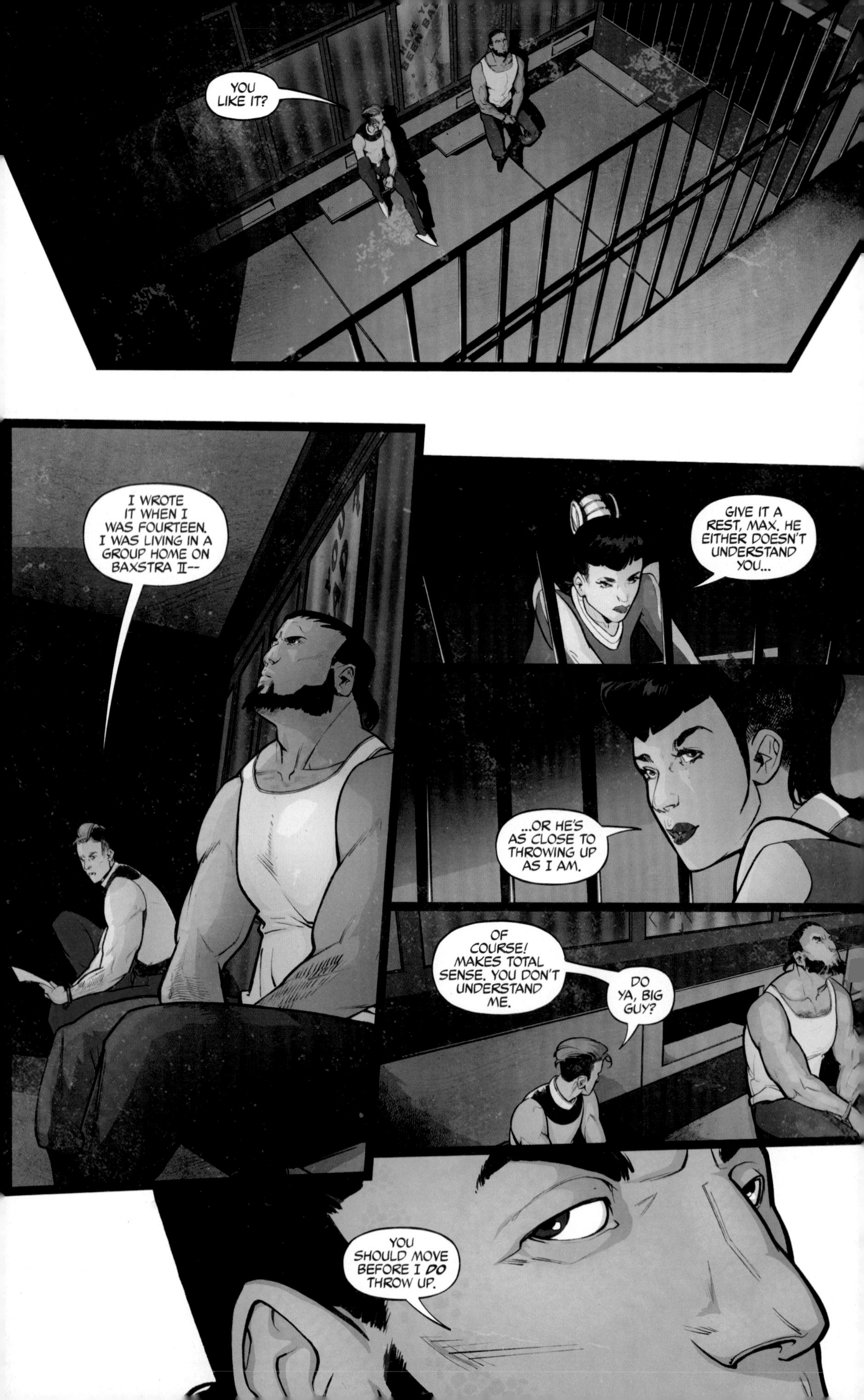
YOU LIKE IT?
I WROTE IT WHEN I WAS FOURTEEN. I WAS LIVING IN A GROUP HOME ON BAXSTRA II--
GIVE IT A REST, MAX. HE EITHER DOESN'T UNDERSTAND YOU...
...OR HE'S AS CLOSE TO THROWING UP AS I AM.
OF COURSE! MAKES TOTAL SENSE. YOU DON'T UNDERSTAND ME.
DO YA, BIG GUY?
YOU SHOULD MOVE BEFORE I *DO* THROW UP.

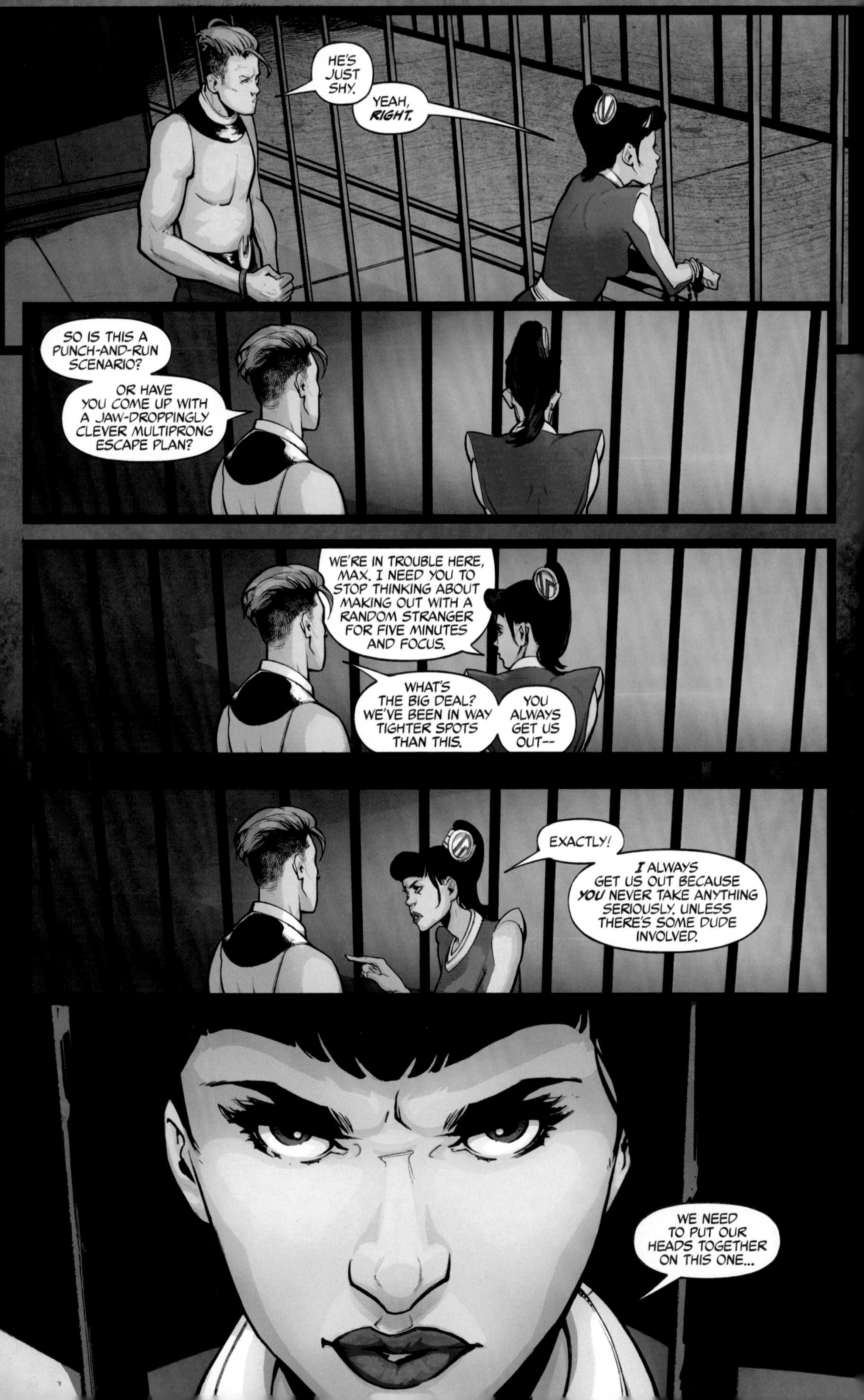
HE'S JUST SHY.
YEAH, RIGHT.
SO IS THIS A PUNCH-AND-RUN SCENARIO?
OR HAVE YOU COME UP WITH A JAW-DROPPINGLY CLEVER MULTIPRONG ESCAPE PLAN?
WE'RE IN TROUBLE HERE, MAX. I NEED YOU TO STOP THINKING ABOUT MAKING OUT WITH A RANDOM STRANGER FOR FIVE MINUTES AND FOCUS.
WHAT'S THE BIG DEAL? WE'VE BEEN IN WAY TIGHTER SPOTS THAN THIS.
YOU ALWAYS GET US OUT--
EXACTLY!
I ALWAYS GET US OUT BECAUSE YOU NEVER TAKE ANYTHING SERIOUSLY. UNLESS THERE'S SOME DUDE INVOLVED.
WE NEED TO PUT OUR HEADS TOGETHER ON THIS ONE...

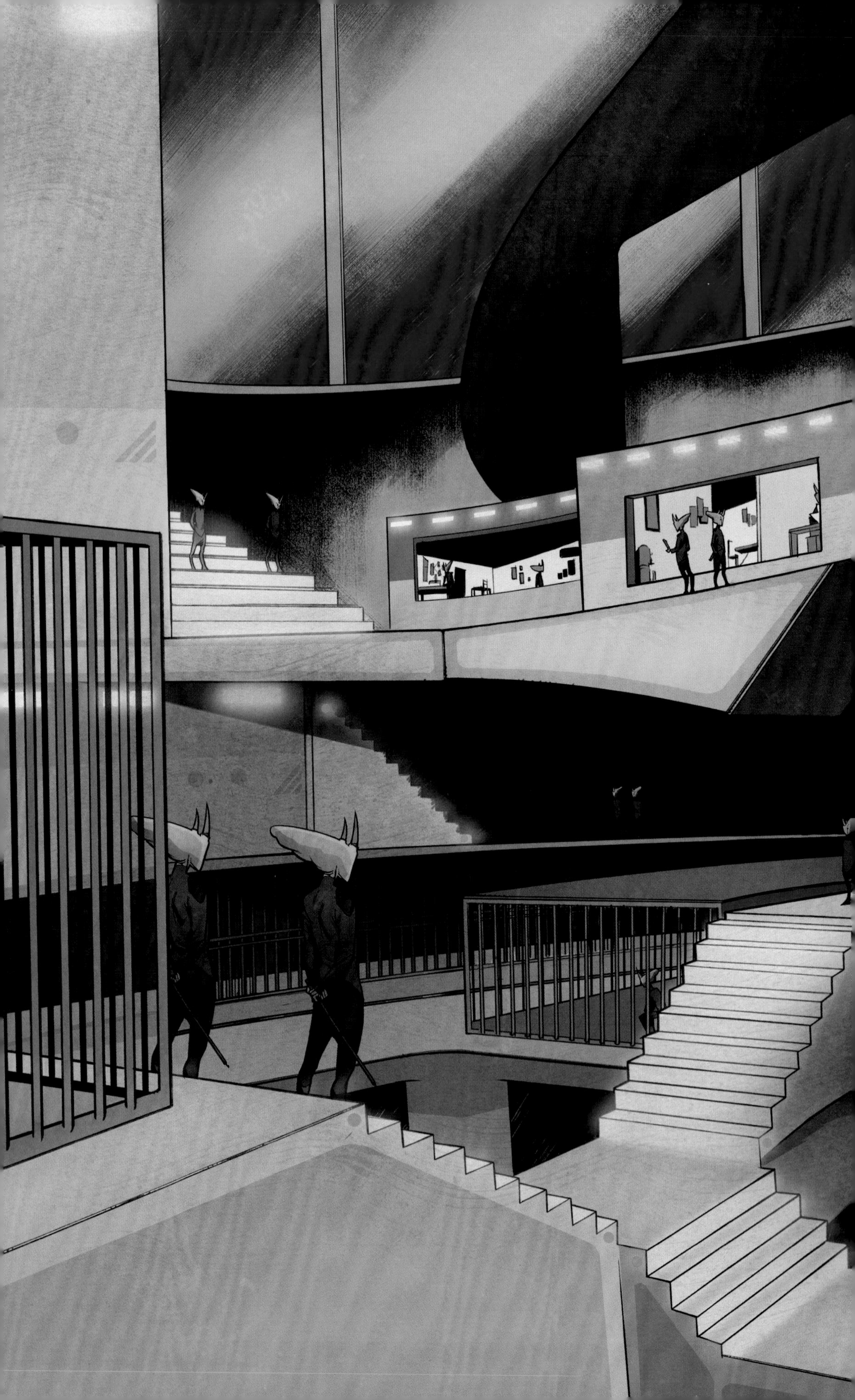

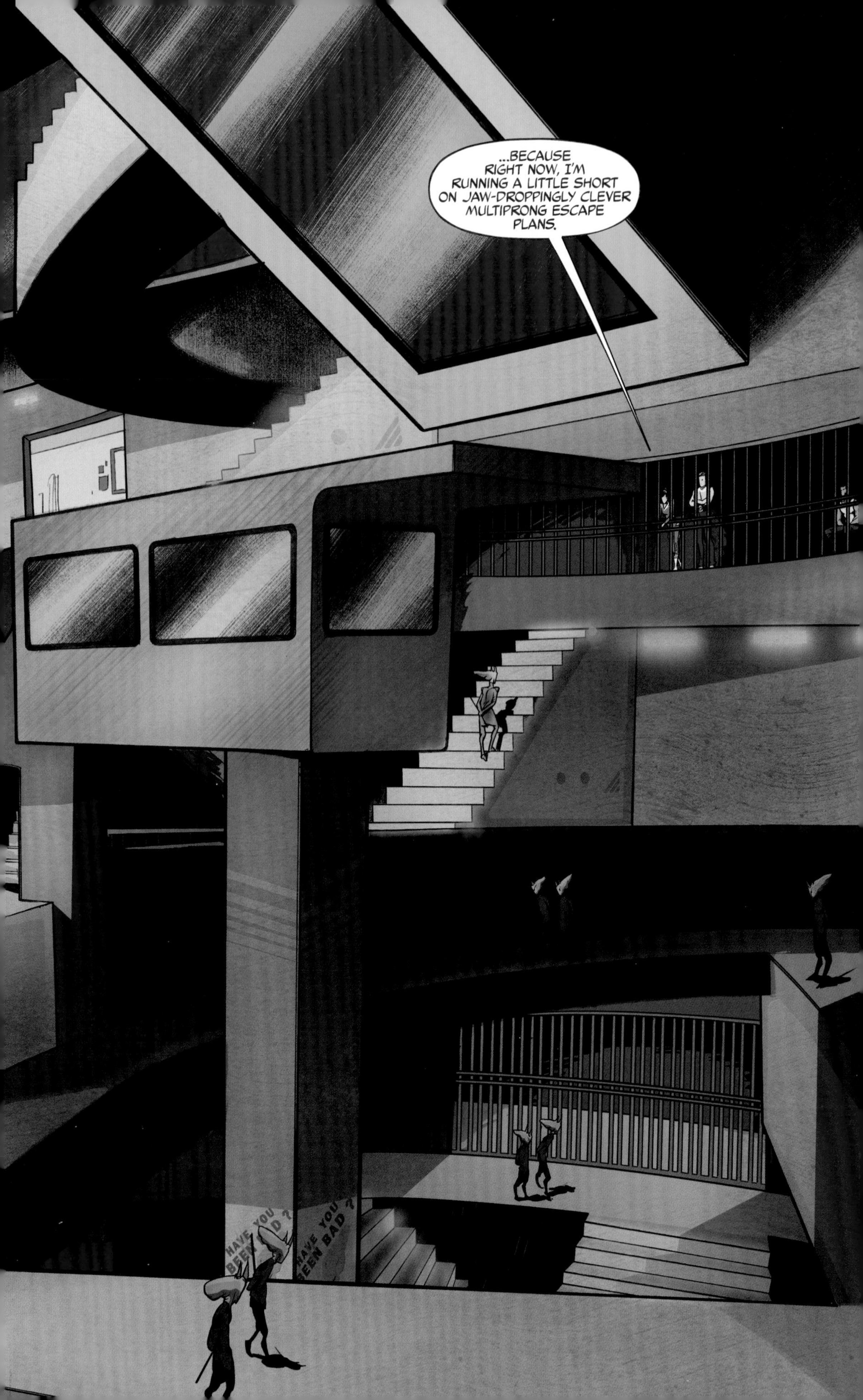
...BECAUSE RIGHT NOW, I'M RUNNING A LITTLE SHORT ON JAW-DROPPINGLY CLEVER MULTIPRONG ESCAPE PLANS.
HAVE YOU BEEN BAD ?

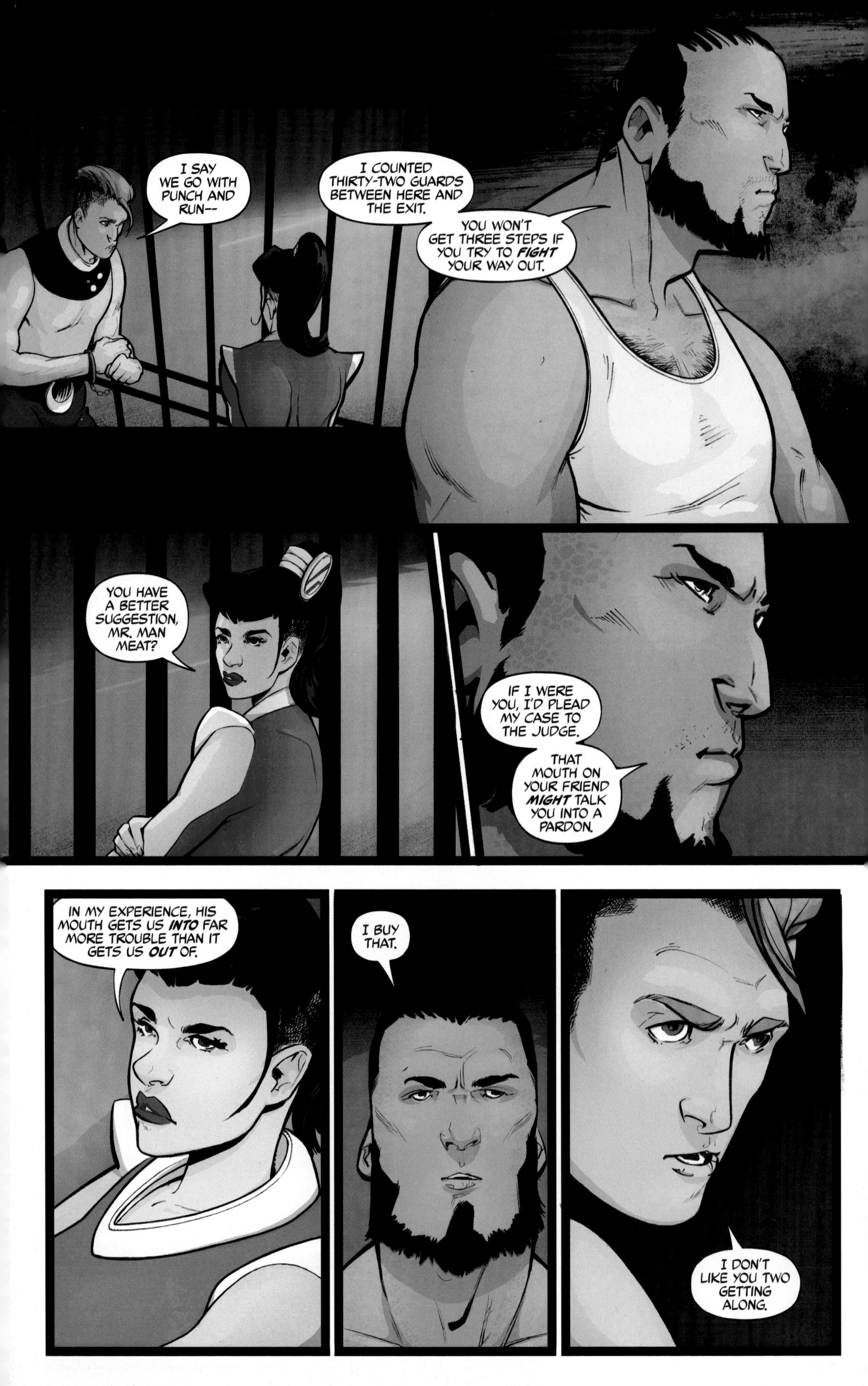
I SAY WE GO WITH PUNCH AND RUN--
I COUNTED THIRTY-TWO GUARDS BETWEEN HERE AND THE EXIT.
YOU WON'T GET THREE STEPS IF YOU TRY TO *FIGHT* YOUR WAY OUT.
YOU HAVE A BETTER SUGGESTION, MR. MAN MEAT?
IF I WERE YOU, I'D PLEAD MY CASE TO THE JUDGE.
THAT MOUTH ON YOUR FRIEND *MIGHT* TALK YOU INTO A PARDON.
IN MY EXPERIENCE, HIS MOUTH GETS US *INTO* FAR MORE TROUBLE THAN IT GETS US *OUT* OF.
I BUY THAT.
I DON'T LIKE YOU TWO GETTING ALONG.

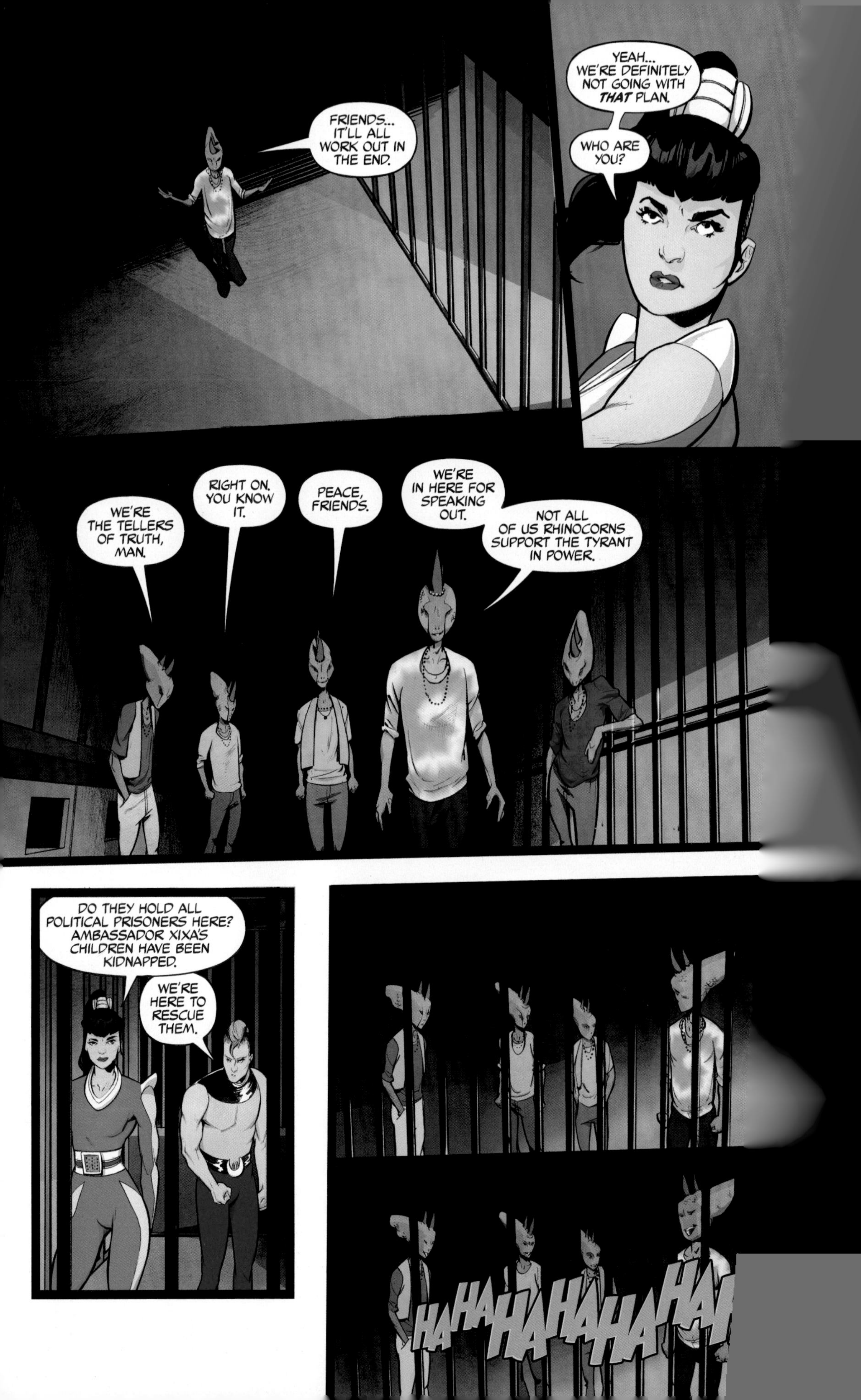
FRIENDS... IT'LL ALL WORK OUT IN THE END.
YEAH... WE'RE DEFINITELY NOT GOING WITH THAT PLAN.
WHO ARE YOU?
WE'RE THE TELLERS OF TRUTH, MAN.
RIGHT ON. YOU KNOW IT.
PEACE, FRIENDS.
WE'RE IN HERE FOR SPEAKING OUT.
NOT ALL OF US RHINOCORNS SUPPORT THE TYRANT IN POWER.
DO THEY HOLD ALL POLITICAL PRISONERS HERE? AMBASSADOR XIXA'S CHILDREN HAVE BEEN KIDNAPPED.
WE'RE HERE TO RESCUE THEM.
HAHAHAHAHAHAHAHA

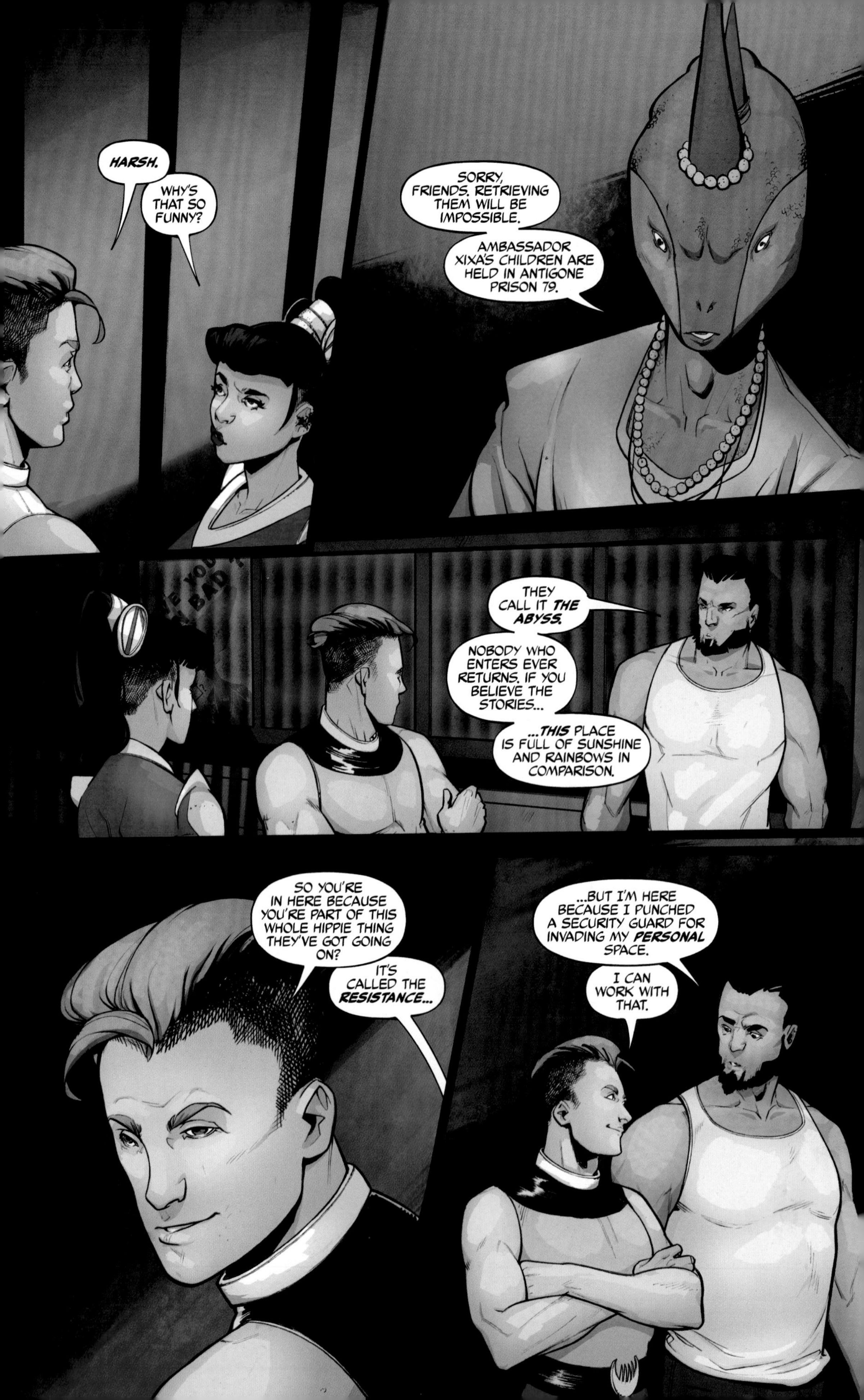
HARSH.
WHY'S THAT SO FUNNY?
SORRY, FRIENDS. RETRIEVING THEM WILL BE IMPOSSIBLE.
AMBASSADOR XIXA'S CHILDREN ARE HELD IN ANTIGONE PRISON 79.
THEY CALL IT THE ABYSS.
NOBODY WHO ENTERS EVER RETURNS. IF YOU BELIEVE THE STORIES...
...THIS PLACE IS FULL OF SUNSHINE AND RAINBOWS IN COMPARISON.
SO YOU'RE IN HERE BECAUSE YOU'RE PART OF THIS WHOLE HIPPIE THING THEY'VE GOT GOING ON?
IT'S CALLED THE RESISTANCE...
...BUT I'M HERE BECAUSE I PUNCHED A SECURITY GUARD FOR INVADING MY PERSONAL SPACE.
I CAN WORK WITH THAT.

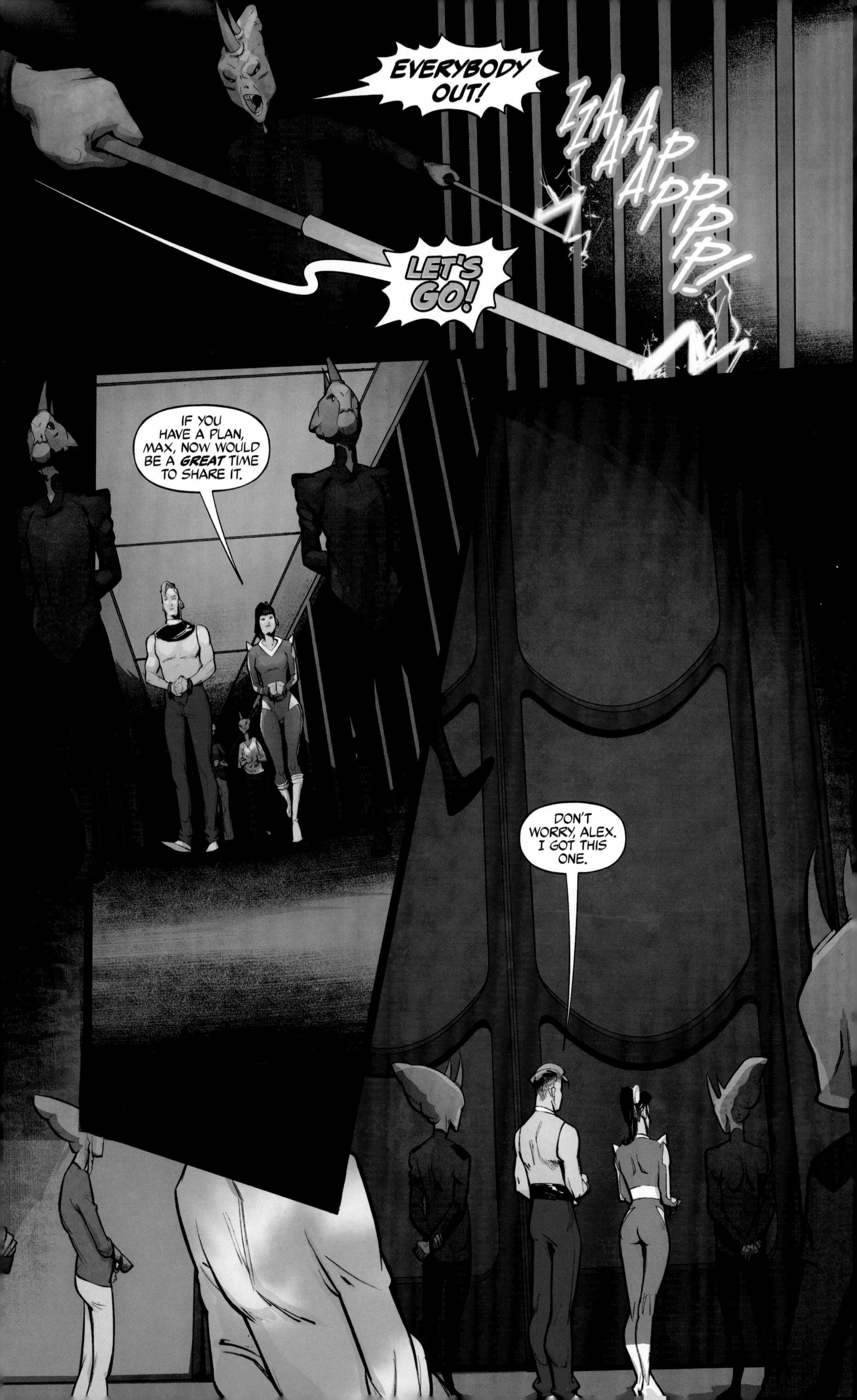
EVERYBODY OUT!
ZZAAAAPPPP!
LET'S GO!
IF YOU HAVE A PLAN, MAX, NOW WOULD BE A **GREAT** TIME TO SHARE IT.
DON'T WORRY, ALEX. I GOT THIS ONE.

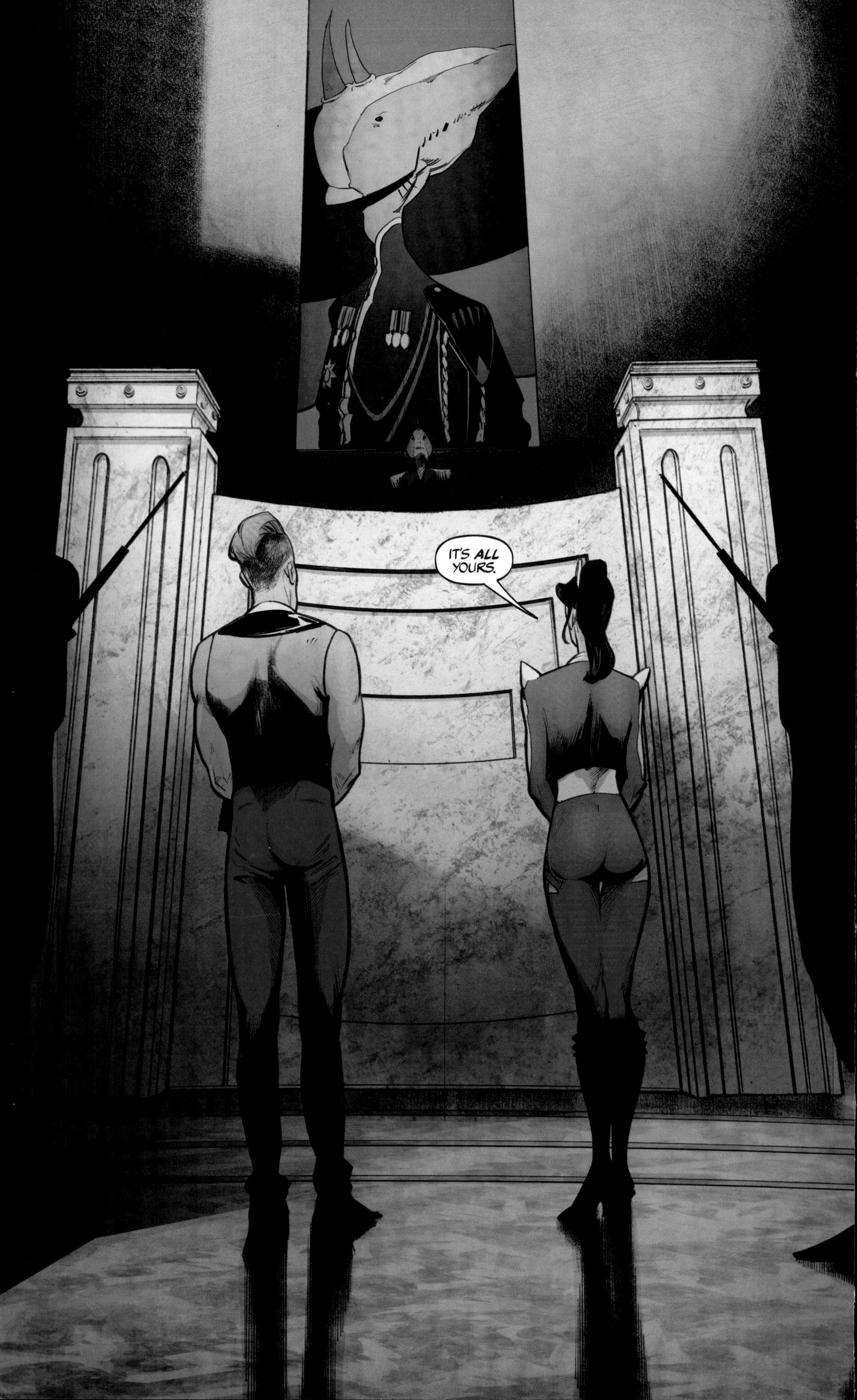
IT'S ALL YOURS.

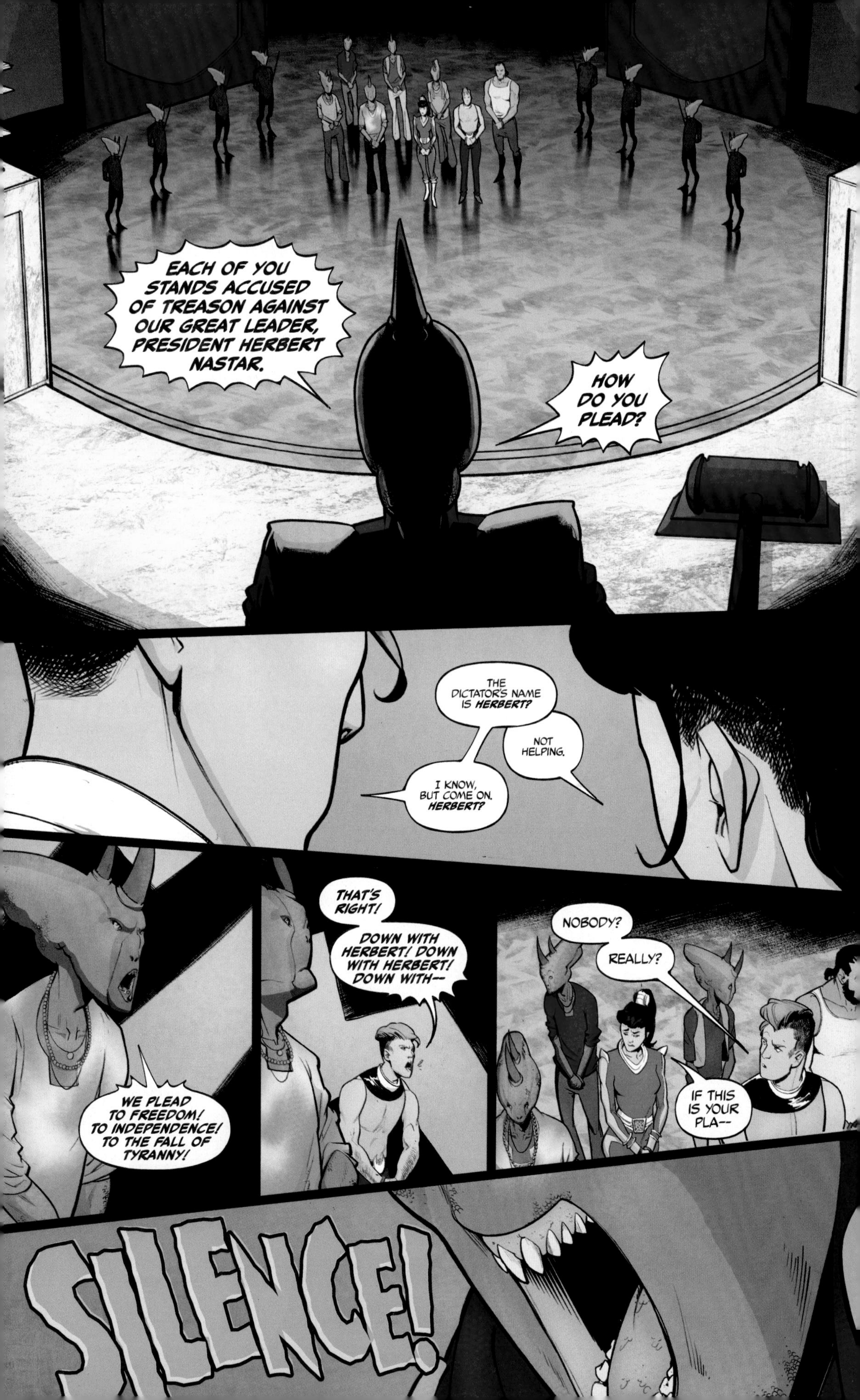
EACH OF YOU STANDS ACCUSED OF TREASON AGAINST OUR GREAT LEADER, PRESIDENT HERBERT NASTAR.
HOW DO YOU PLEAD?
THE DICTATOR'S NAME IS HERBERT?
NOT HELPING.
I KNOW, BUT COME ON. HERBERT?
WE PLEAD TO FREEDOM! TO INDEPENDENCE! TO THE FALL OF TYRANNY!
THAT'S RIGHT!
DOWN WITH HERBERT! DOWN WITH HERBERT! DOWN WITH--
NOBODY?
REALLY?
IF THIS IS YOUR PLA--
SILENCE!

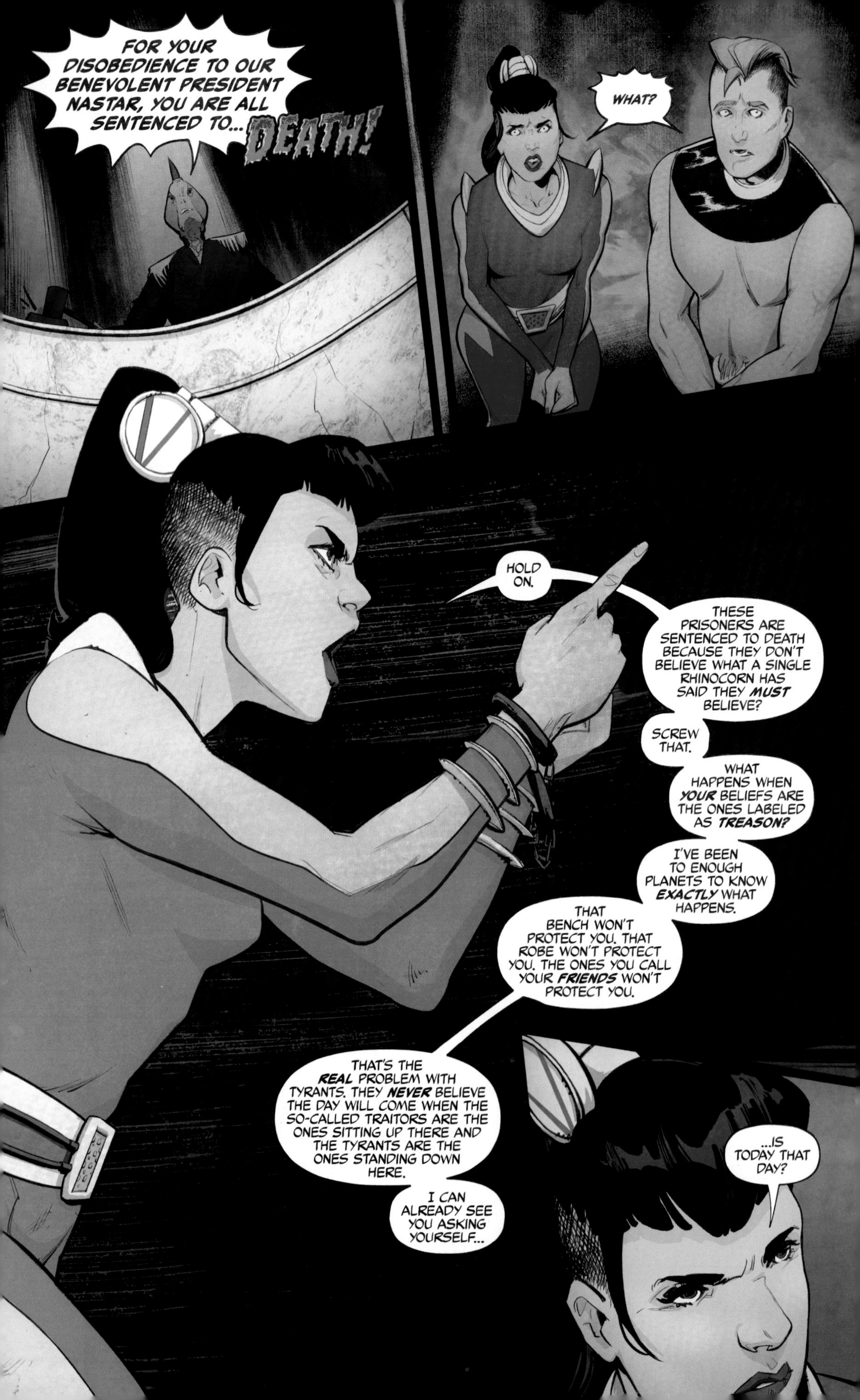
FOR YOUR DISOBEDIENCE TO OUR BENEVOLENT PRESIDENT NASTAR, YOU ARE ALL SENTENCED TO... DEATH!
WHAT?
HOLD ON.
THESE PRISONERS ARE SENTENCED TO DEATH BECAUSE THEY DON'T BELIEVE WHAT A SINGLE RHINOCORN HAS SAID THEY MUST BELIEVE?
SCREW THAT.
WHAT HAPPENS WHEN YOUR BELIEFS ARE THE ONES LABELED AS TREASON?
I'VE BEEN TO ENOUGH PLANETS TO KNOW EXACTLY WHAT HAPPENS.
THAT BENCH WON'T PROTECT YOU. THAT ROBE WON'T PROTECT YOU. THE ONES YOU CALL YOUR FRIENDS WON'T PROTECT YOU.
THAT'S THE REAL PROBLEM WITH TYRANTS. THEY NEVER BELIEVE THE DAY WILL COME WHEN THE SO-CALLED TRAITORS ARE THE ONES SITTING UP THERE AND THE TYRANTS ARE THE ONES STANDING DOWN HERE.
I CAN ALREADY SEE YOU ASKING YOURSELF...
...IS TODAY THAT DAY?

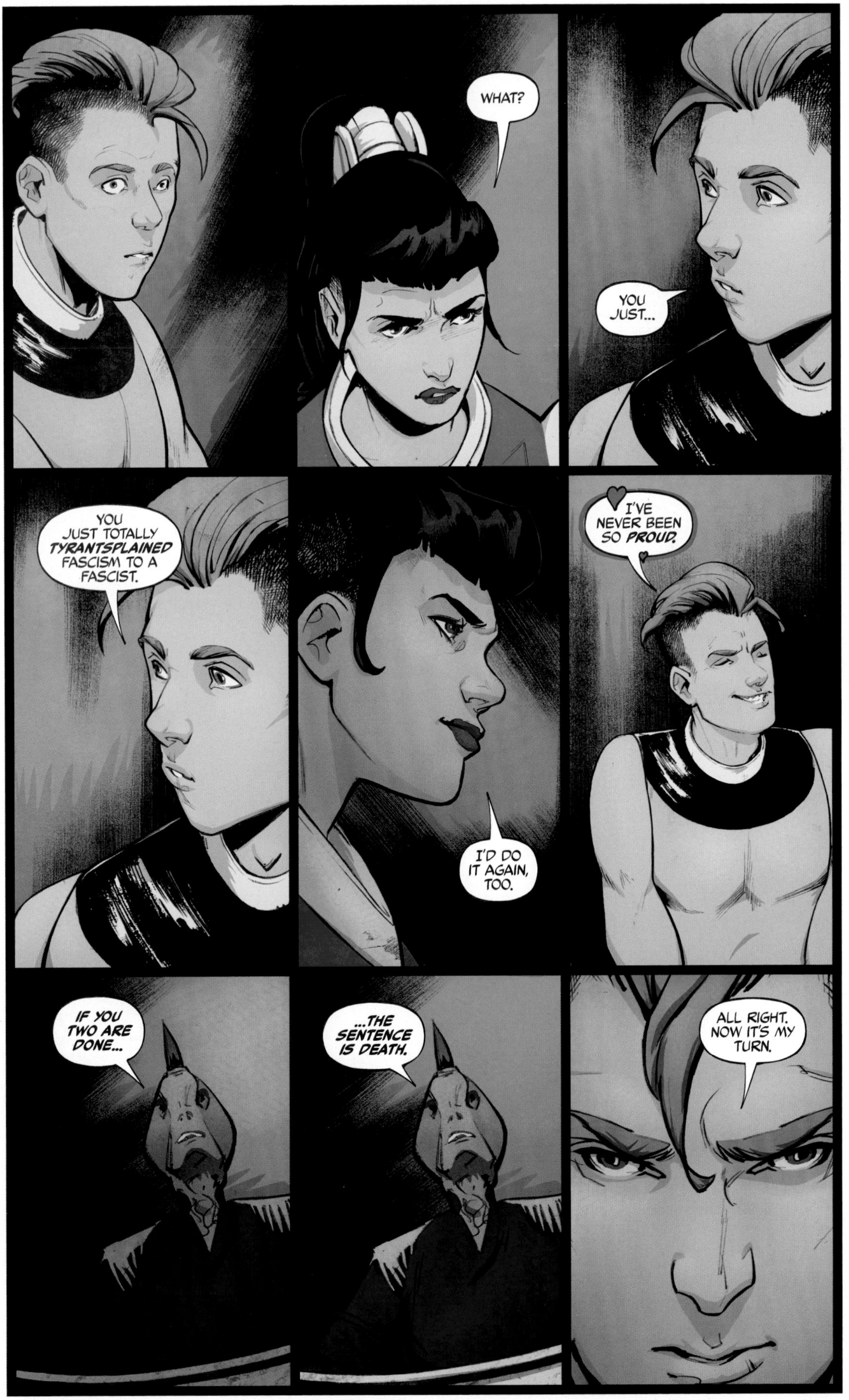
WHAT?
YOU JUST...
YOU JUST TOTALLY *TYRANTSPLAINED* FASCISM TO A FASCIST.
I'D DO IT AGAIN, TOO.
I'VE NEVER BEEN SO *PROUD.*
IF YOU TWO ARE DONE...
...THE SENTENCE IS DEATH.
ALL RIGHT. NOW IT'S MY TURN.

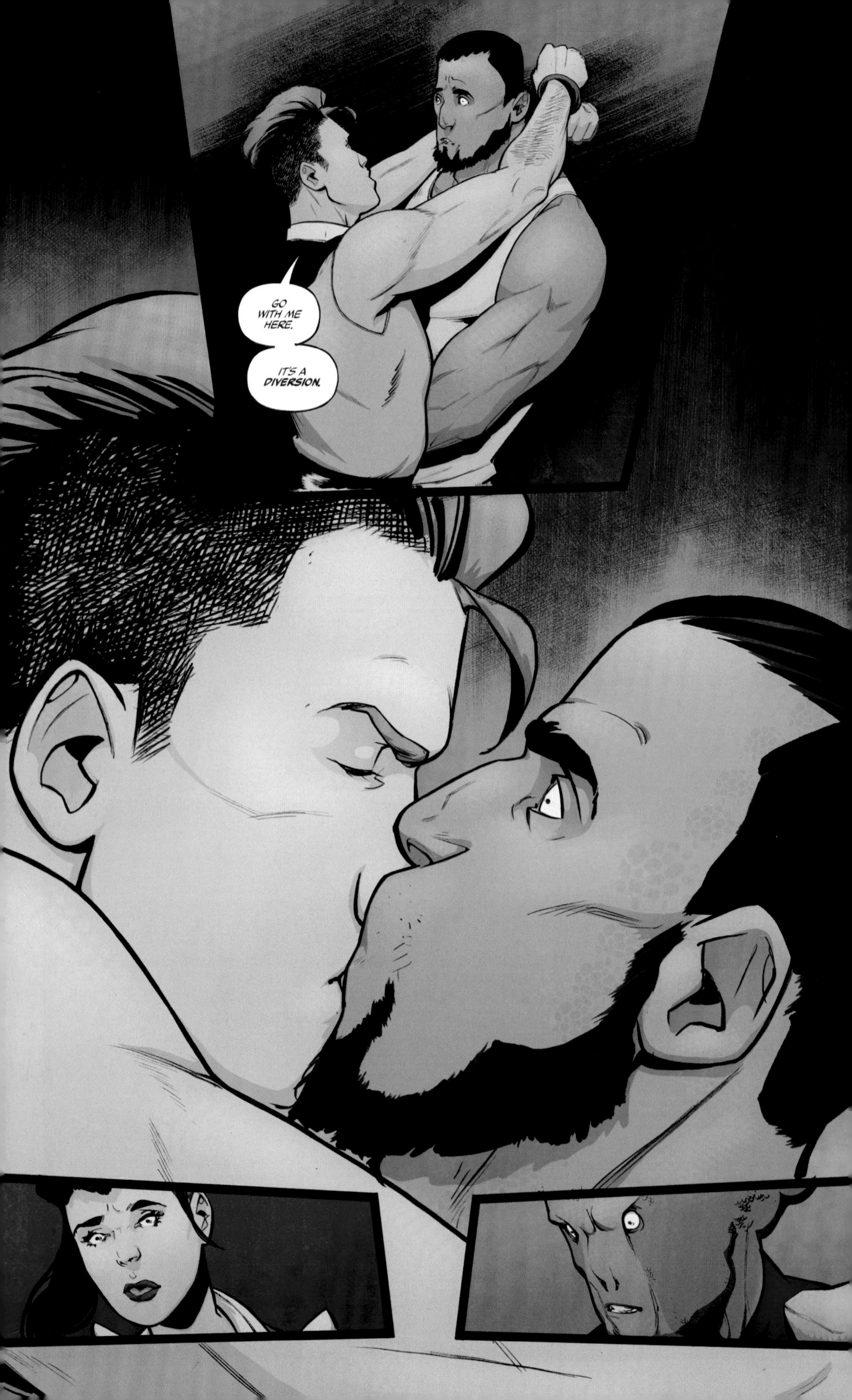
GO WITH ME HERE.
IT'S A DIVERSION.

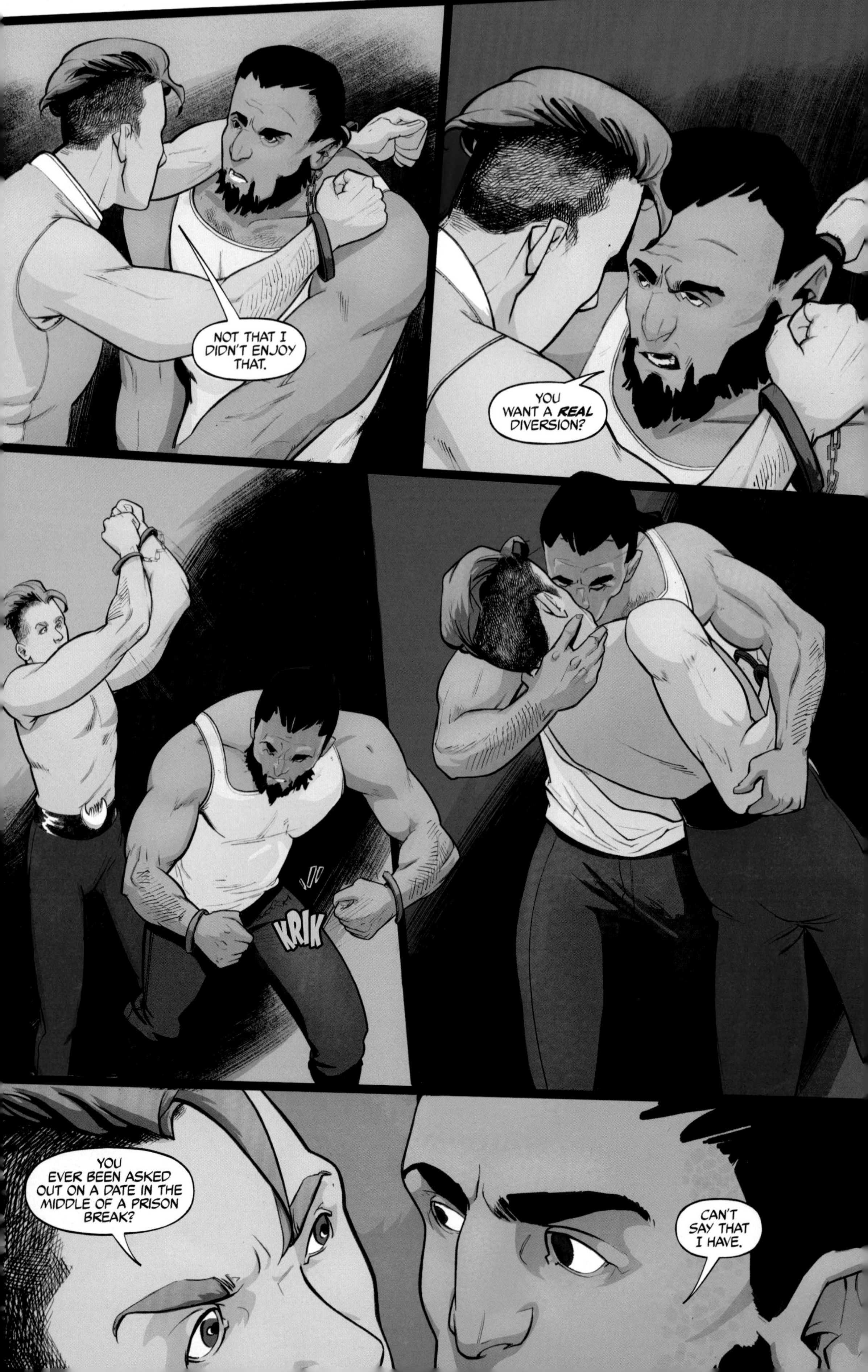
NOT THAT I DIDN'T ENJOY THAT.
YOU WANT A REAL DIVERSION?
KRIK
YOU EVER BEEN ASKED OUT ON A DATE IN THE MIDDLE OF A PRISON BREAK?
CAN'T SAY THAT I HAVE.

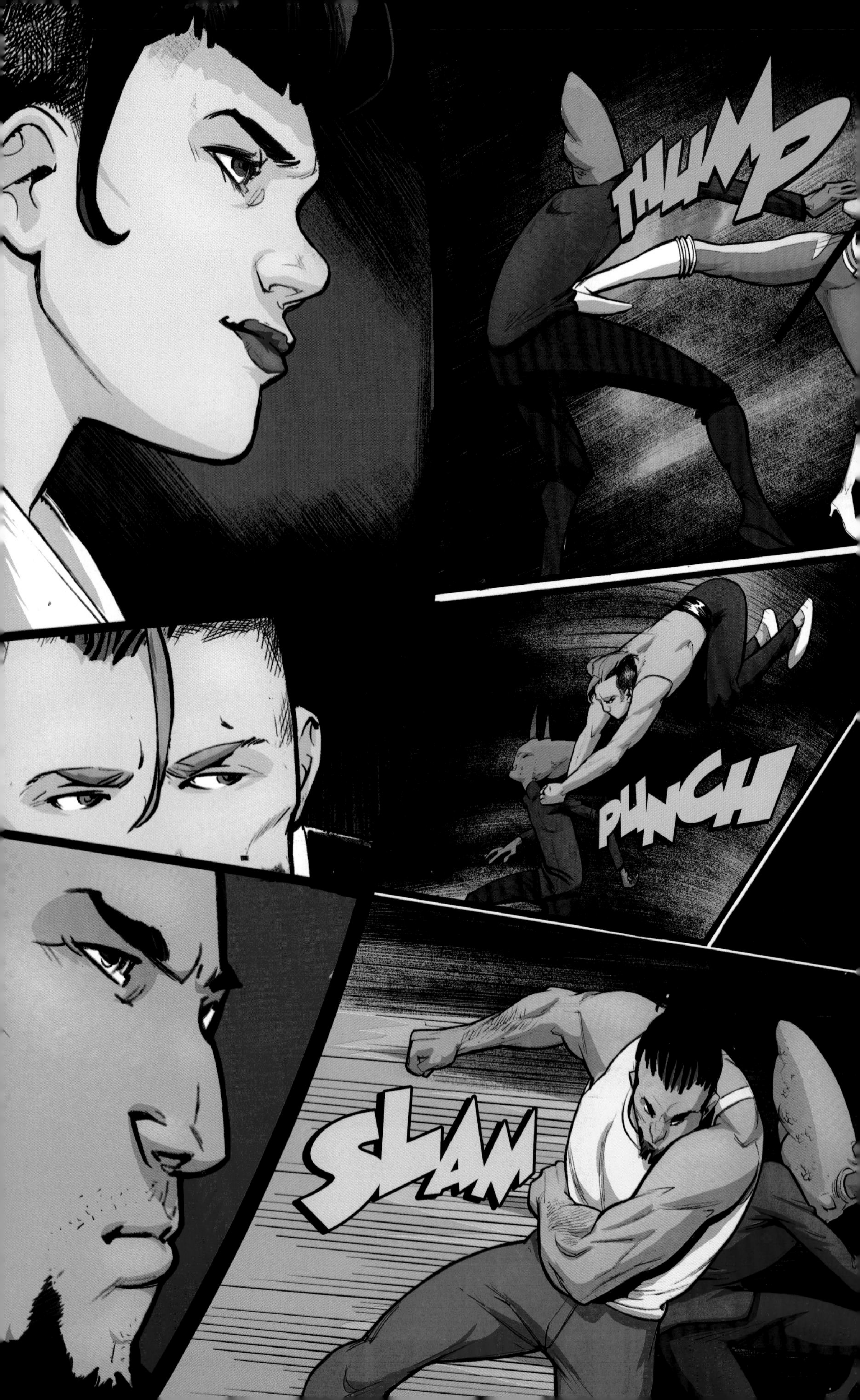
THUMP
PUNCH
SLAM

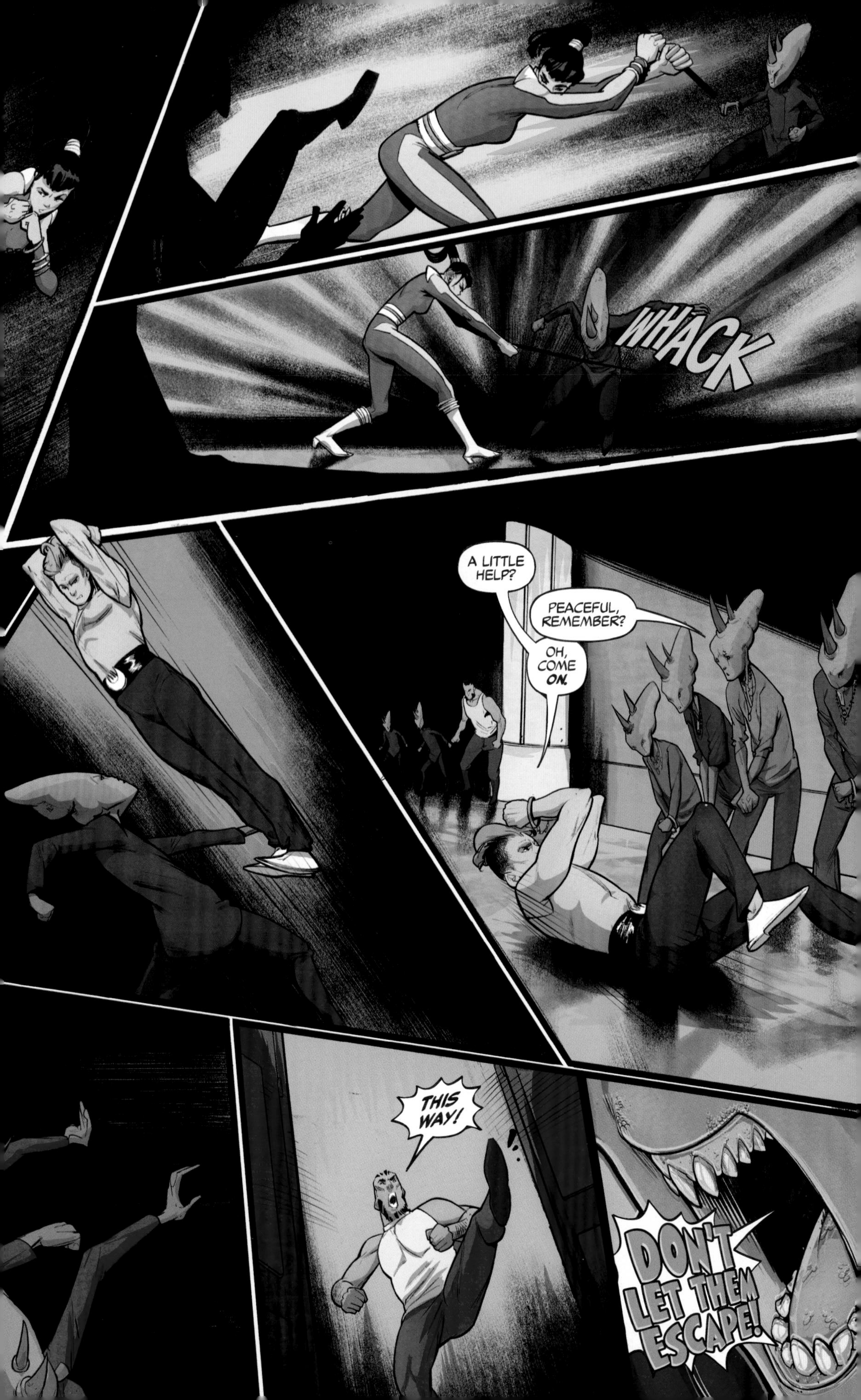
WHACK
A LITTLE HELP?
PEACEFUL, REMEMBER?
OH, COME ON.
THIS WAY!
DON'T LET THEM ESCAPE!

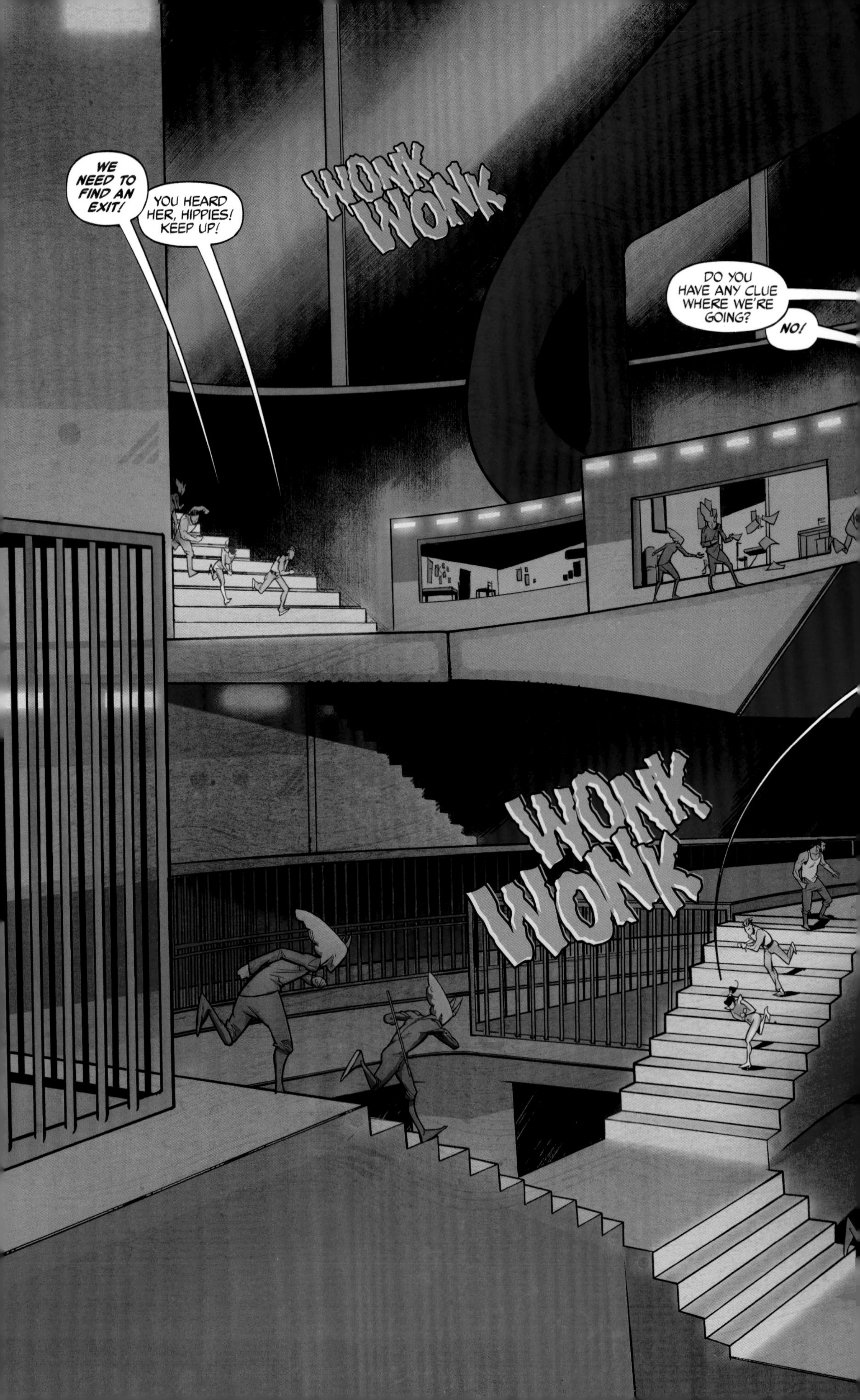
WE NEED TO FIND AN EXIT!
YOU HEARD HER, HIPPIES! KEEP UP!
WONK WONK
DO YOU HAVE ANY CLUE WHERE WE'RE GOING?
NO!
WONK WONK

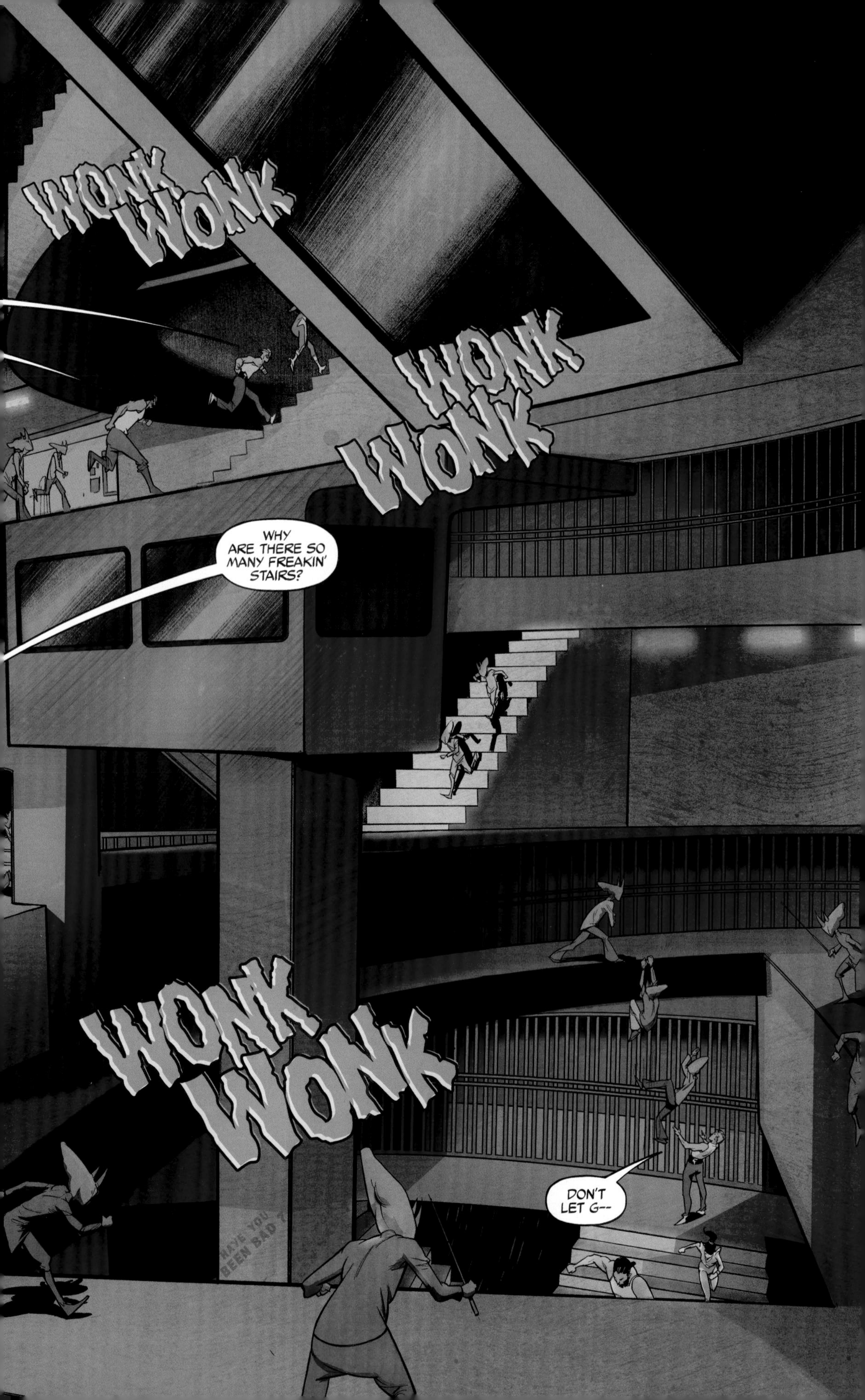
WONK WONK
WONK WONK
WHY ARE THERE SO MANY FREAKIN' STAIRS?
WONK WONK
HAVE YOU BEEN BAD ?
DON'T LET G--

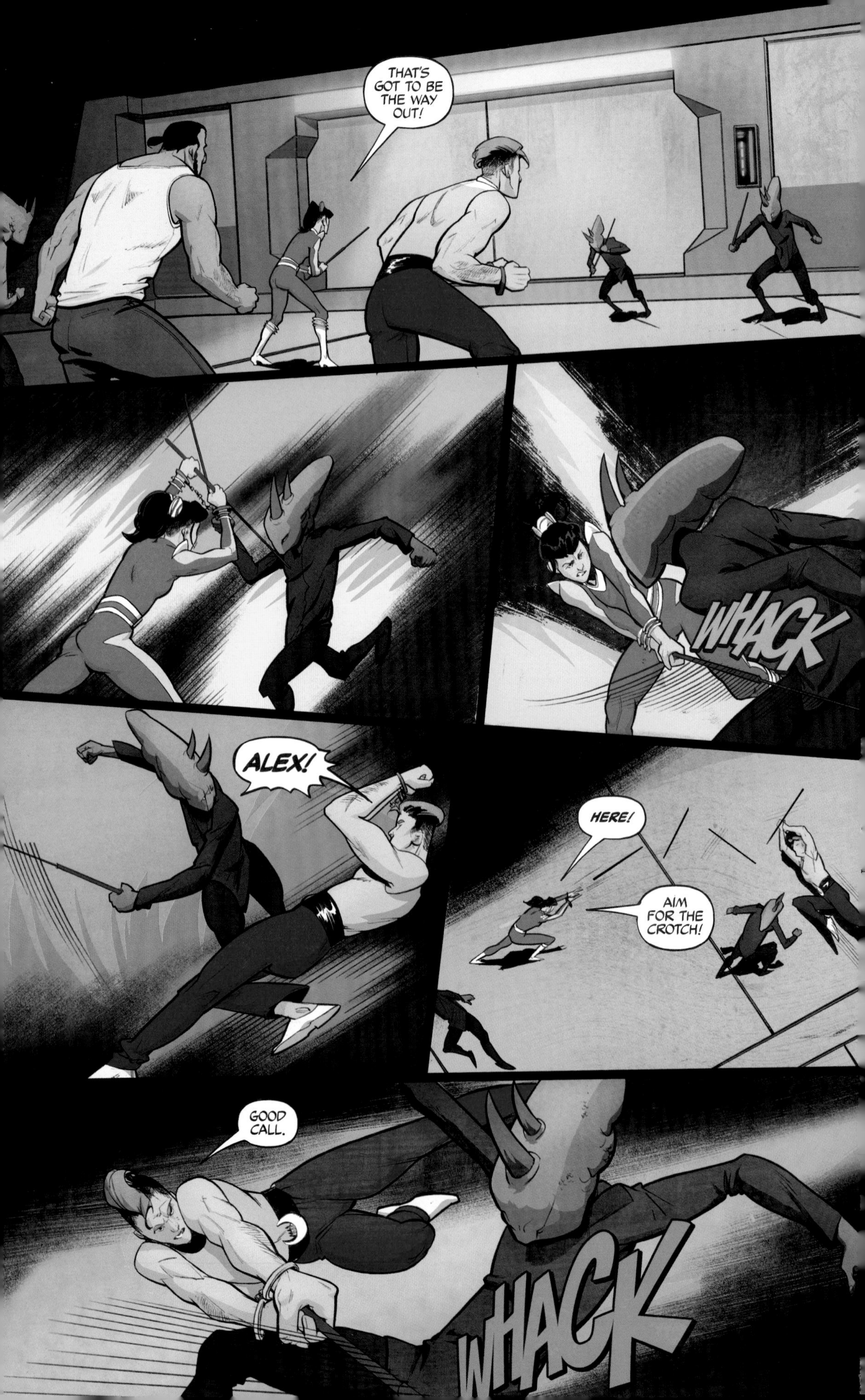
THAT'S GOT TO BE THE WAY OUT!
WHACK
ALEX!
HERE!
AIM FOR THE CROTCH!
GOOD CALL.
WHACK

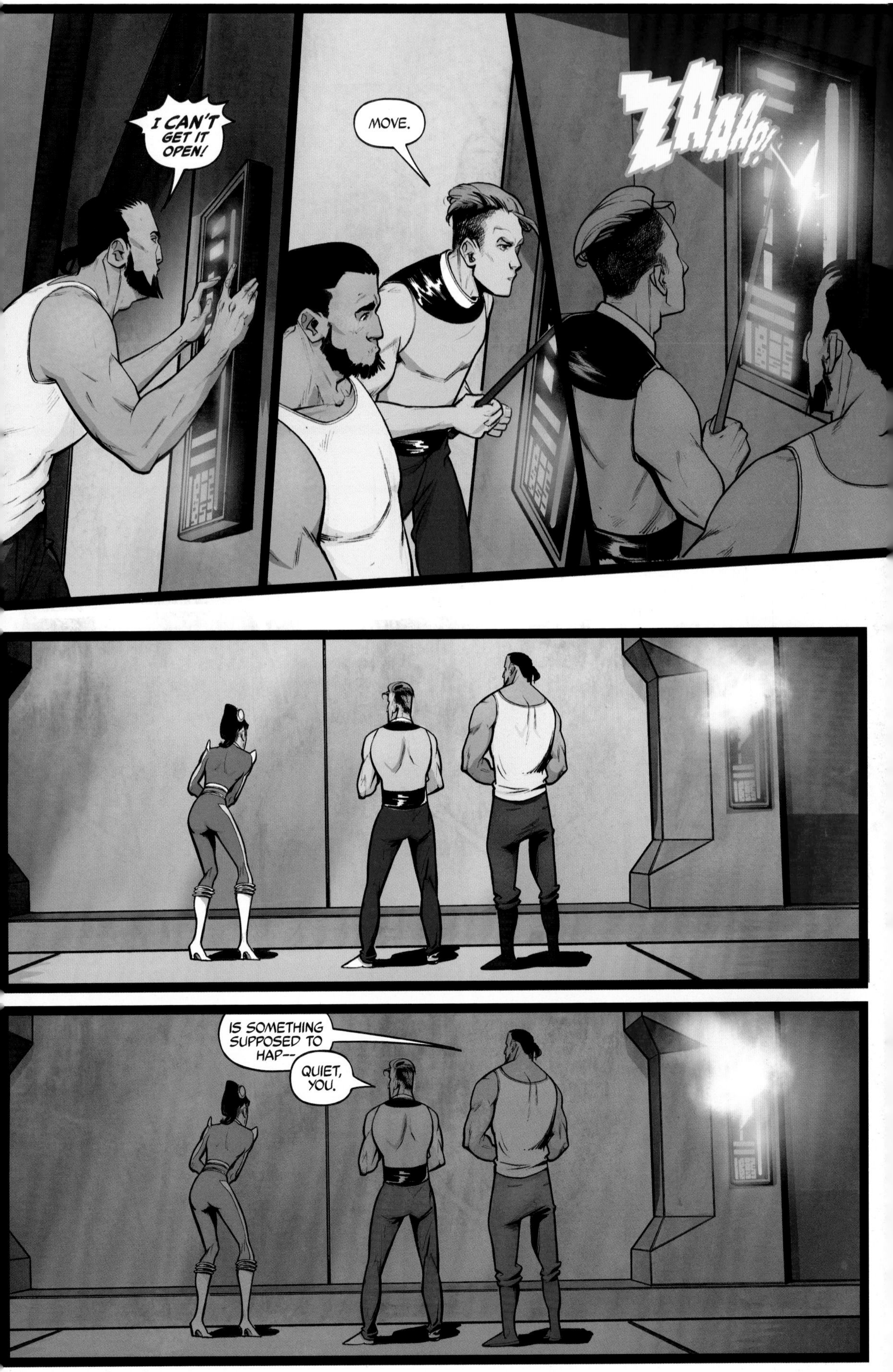
I CAN'T GET IT OPEN!
MOVE.
ZAAAP!
IS SOMETHING SUPPOSED TO HAP--
QUIET, YOU.

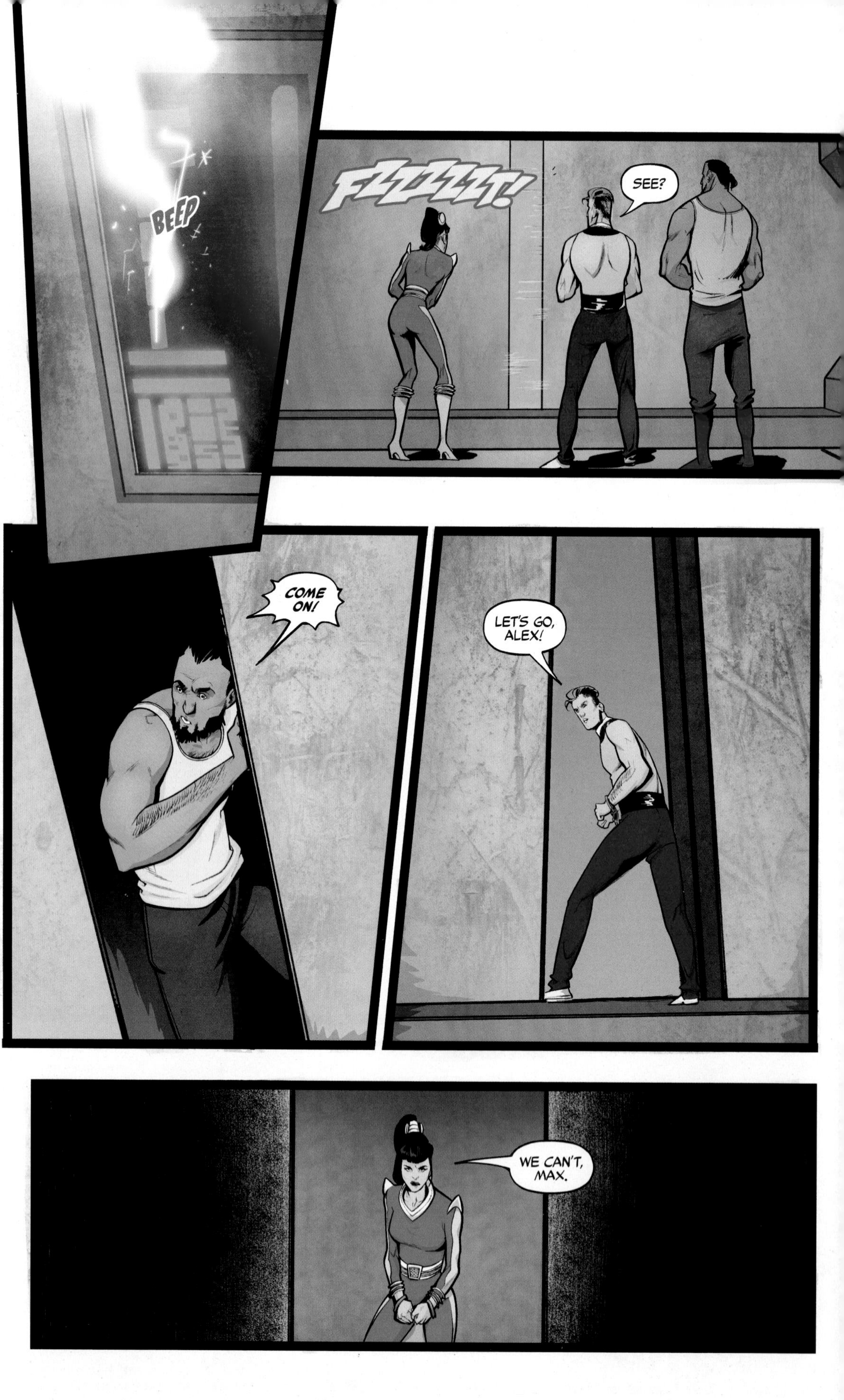
BEEP
FZZZZZT!
SEE?
COME ON!
LET'S GO, ALEX!
WE CAN'T, MAX.

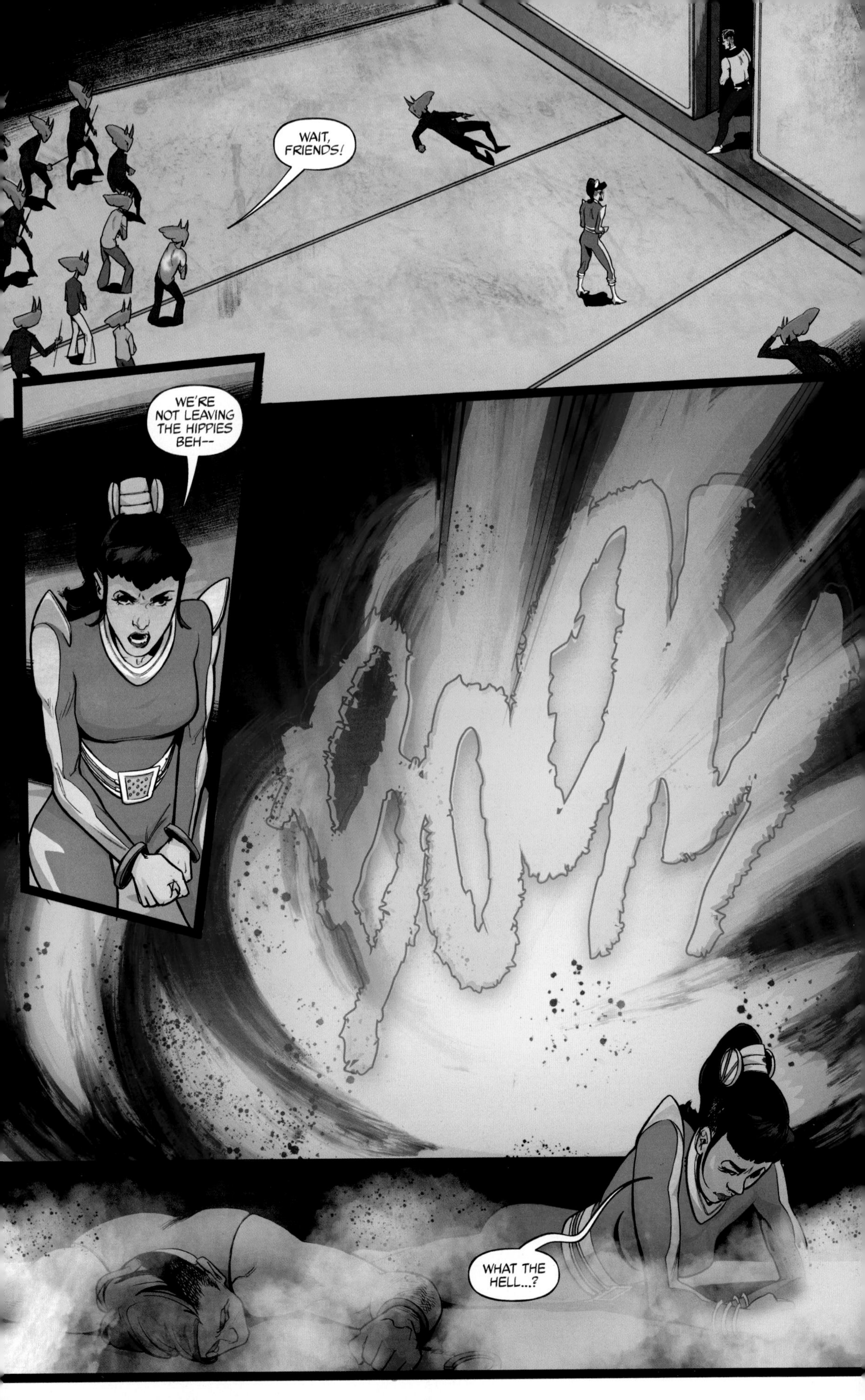
WAIT, FRIENDS!
WE'RE NOT LEAVING THE HIPPIES BEH--
WHAT THE HELL...?

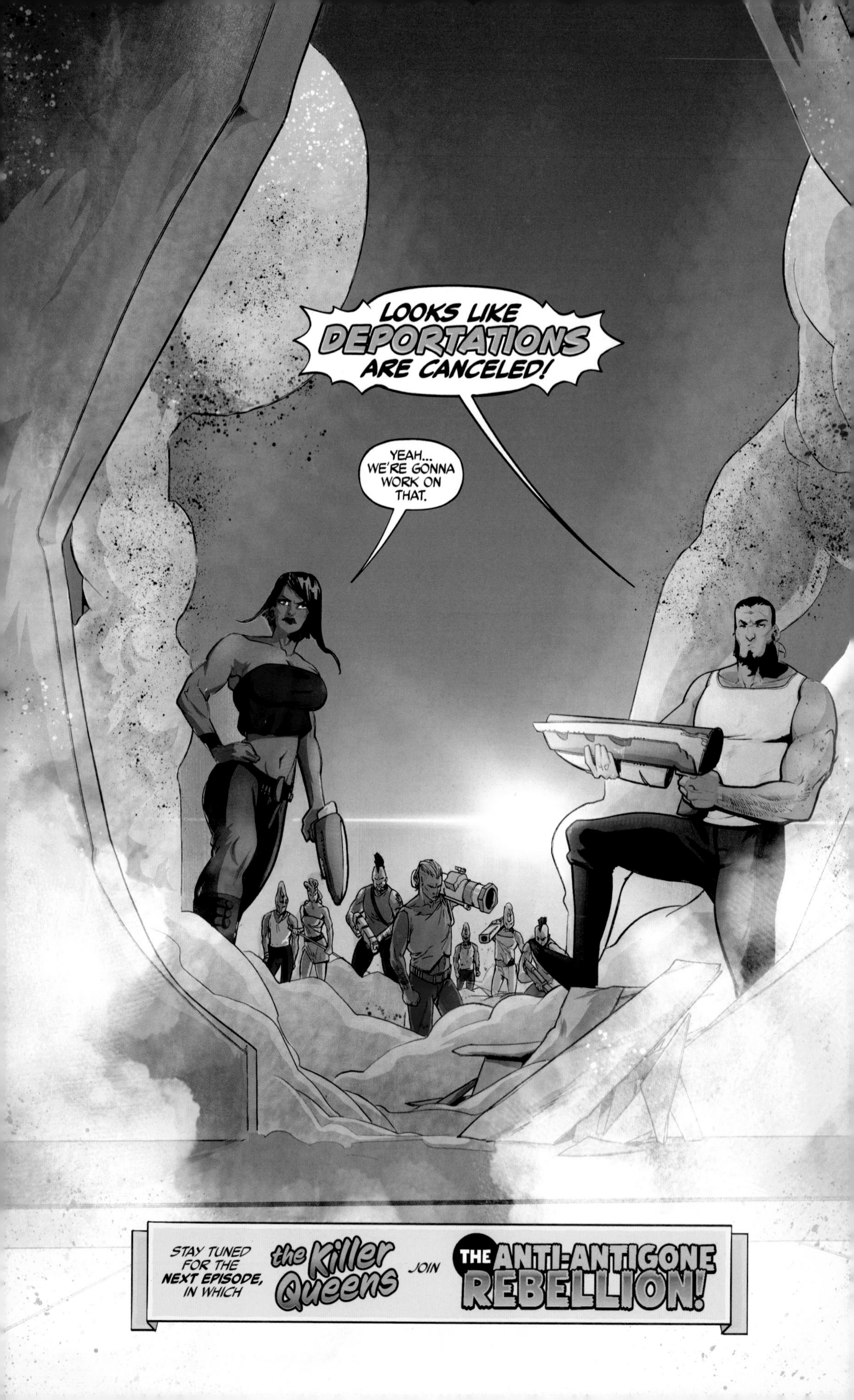
LOOKS LIKE DEPORTATIONS ARE CANCELED!
YEAH... WE'RE GONNA WORK ON THAT.
STAY TUNED FOR THE NEXT EPISODE, IN WHICH the Killer Queens JOIN THE ANTI-ANTIGONE REBELLION!

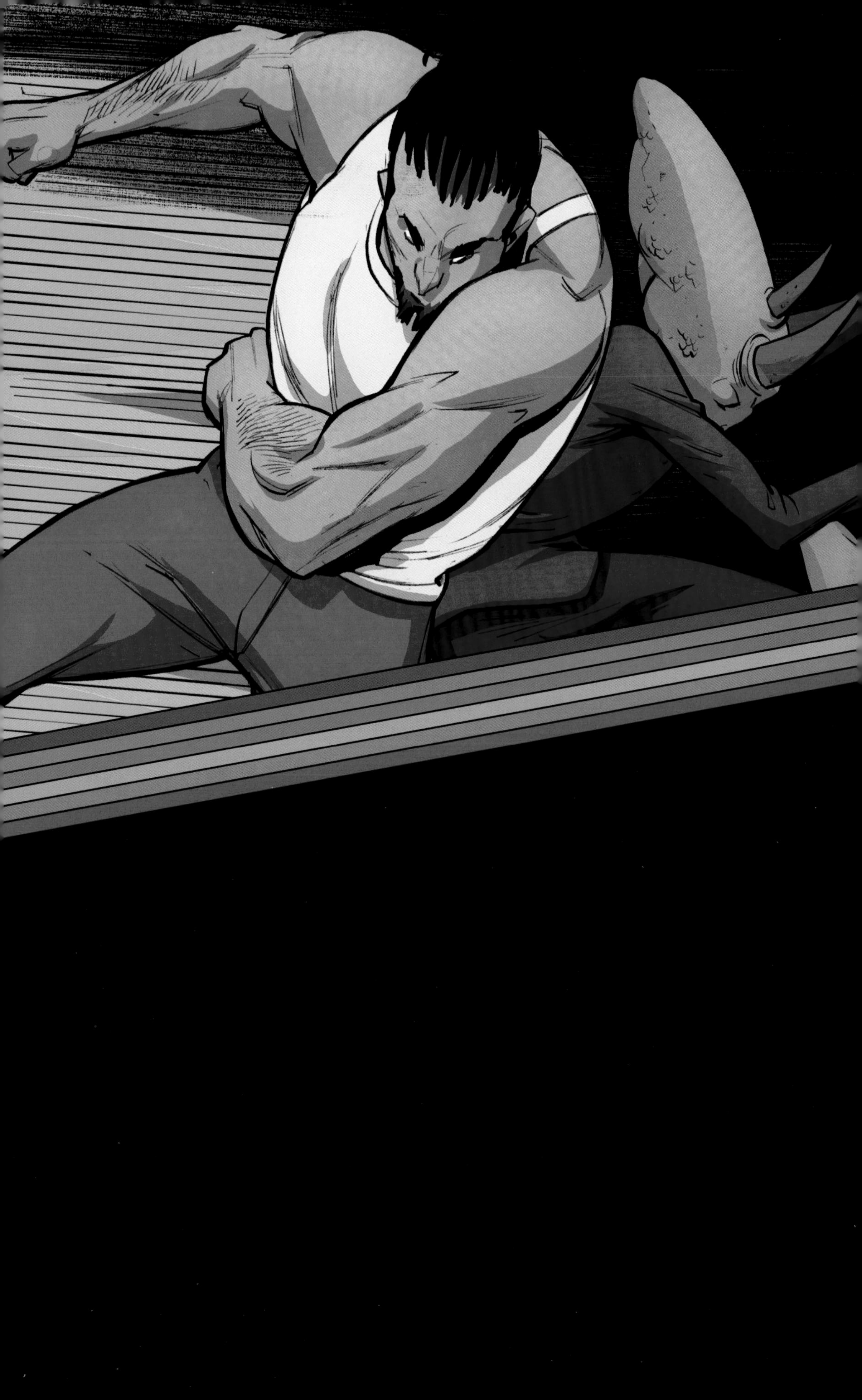

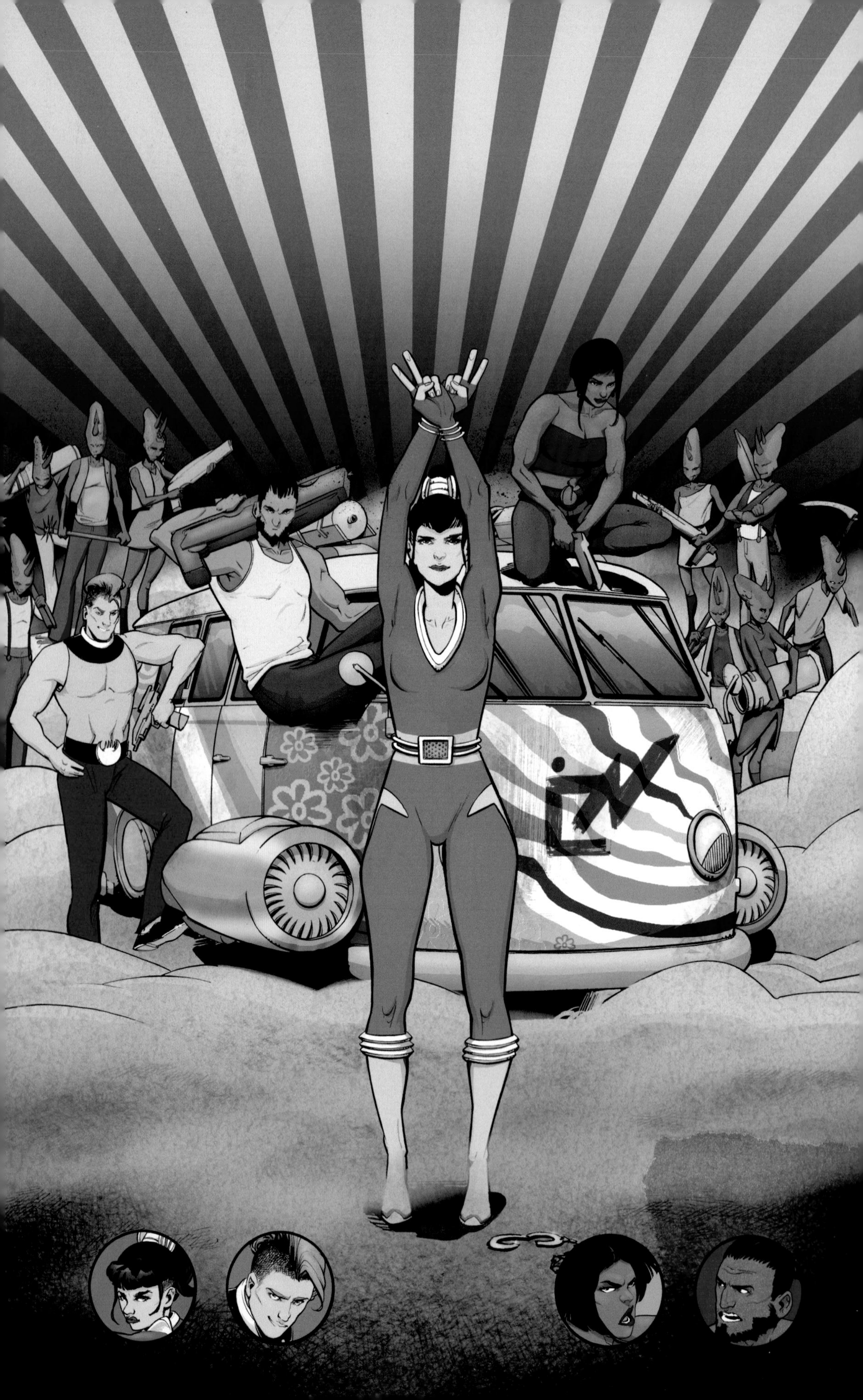

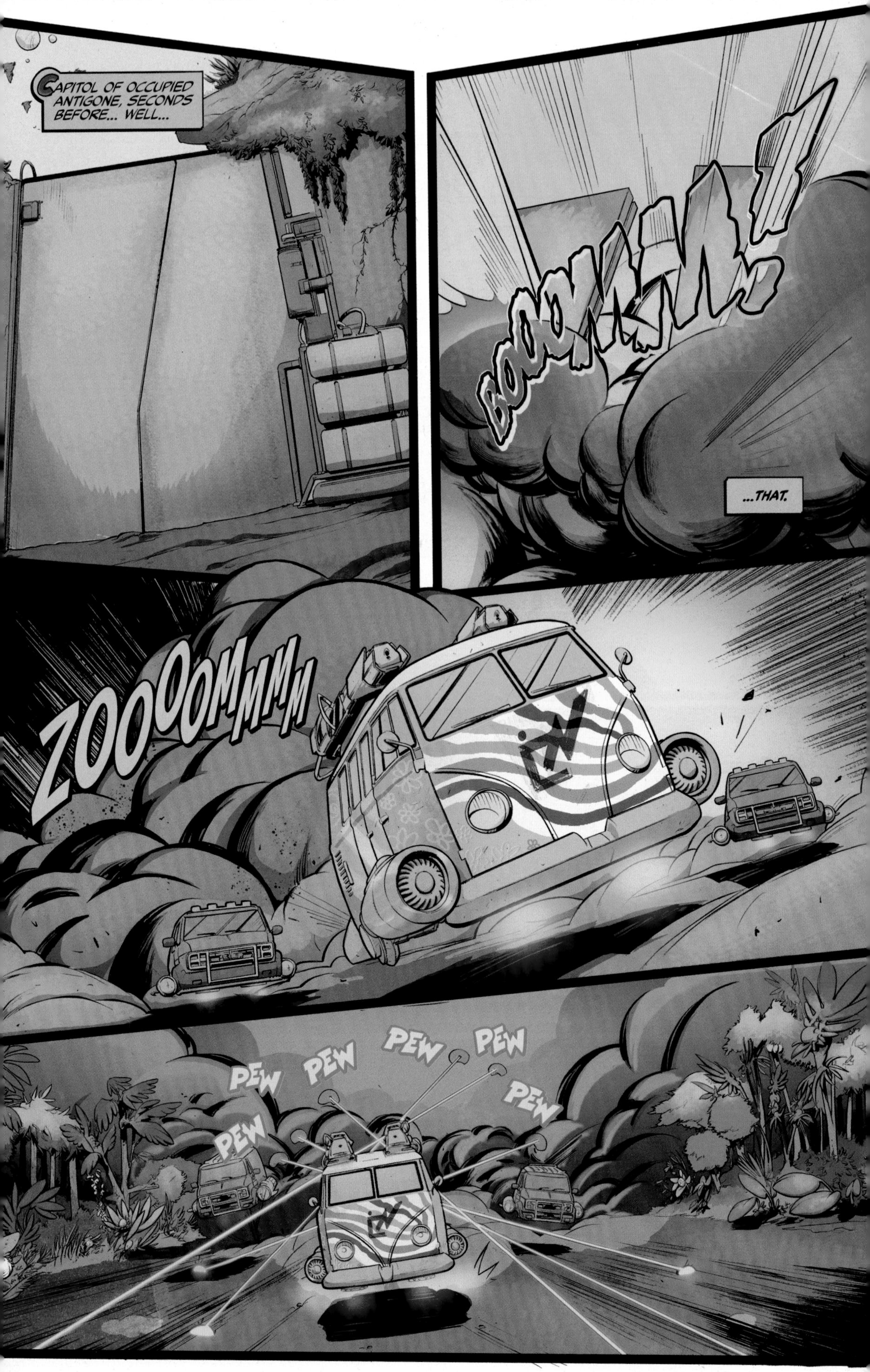
CAPITOL OF OCCUPIED ANTIGONE, SECONDS BEFORE... WELL...
BOOOOOM!
...THAT.
ZOOOOOMMMM
PEW
PEW
PEW
PEW
PEW
PEW

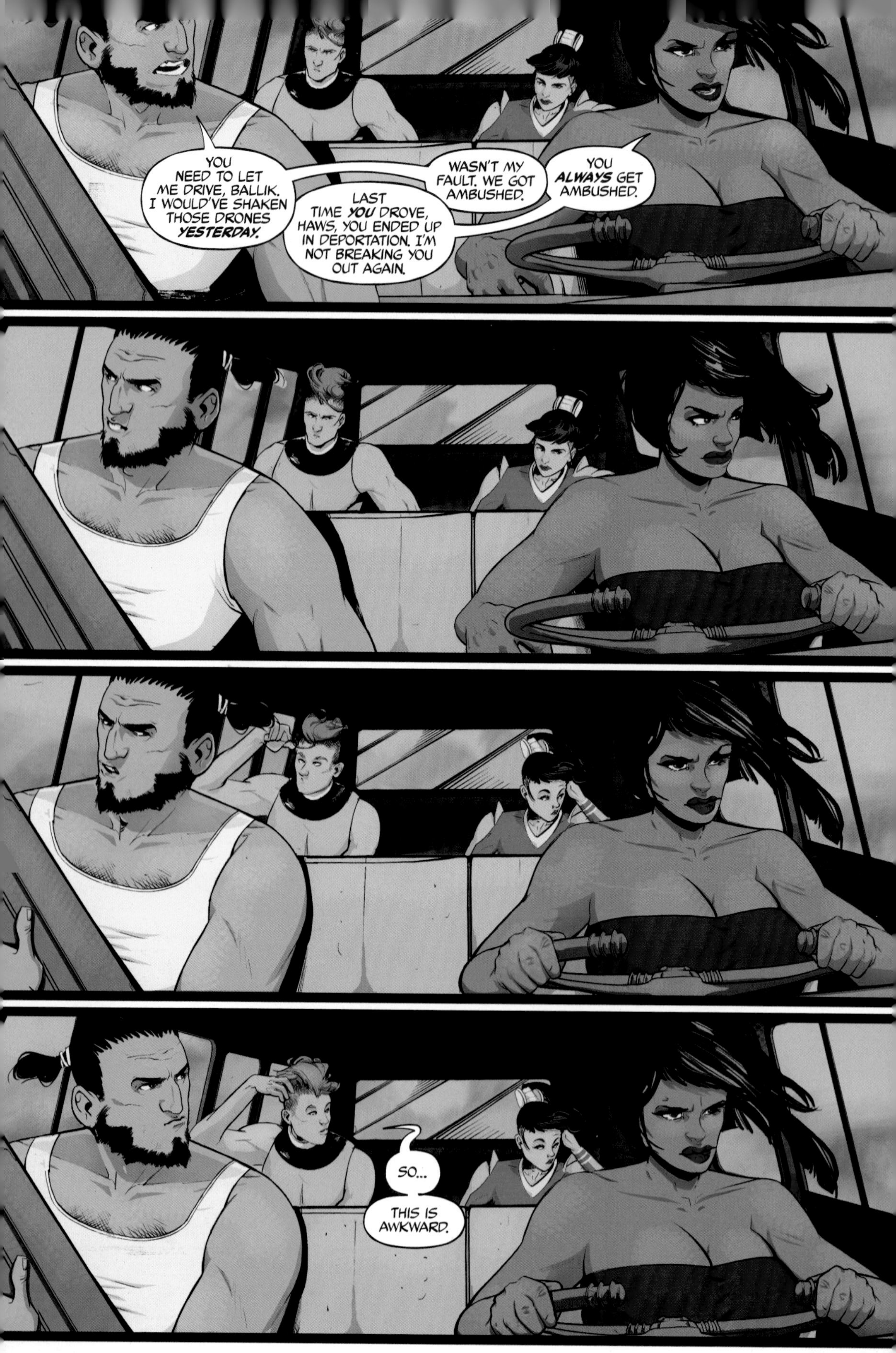
YOU NEED TO LET ME DRIVE, BALLIK. I WOULD'VE SHAKEN THOSE DRONES YESTERDAY.
LAST TIME YOU DROVE, HAWS, YOU ENDED UP IN DEPORTATION. I'M NOT BREAKING YOU OUT AGAIN.
WASN'T MY FAULT. WE GOT AMBUSHED.
YOU ALWAYS GET AMBUSHED.
SO...
THIS IS AWKWARD.

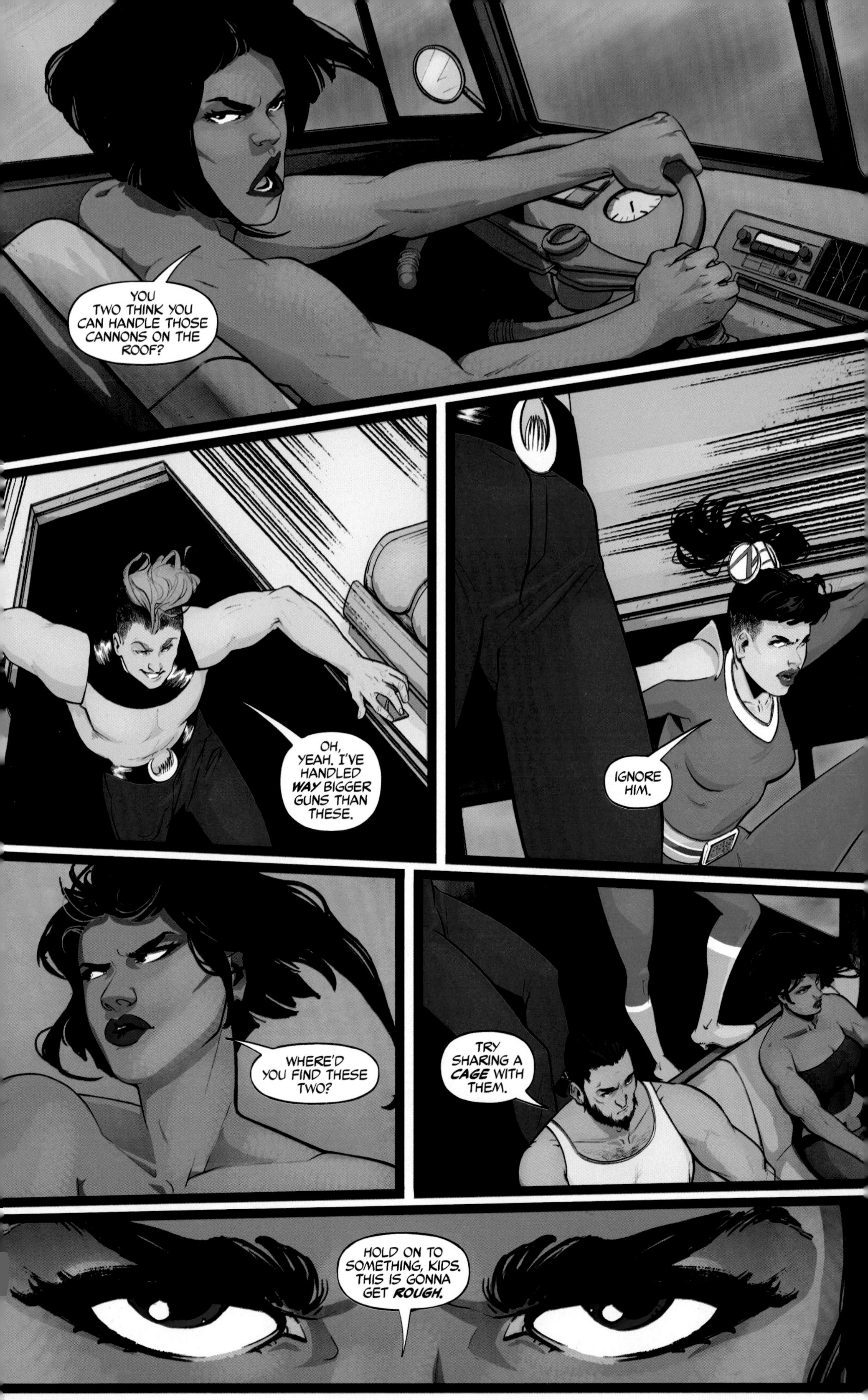
YOU TWO THINK YOU CAN HANDLE THOSE CANNONS ON THE ROOF?
OH, YEAH. I'VE HANDLED WAY BIGGER GUNS THAN THESE.
IGNORE HIM.
WHERE'D YOU FIND THESE TWO?
TRY SHARING A CAGE WITH THEM.
HOLD ON TO SOMETHING, KIDS. THIS IS GONNA GET ROUGH.

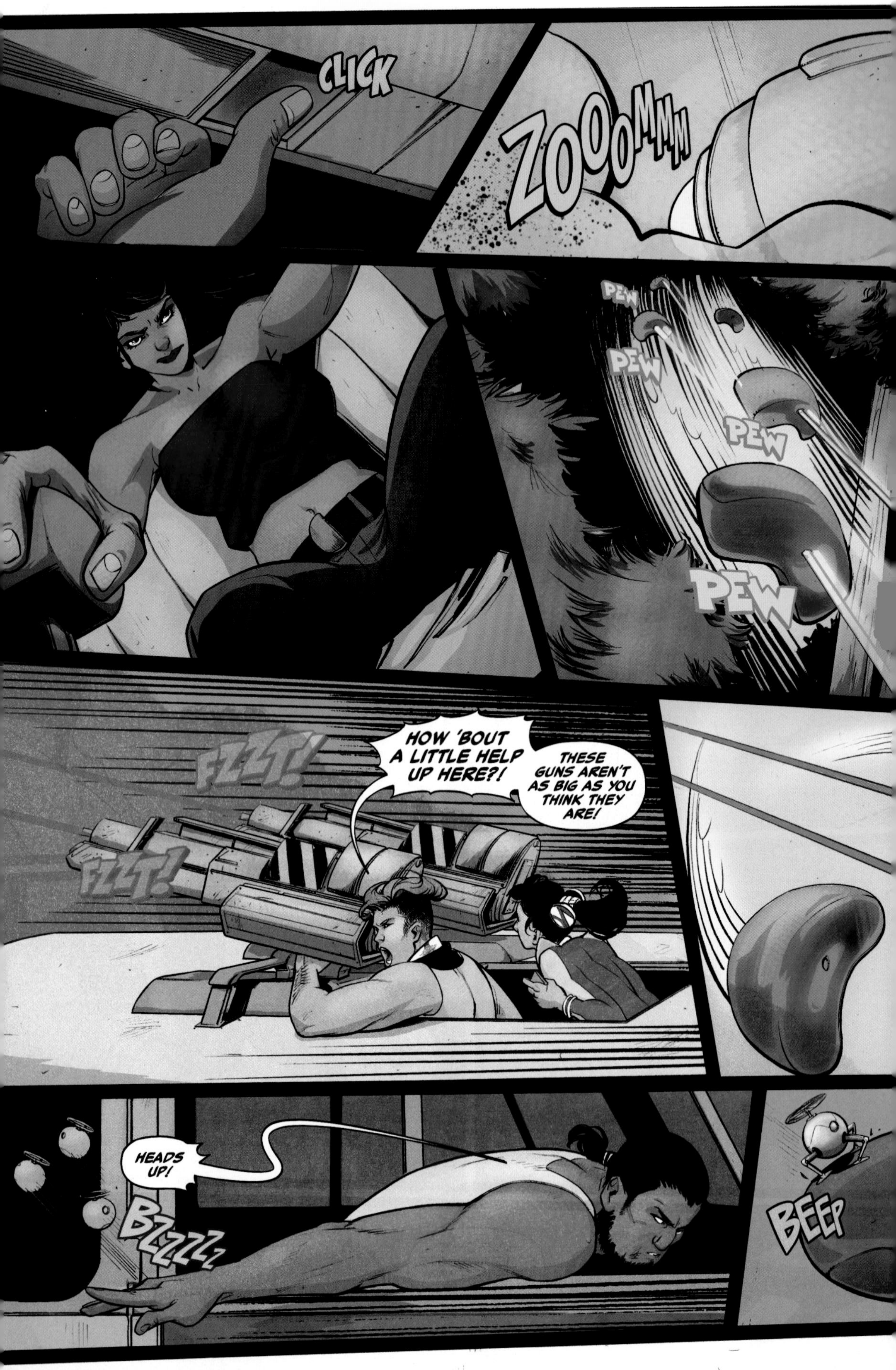
CLICK
ZOOOMMMM
PEW
PEW
PEW
PEW
FZZT!
FZZT!
HOW 'BOUT A LITTLE HELP UP HERE?!
THESE GUNS AREN'T AS BIG AS YOU THINK THEY ARE!
HEADS UP!
BZZZZZ
BEEP

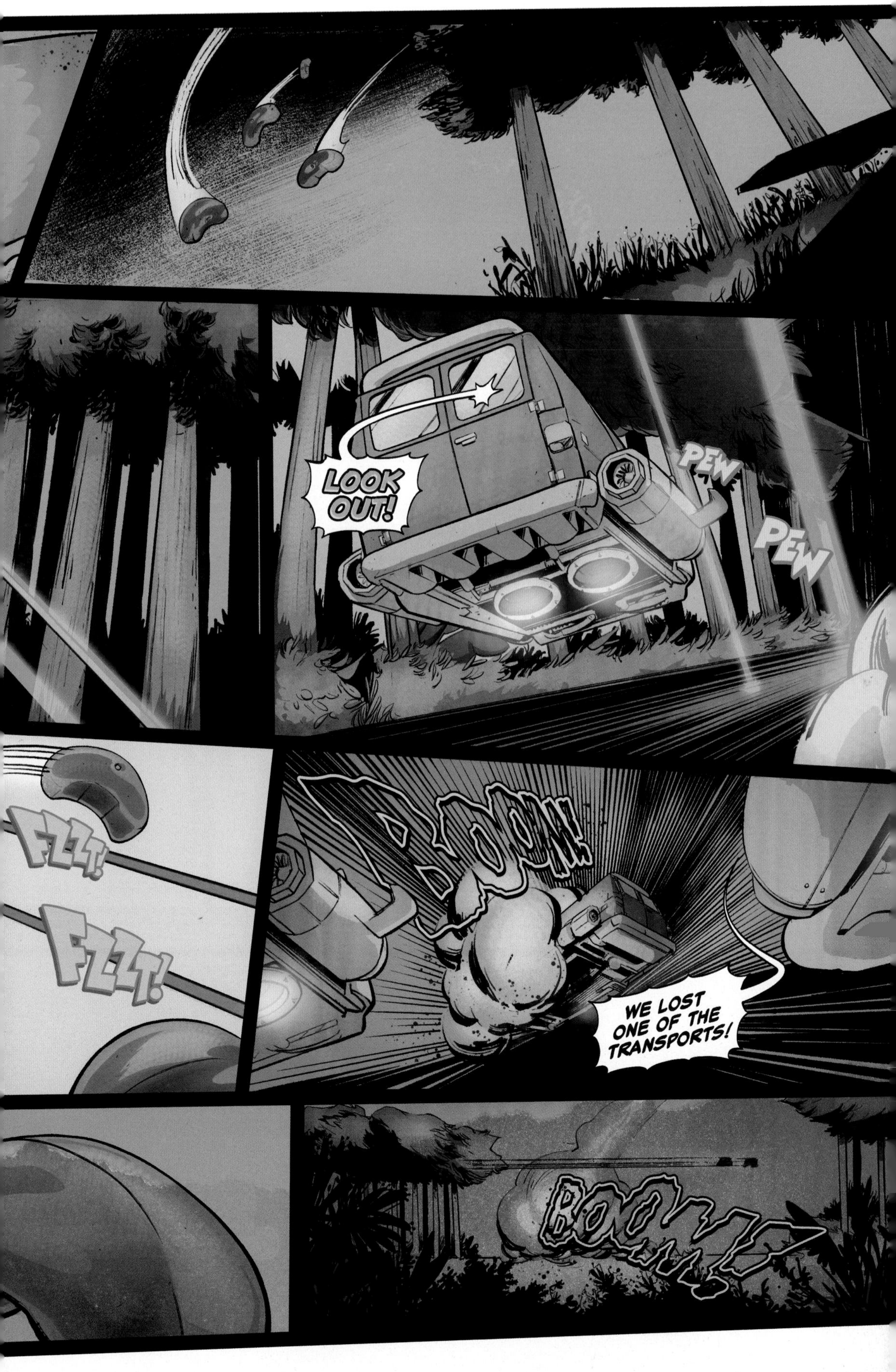
LOOK OUT!
PEW
PEW
FZZT!
FZZT!
BOOOM!
WE LOST ONE OF THE TRANSPORTS!
BOOOM!

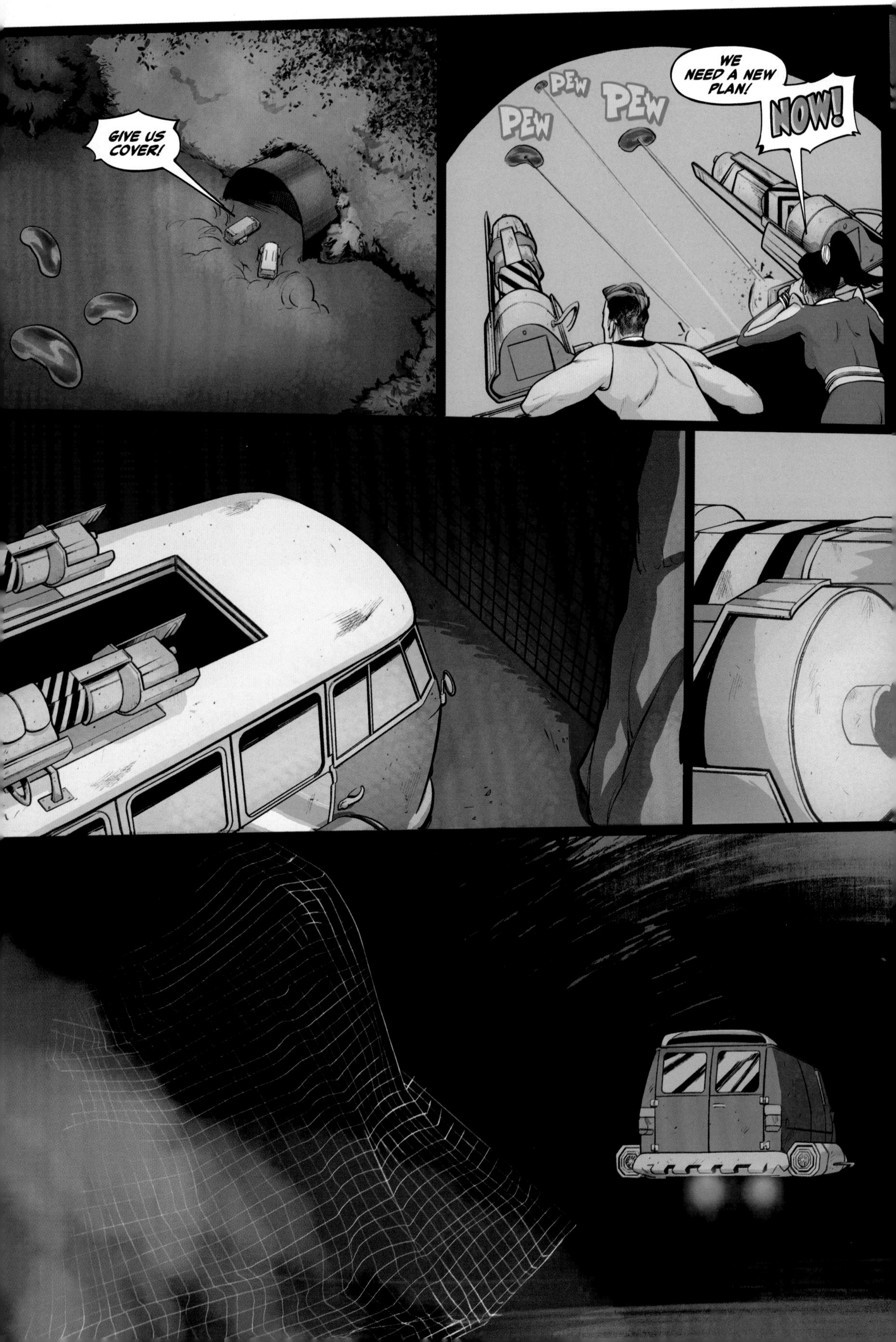
GIVE US COVER!
PEW
PEW
PEW
WE NEED A NEW PLAN!
NOW!

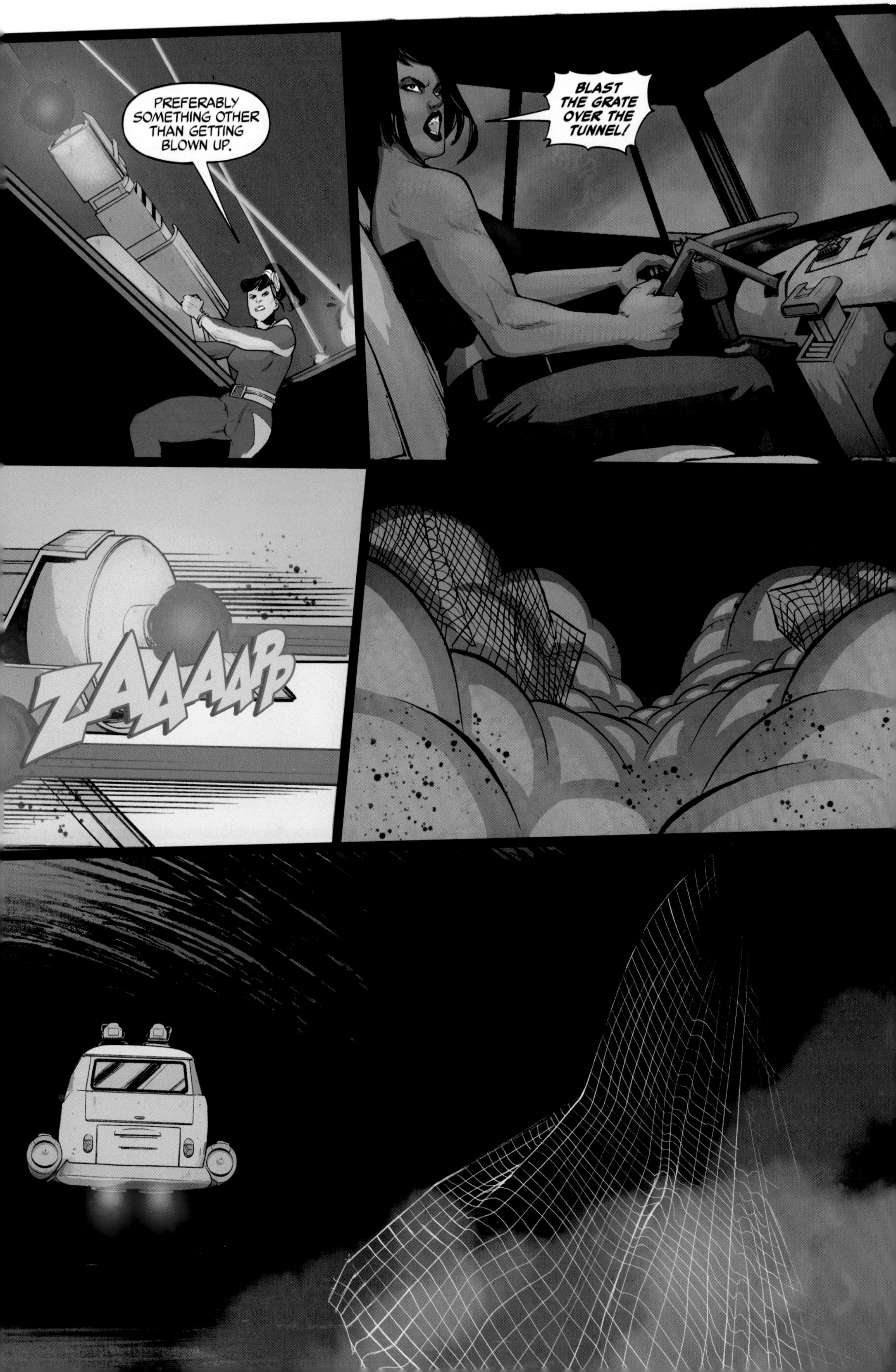
PREFERABLY SOMETHING OTHER THAN GETTING BLOWN UP.
BLAST THE GRATE OVER THE TUNNEL!
ZAAAAP

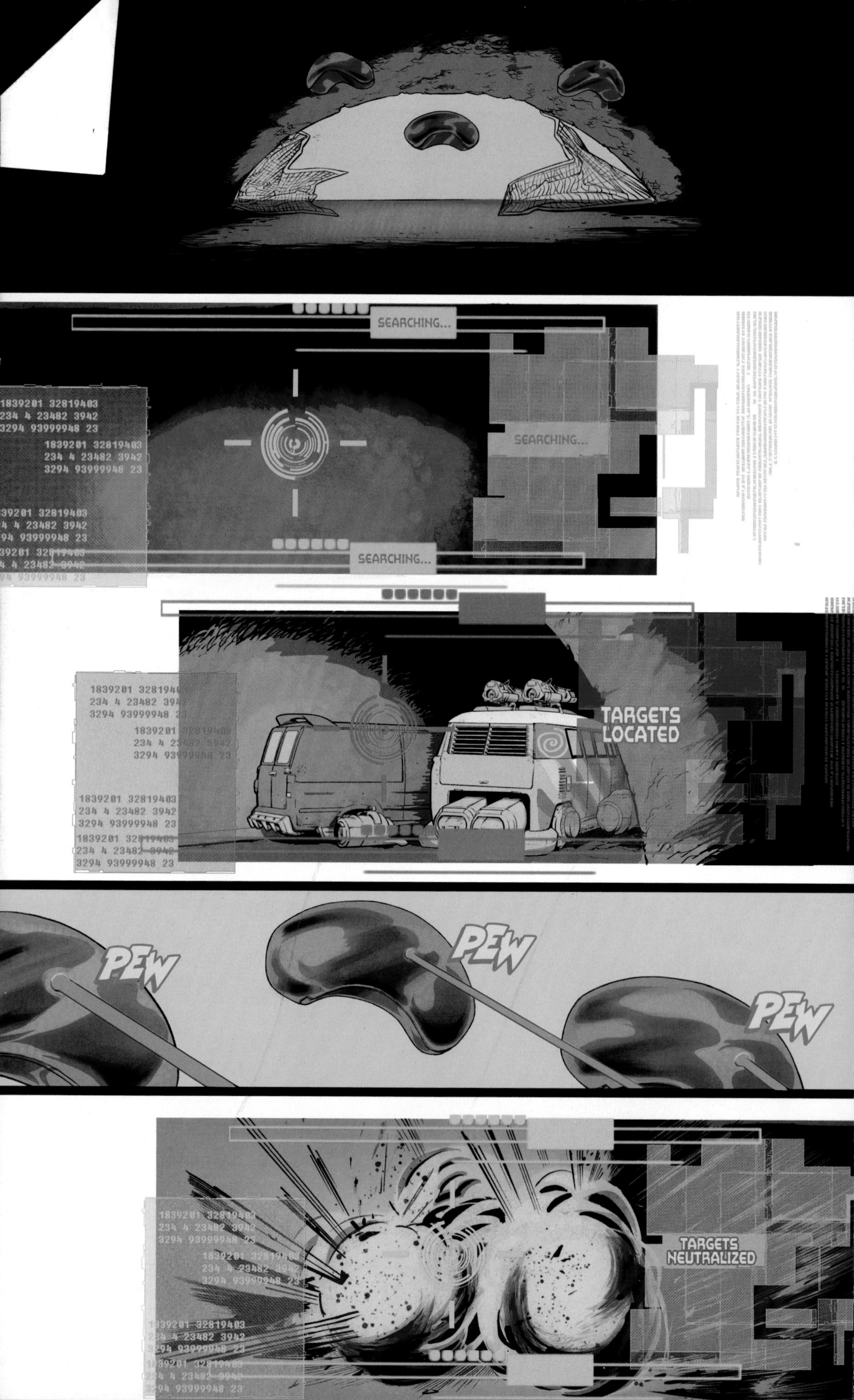

SEARCHING...
SEARCHING...
SEARCHING...
TARGETS LOCATED
PEW
PEW
PEW
TARGETS NEUTRALIZED

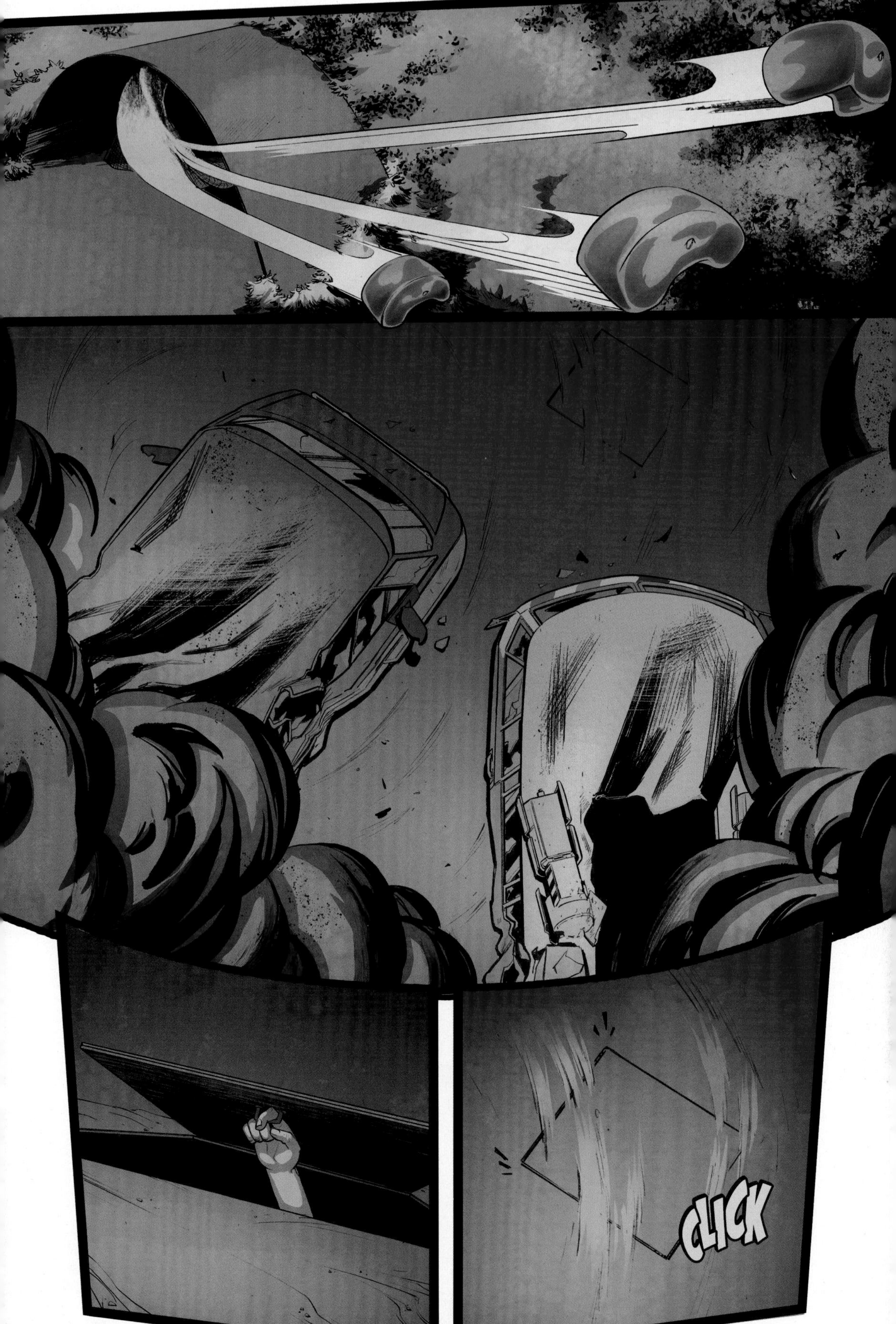
CLICK

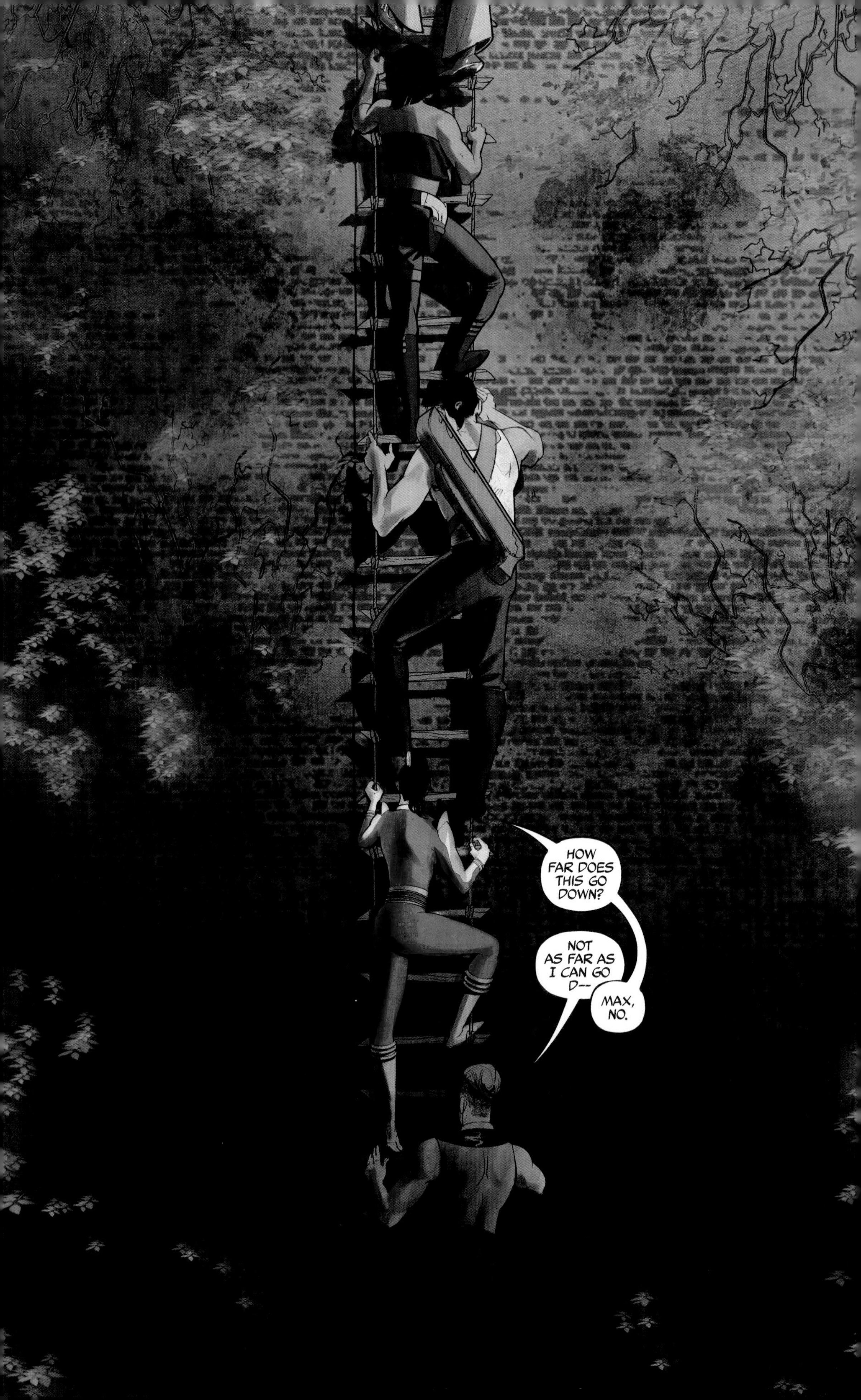
HOW FAR DOES THIS GO DOWN?
NOT AS FAR AS I CAN GO D--
MAX, NO.

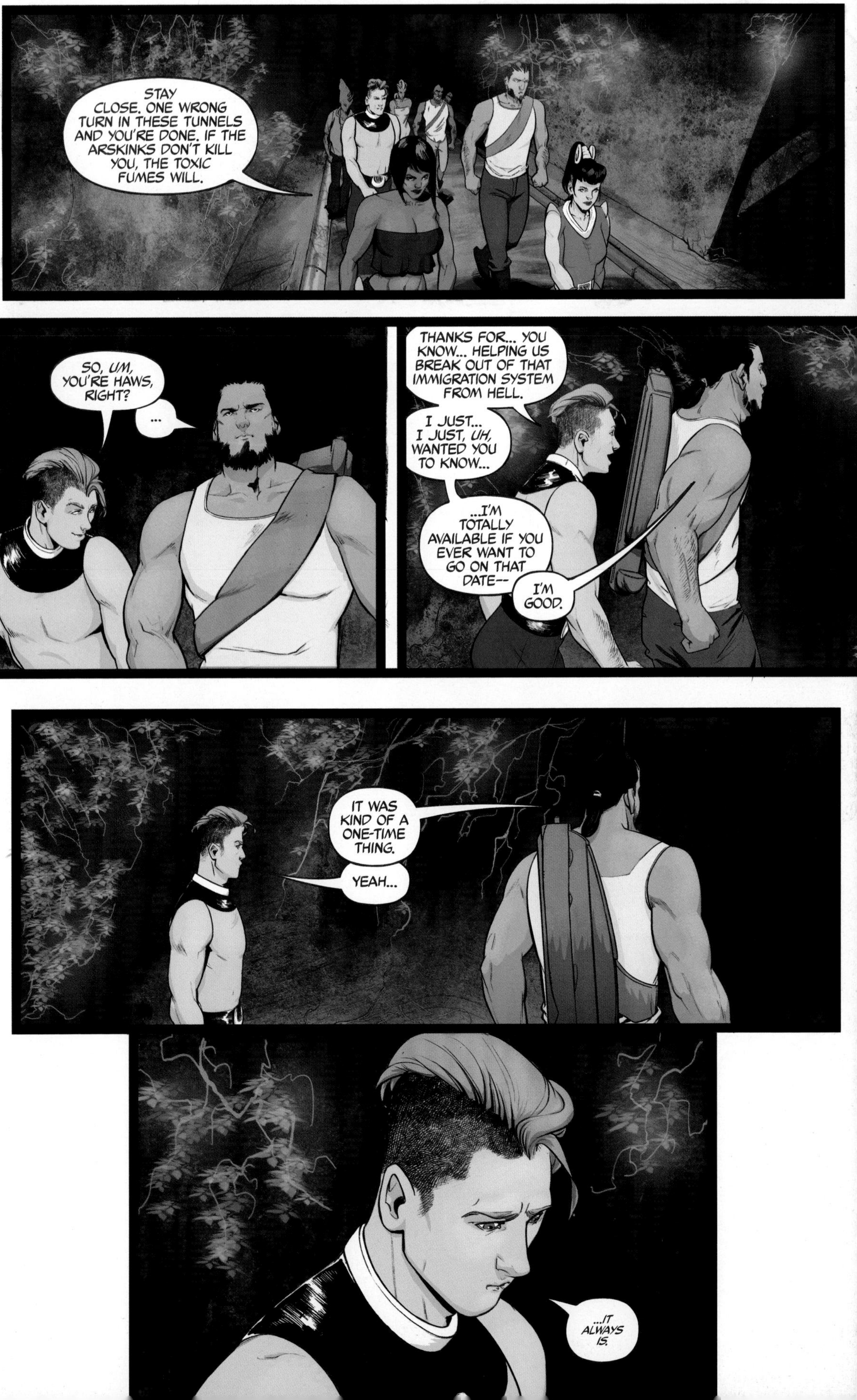
STAY CLOSE. ONE WRONG TURN IN THESE TUNNELS AND YOU'RE DONE. IF THE ARSKINKS DON'T KILL YOU, THE TOXIC FUMES WILL.
SO, *UM*, YOU'RE HAWS, RIGHT?
...
THANKS FOR... YOU KNOW... HELPING US BREAK OUT OF THAT IMMIGRATION SYSTEM FROM HELL.
I JUST... I JUST, *UH*, WANTED YOU TO KNOW...
...I'M TOTALLY AVAILABLE IF YOU EVER WANT TO GO ON THAT DATE--
I'M GOOD.
IT WAS KIND OF A ONE-TIME THING.
YEAH...
...IT ALWAYS IS.

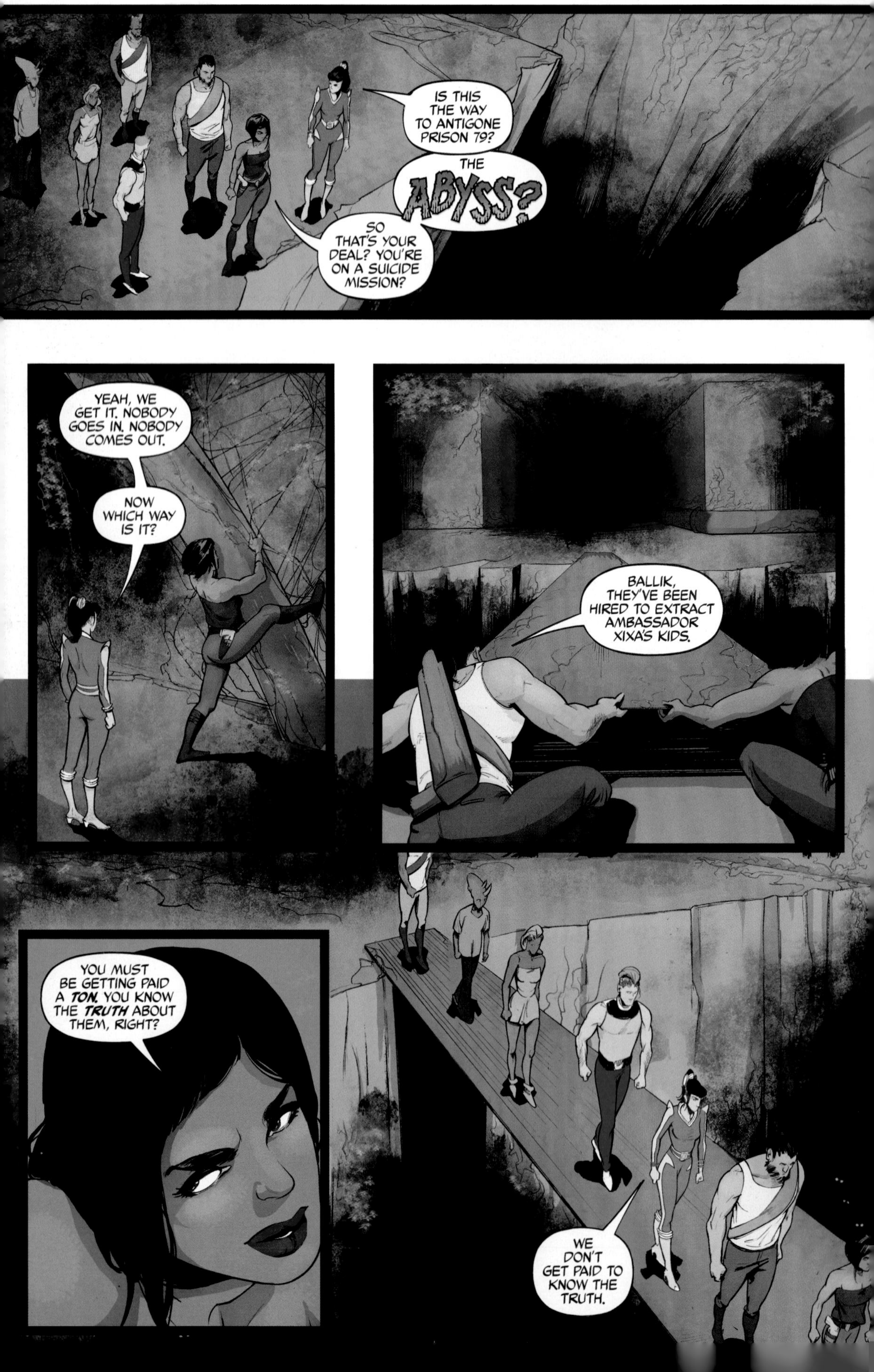
IS THIS THE WAY TO ANTIGONE PRISON 79?
THE ABYSS?
SO THAT'S YOUR DEAL? YOU'RE ON A SUICIDE MISSION?
YEAH, WE GET IT. NOBODY GOES IN. NOBODY COMES OUT.
NOW WHICH WAY IS IT?
BALLIK, THEY'VE BEEN HIRED TO EXTRACT AMBASSADOR XIXA'S KIDS.
YOU MUST BE GETTING PAID A TON. YOU KNOW THE TRUTH ABOUT THEM, RIGHT?
WE DON'T GET PAID TO KNOW THE TRUTH.

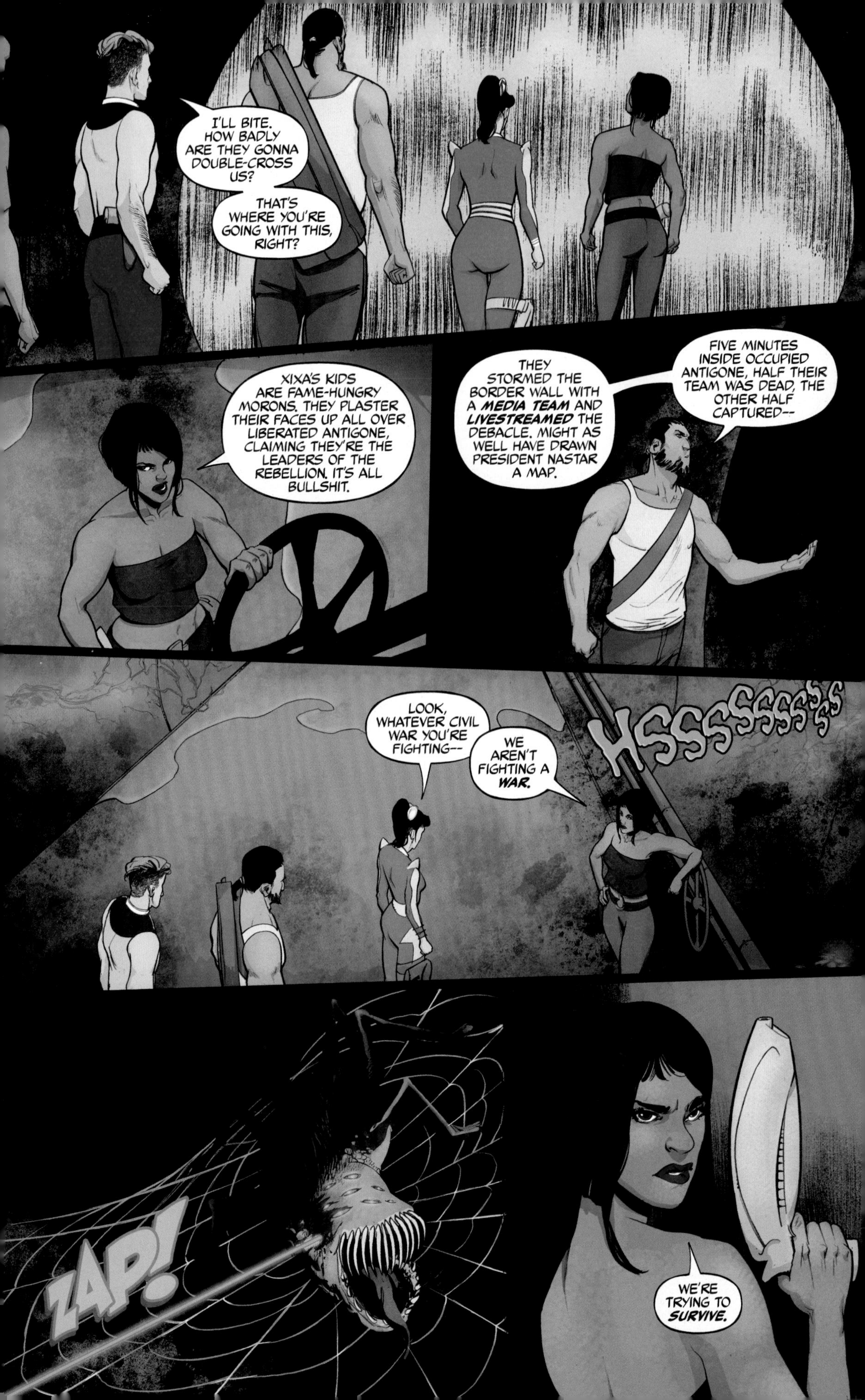

I'LL BITE. HOW BADLY ARE THEY GONNA DOUBLE-CROSS US?
THAT'S WHERE YOU'RE GOING WITH THIS, RIGHT?
XIXA'S KIDS ARE FAME-HUNGRY MORONS. THEY PLASTER THEIR FACES UP ALL OVER LIBERATED ANTIGONE, CLAIMING THEY'RE THE LEADERS OF THE REBELLION. IT'S ALL BULLSHIT.
THEY STORMED THE BORDER WALL WITH A ***MEDIA TEAM*** AND ***LIVESTREAMED*** THE DEBACLE. MIGHT AS WELL HAVE DRAWN PRESIDENT NASTAR A MAP.
FIVE MINUTES INSIDE OCCUPIED ANTIGONE, HALF THEIR TEAM WAS DEAD, THE OTHER HALF CAPTURED--
LOOK, WHATEVER CIVIL WAR YOU'RE FIGHTING--
WE AREN'T FIGHTING A ***WAR.***
HSSSSSSSSSS
ZAP!
WE'RE TRYING TO ***SURVIVE.***

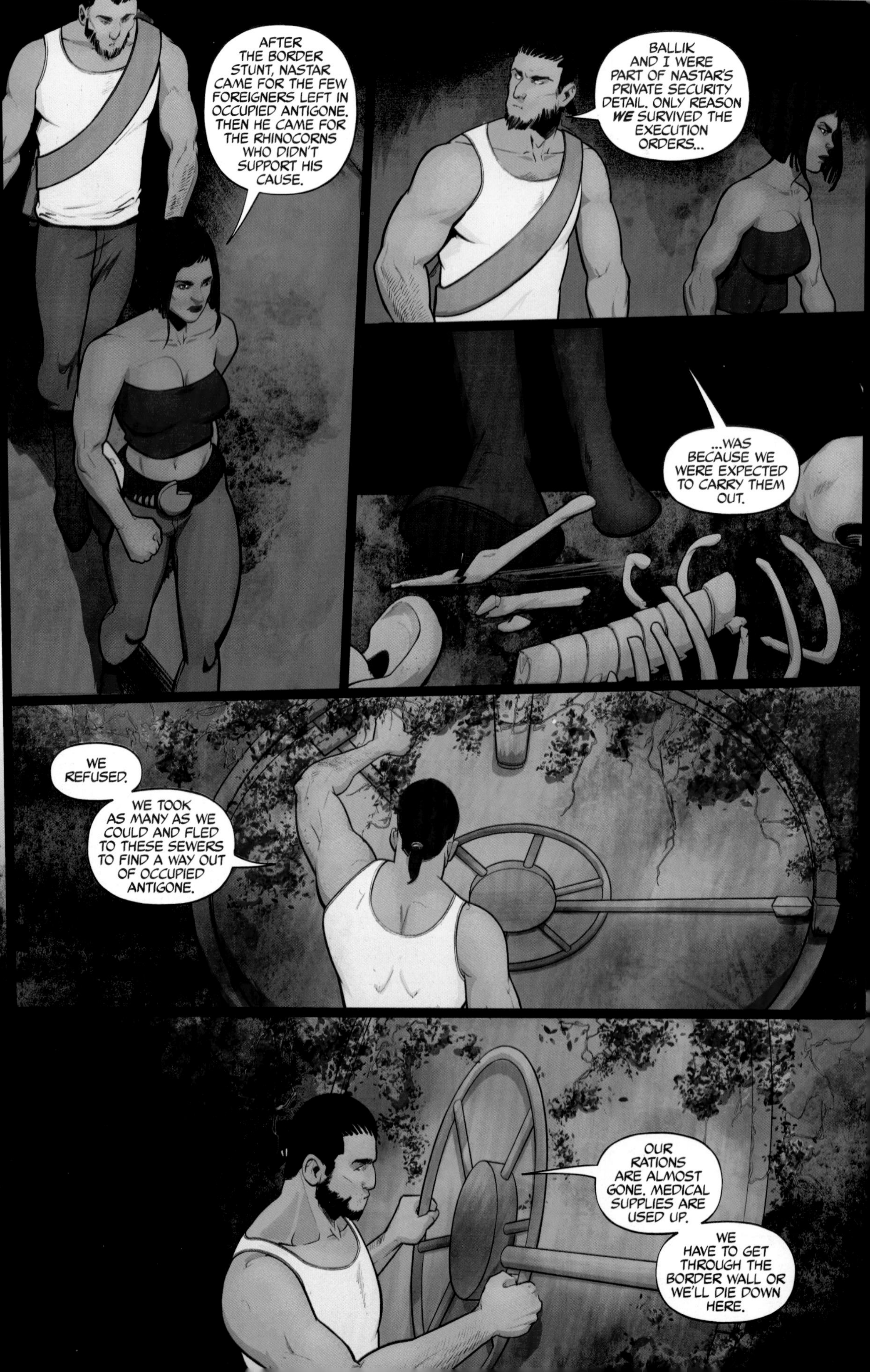
AFTER THE BORDER STUNT, NASTAR CAME FOR THE FEW FOREIGNERS LEFT IN OCCUPIED ANTIGONE. THEN HE CAME FOR THE RHINOCORNS WHO DIDN'T SUPPORT HIS CAUSE.
BALLIK AND I WERE PART OF NASTAR'S PRIVATE SECURITY DETAIL. ONLY REASON *WE* SURVIVED THE EXECUTION ORDERS...
...WAS BECAUSE WE WERE EXPECTED TO CARRY THEM OUT.
WE REFUSED.
WE TOOK AS MANY AS WE COULD AND FLED TO THESE SEWERS TO FIND A WAY OUT OF OCCUPIED ANTIGONE.
OUR RATIONS ARE ALMOST GONE. MEDICAL SUPPLIES ARE USED UP.
WE HAVE TO GET THROUGH THE BORDER WALL OR WE'LL DIE DOWN HERE.

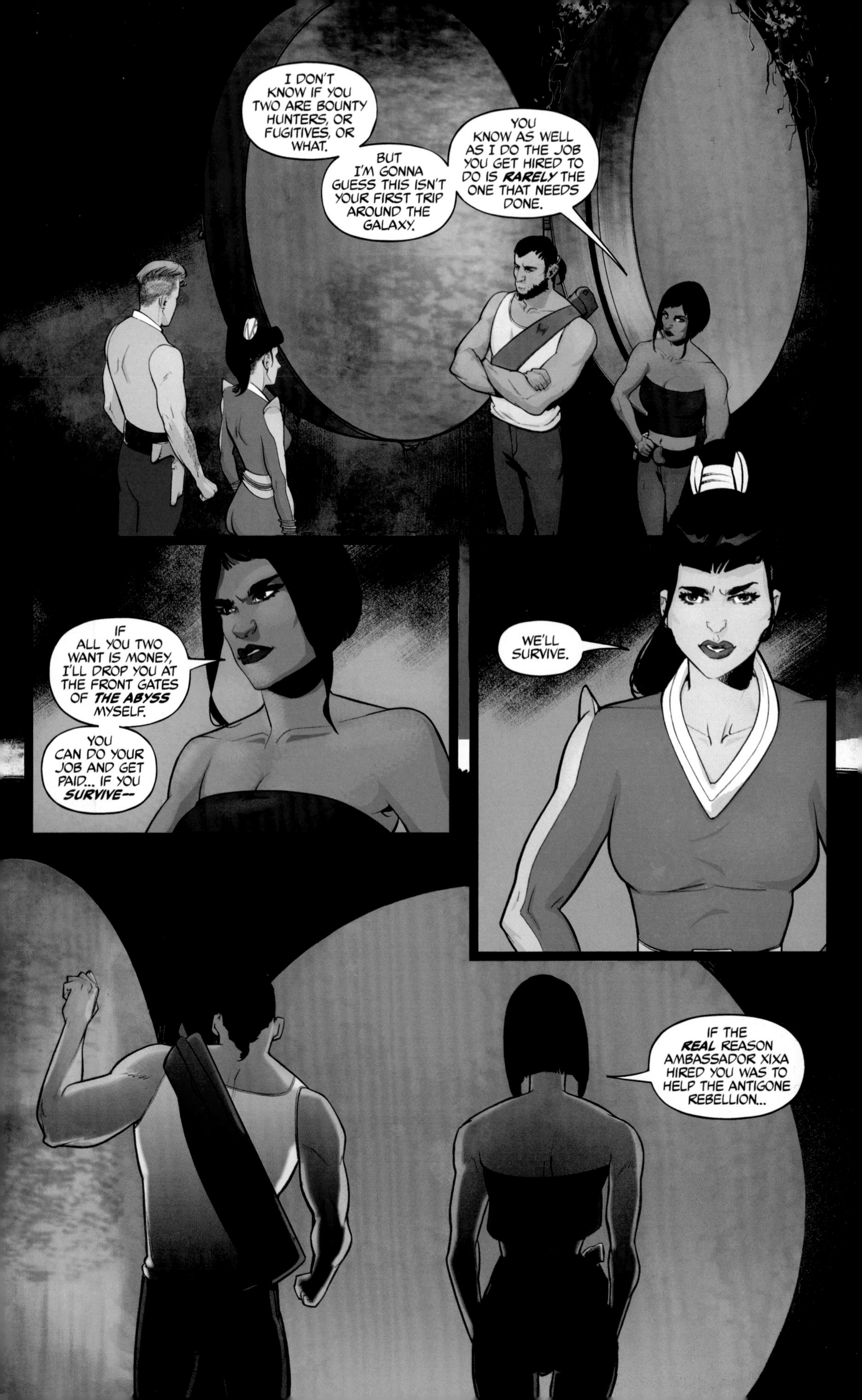
I DON'T KNOW IF YOU TWO ARE BOUNTY HUNTERS, OR FUGITIVES, OR WHAT.
BUT I'M GONNA GUESS THIS ISN'T YOUR FIRST TRIP AROUND THE GALAXY.
YOU KNOW AS WELL AS I DO THE JOB YOU GET HIRED TO DO IS RARELY THE ONE THAT NEEDS DONE.
IF ALL YOU TWO WANT IS MONEY, I'LL DROP YOU AT THE FRONT GATES OF THE ABYSS MYSELF.
YOU CAN DO YOUR JOB AND GET PAID... IF YOU SURVIVE--
WE'LL SURVIVE.
IF THE REAL REASON AMBASSADOR XIXA HIRED YOU WAS TO HELP THE ANTIGONE REBELLION...

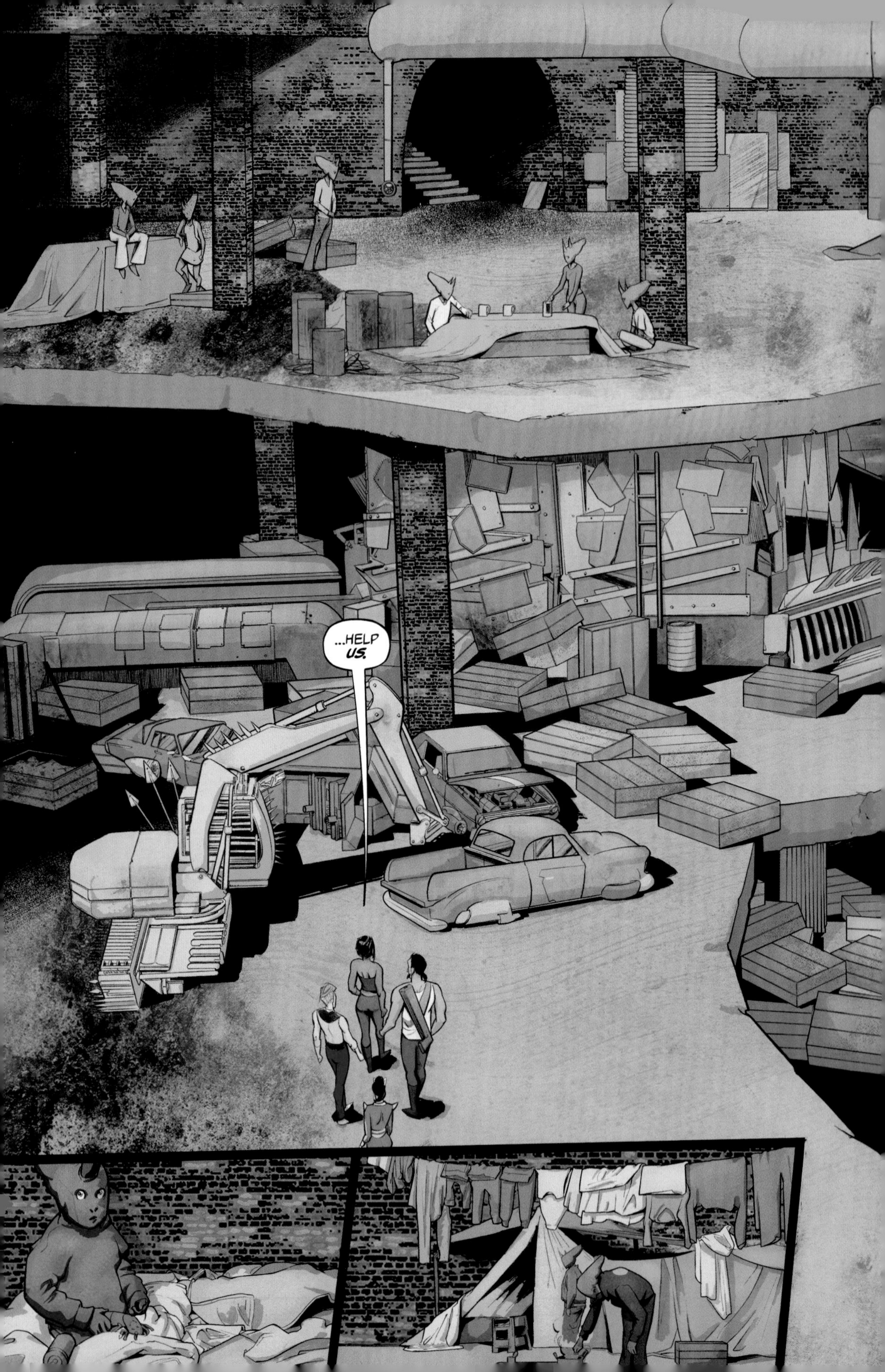
...HELP US.

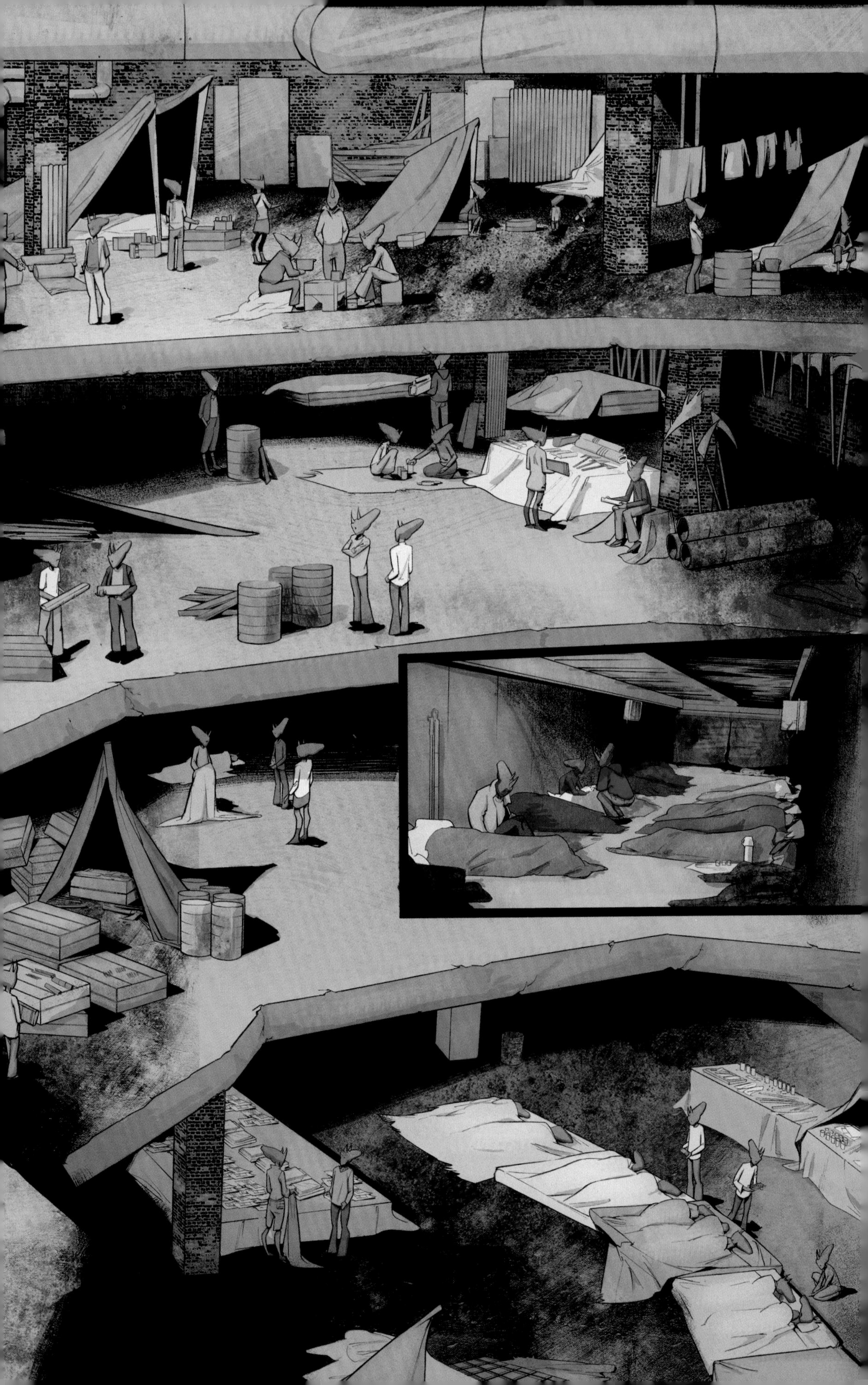

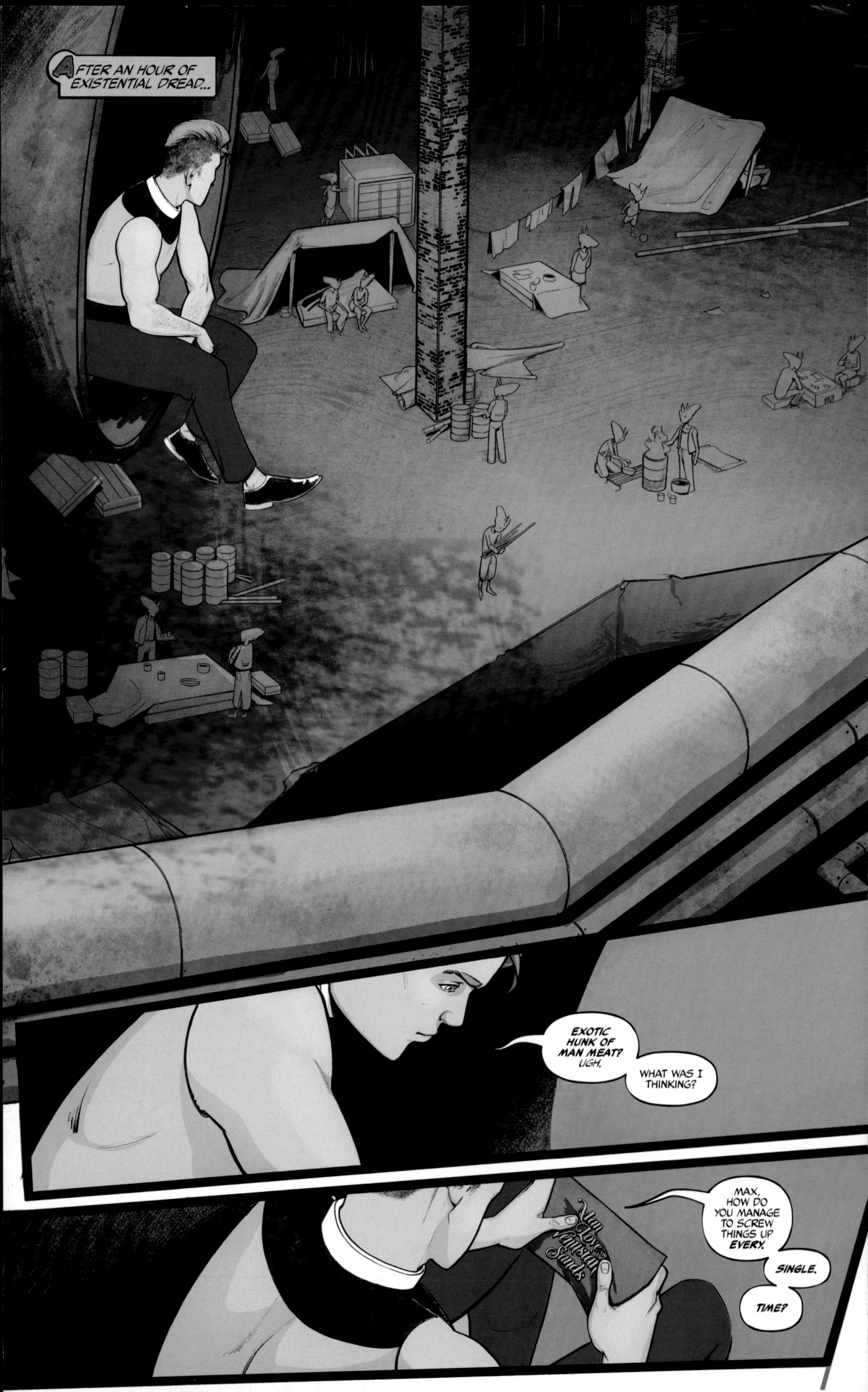

AFTER AN HOUR OF EXISTENTIAL DREAD...
EXOTIC HUNK OF MAN MEAT? UGH.
WHAT WAS I THINKING?
Man Love on the Venusian Sands
MAX, HOW DO YOU MANAGE TO SCREW THINGS UP EVERY.
SINGLE.
TIME?

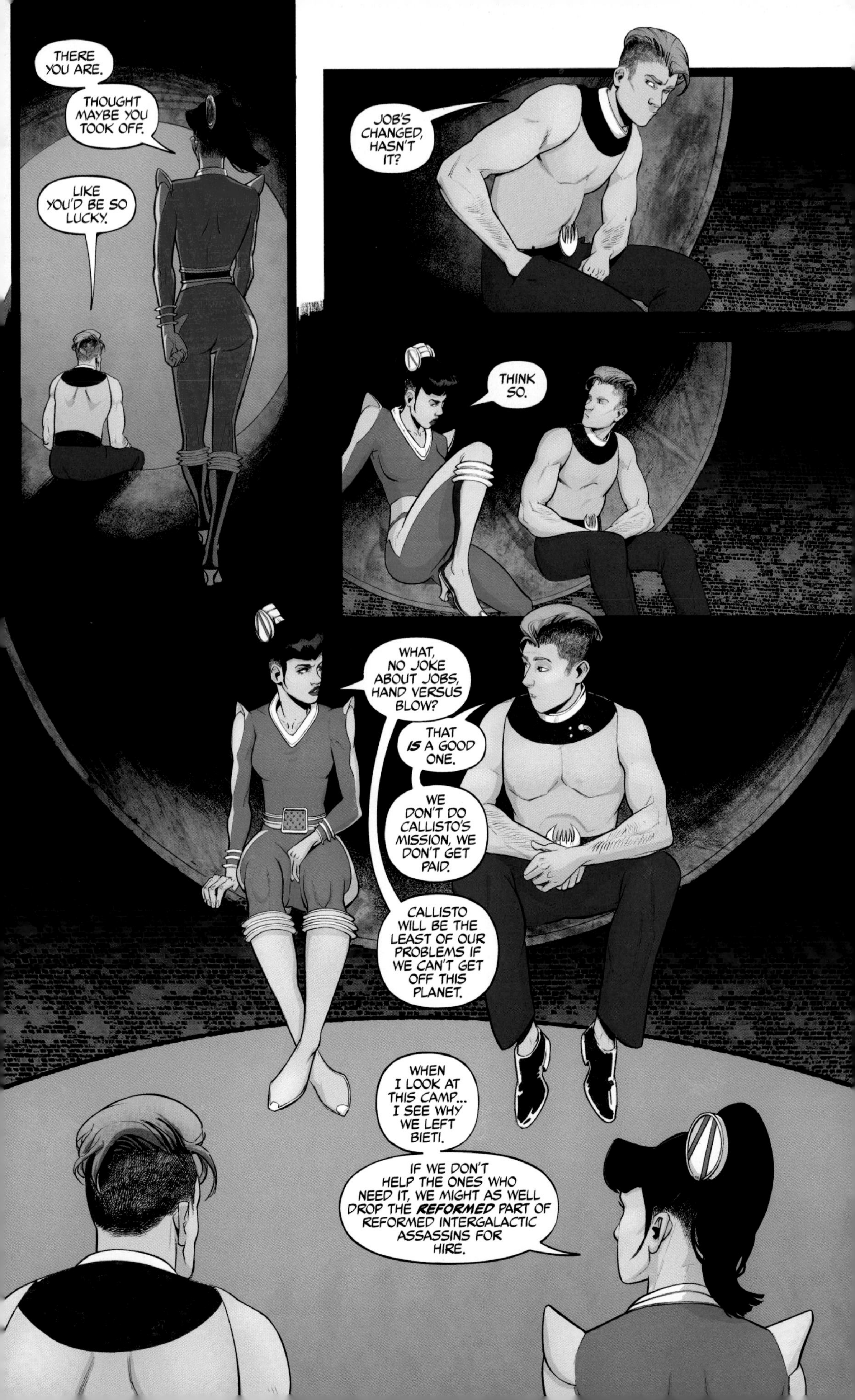
THERE YOU ARE.
THOUGHT MAYBE YOU TOOK OFF.
LIKE YOU'D BE SO LUCKY.
JOB'S CHANGED, HASN'T IT?
THINK SO.
WHAT, NO JOKE ABOUT JOBS, HAND VERSUS BLOW?
THAT *IS* A GOOD ONE.
WE DON'T DO CALLISTO'S MISSION, WE DON'T GET PAID.
CALLISTO WILL BE THE LEAST OF OUR PROBLEMS IF WE CAN'T GET OFF THIS PLANET.
WHEN I LOOK AT THIS CAMP... I SEE WHY WE LEFT BIETI.
IF WE DON'T HELP THE ONES WHO NEED IT, WE MIGHT AS WELL DROP THE ***REFORMED*** PART OF REFORMED INTERGALACTIC ASSASSINS FOR HIRE.

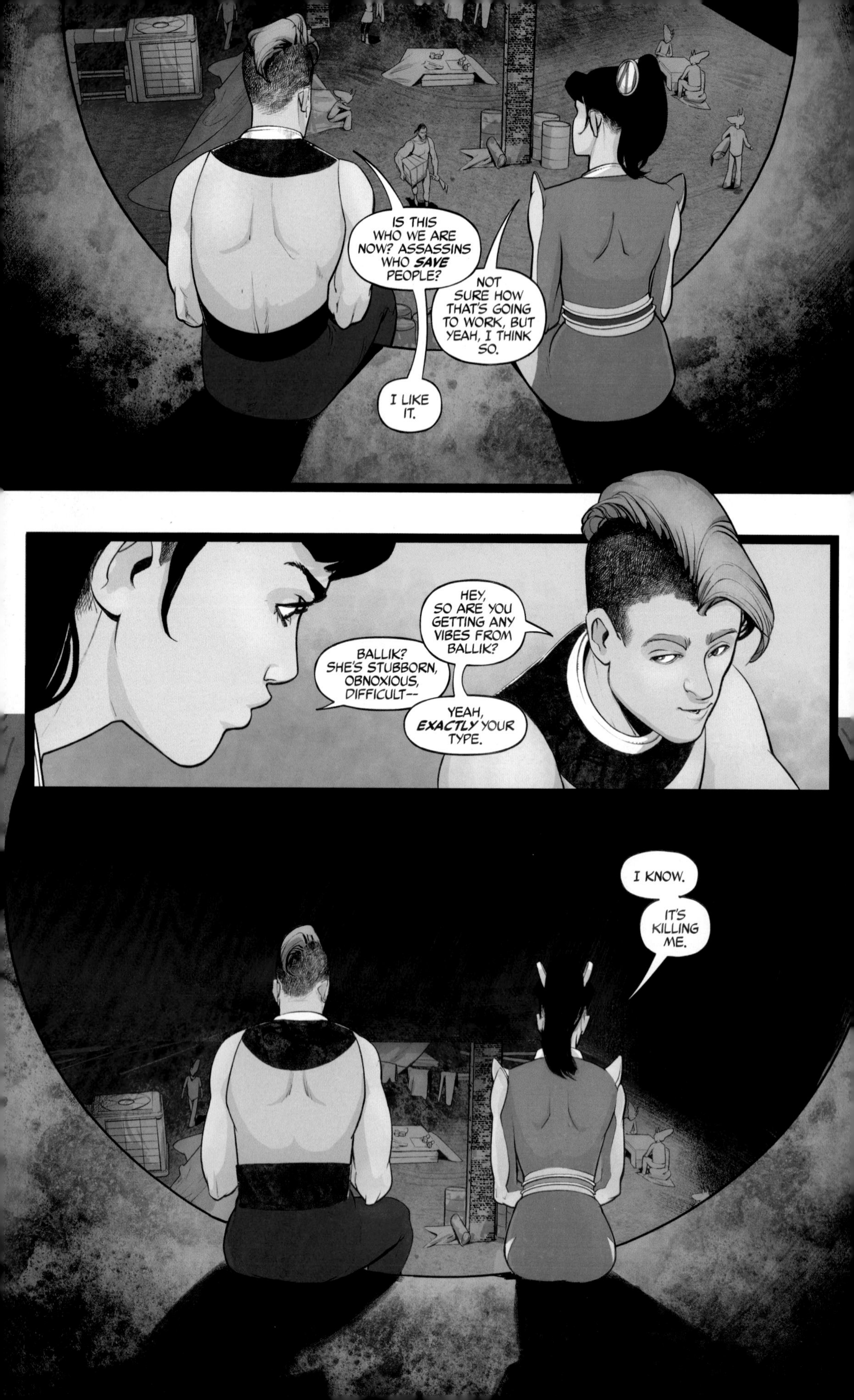
IS THIS WHO WE ARE NOW? ASSASSINS WHO *SAVE* PEOPLE?
NOT SURE HOW THAT'S GOING TO WORK, BUT YEAH, I THINK SO.
I LIKE IT.
HEY, SO ARE YOU GETTING ANY VIBES FROM BALLIK?
BALLIK? SHE'S STUBBORN, OBNOXIOUS, DIFFICULT--
YEAH, ***EXACTLY*** YOUR TYPE.
I KNOW.
IT'S KILLING ME.

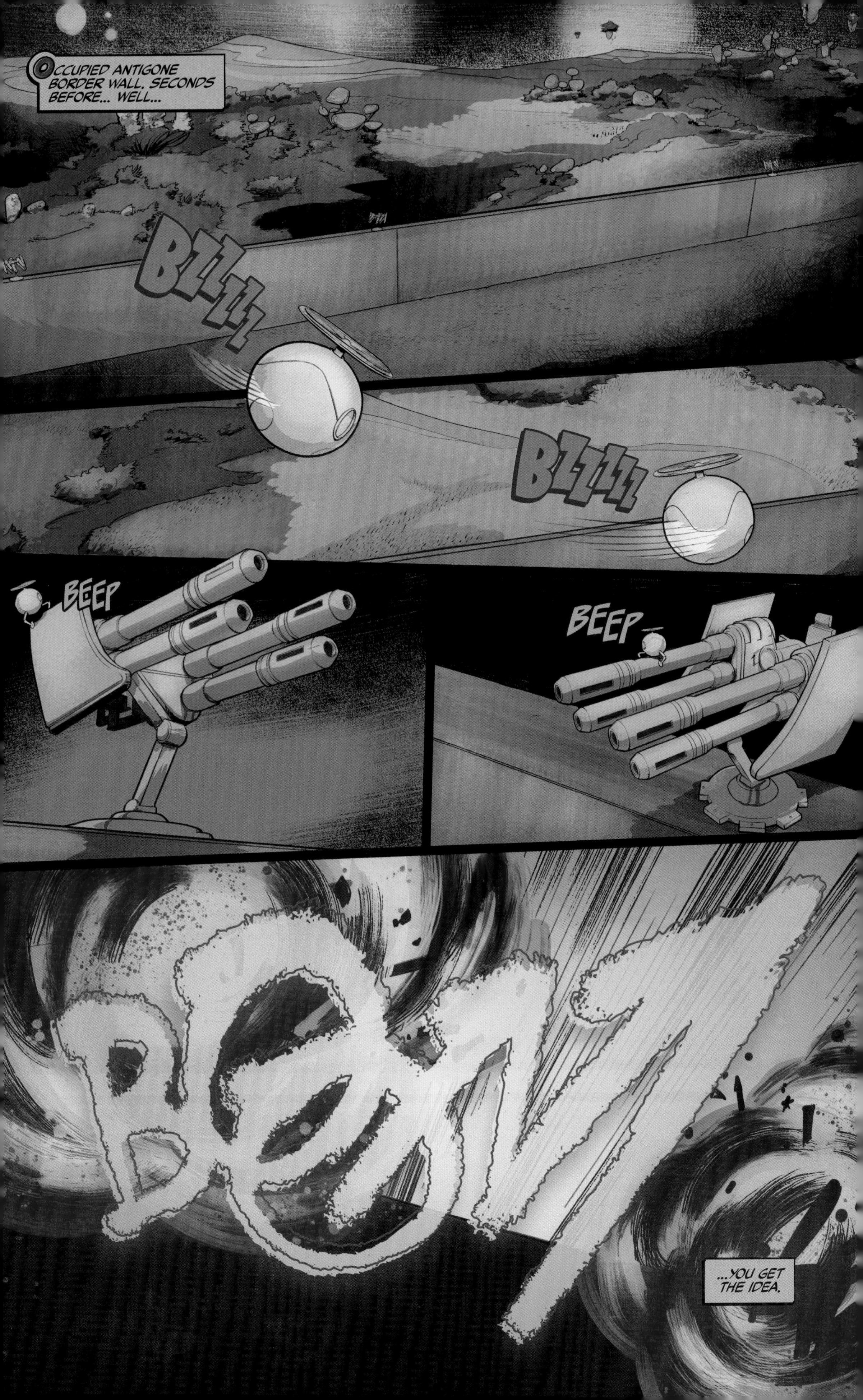
OCCUPIED ANTIGONE BORDER WALL, SECONDS BEFORE... WELL...
BZZZZZ
BZZZZZ
BEEP
BEEP
...YOU GET THE IDEA.

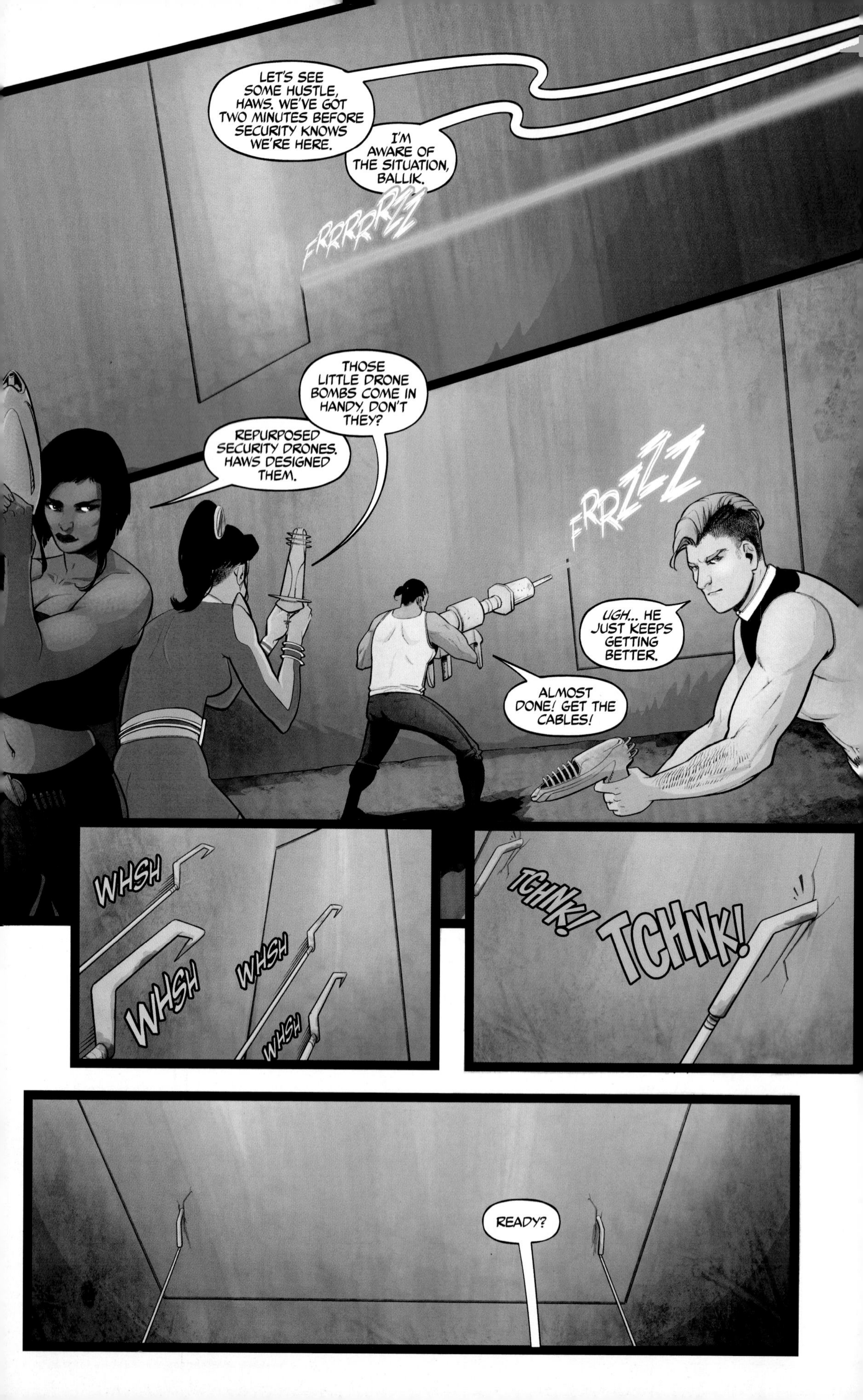
LET'S SEE SOME HUSTLE, HAWS. WE'VE GOT TWO MINUTES BEFORE SECURITY KNOWS WE'RE HERE.
I'M AWARE OF THE SITUATION, BALLIK.
FRRRRRZZZ
THOSE LITTLE DRONE BOMBS COME IN HANDY, DON'T THEY?
REPURPOSED SECURITY DRONES. HAWS DESIGNED THEM.
FRRZZZ
UGH... HE JUST KEEPS GETTING BETTER.
ALMOST DONE! GET THE CABLES!
WHSH
WHSH
WHSH
WHSH
TCHNK!
TCHNK!
READY?

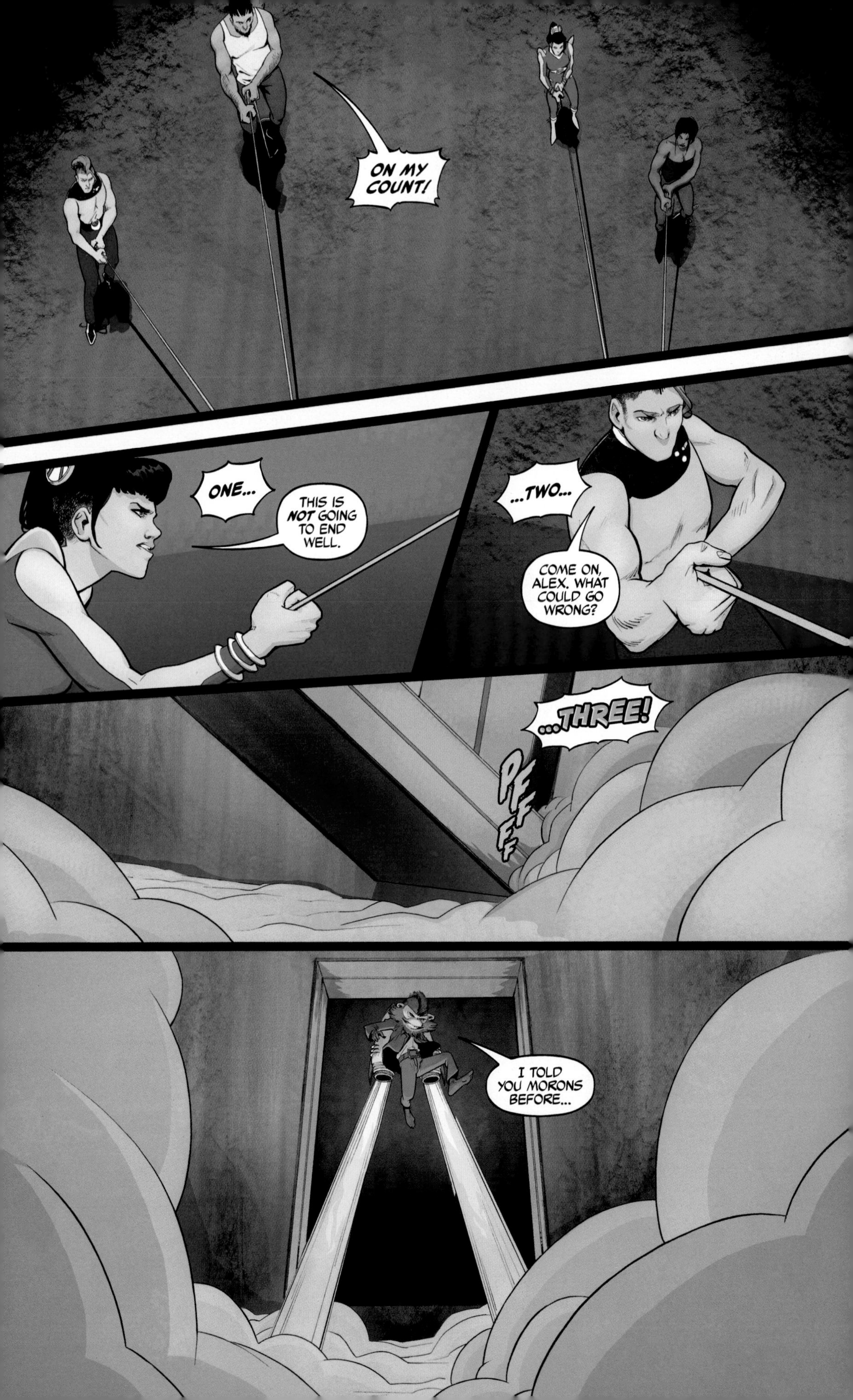
ON MY COUNT!
ONE...
THIS IS NOT GOING TO END WELL.
...TWO...
COME ON, ALEX. WHAT COULD GO WRONG?
...THREE!
PFFFF
I TOLD YOU MORONS BEFORE...

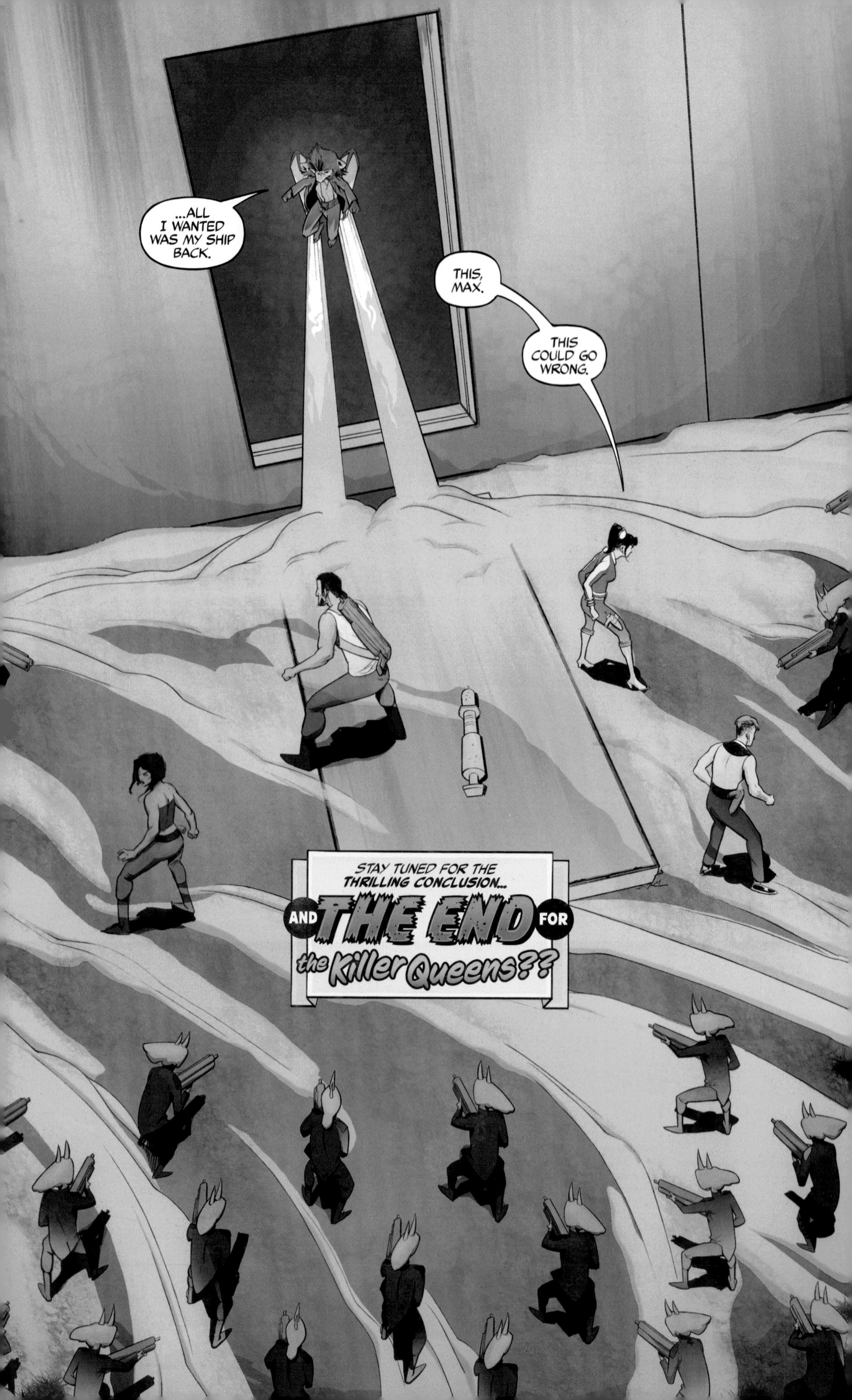
...ALL I WANTED WAS MY SHIP BACK.
THIS, MAX.
THIS COULD GO WRONG.
STAY TUNED FOR THE THRILLING CONCLUSION...
AND THE END FOR the Killer Queens??

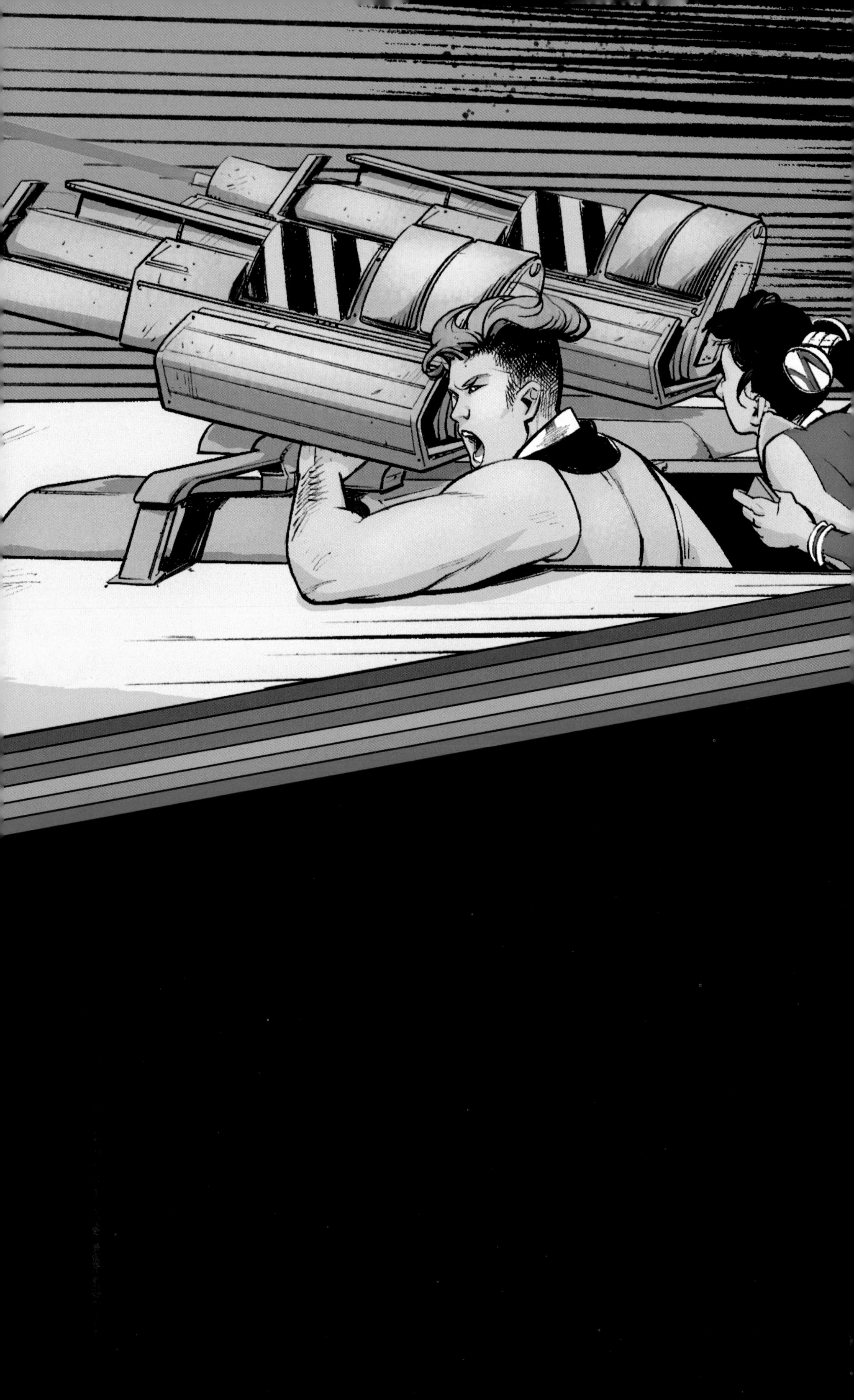

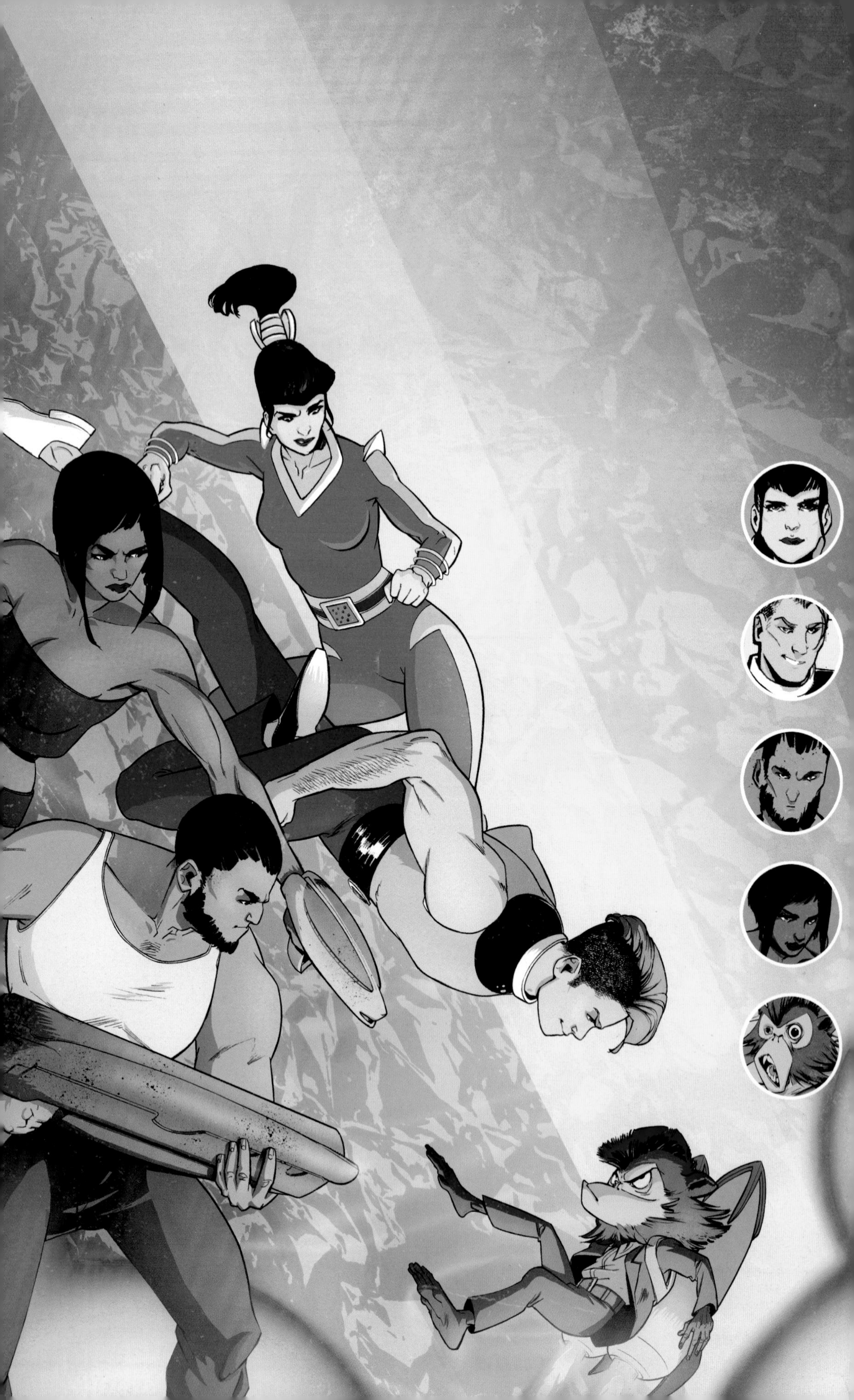

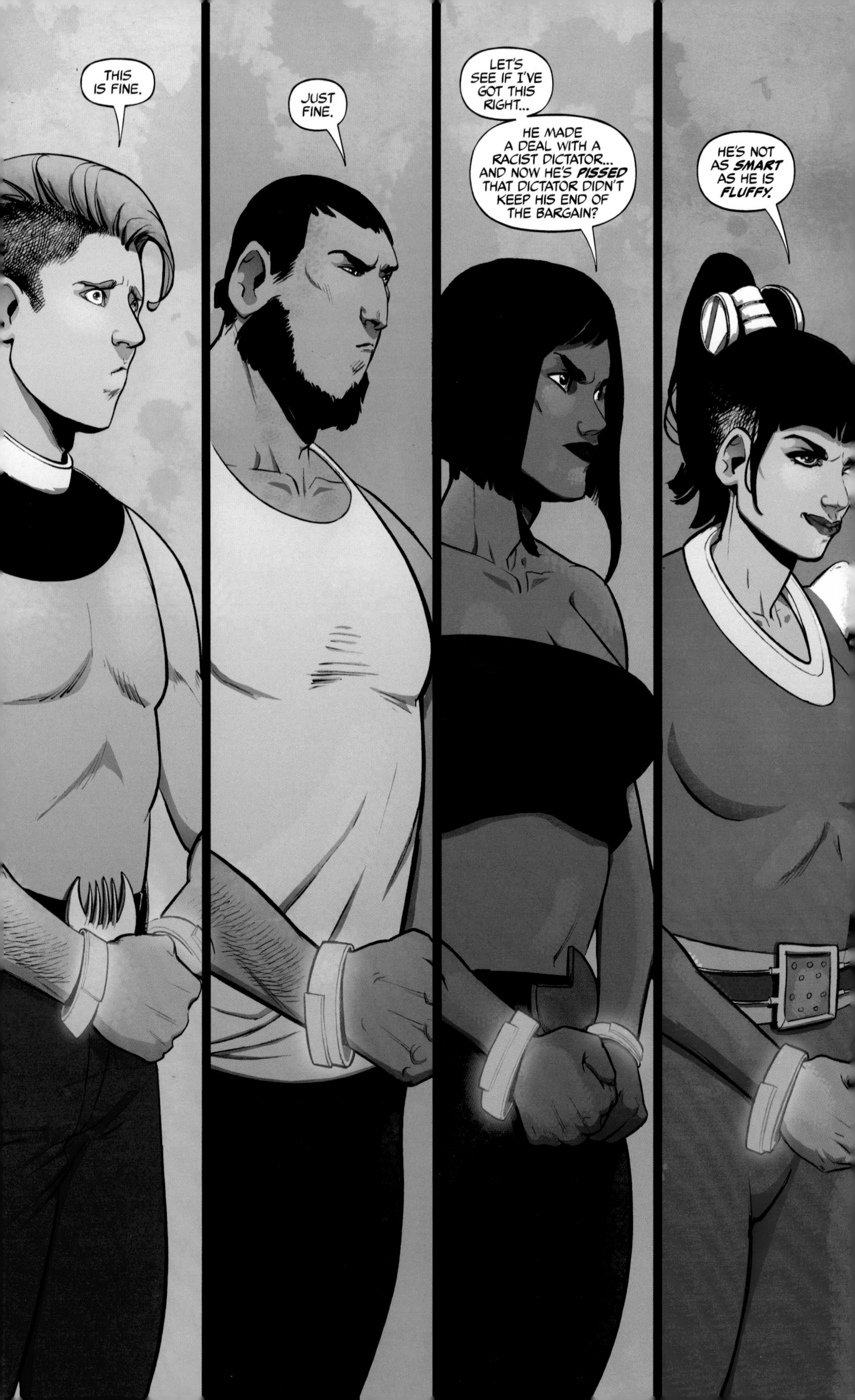
THIS IS FINE.
JUST FINE.
LET'S SEE IF I'VE GOT THIS RIGHT...
HE MADE A DEAL WITH A RACIST DICTATOR... AND NOW HE'S *PISSED* THAT DICTATOR DIDN'T KEEP HIS END OF THE BARGAIN?
HE'S NOT AS *SMART* AS HE IS *FLUFFY*.

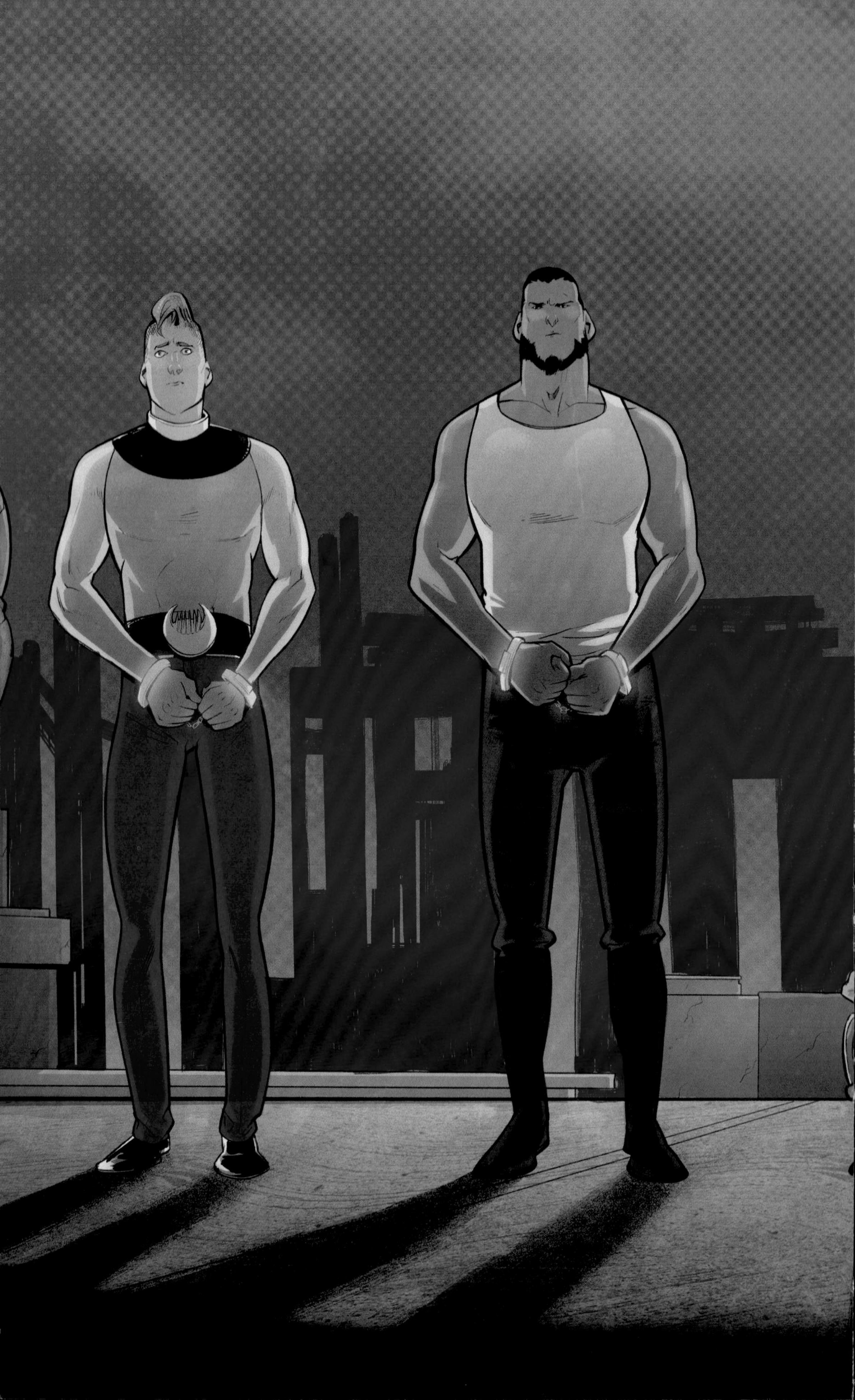

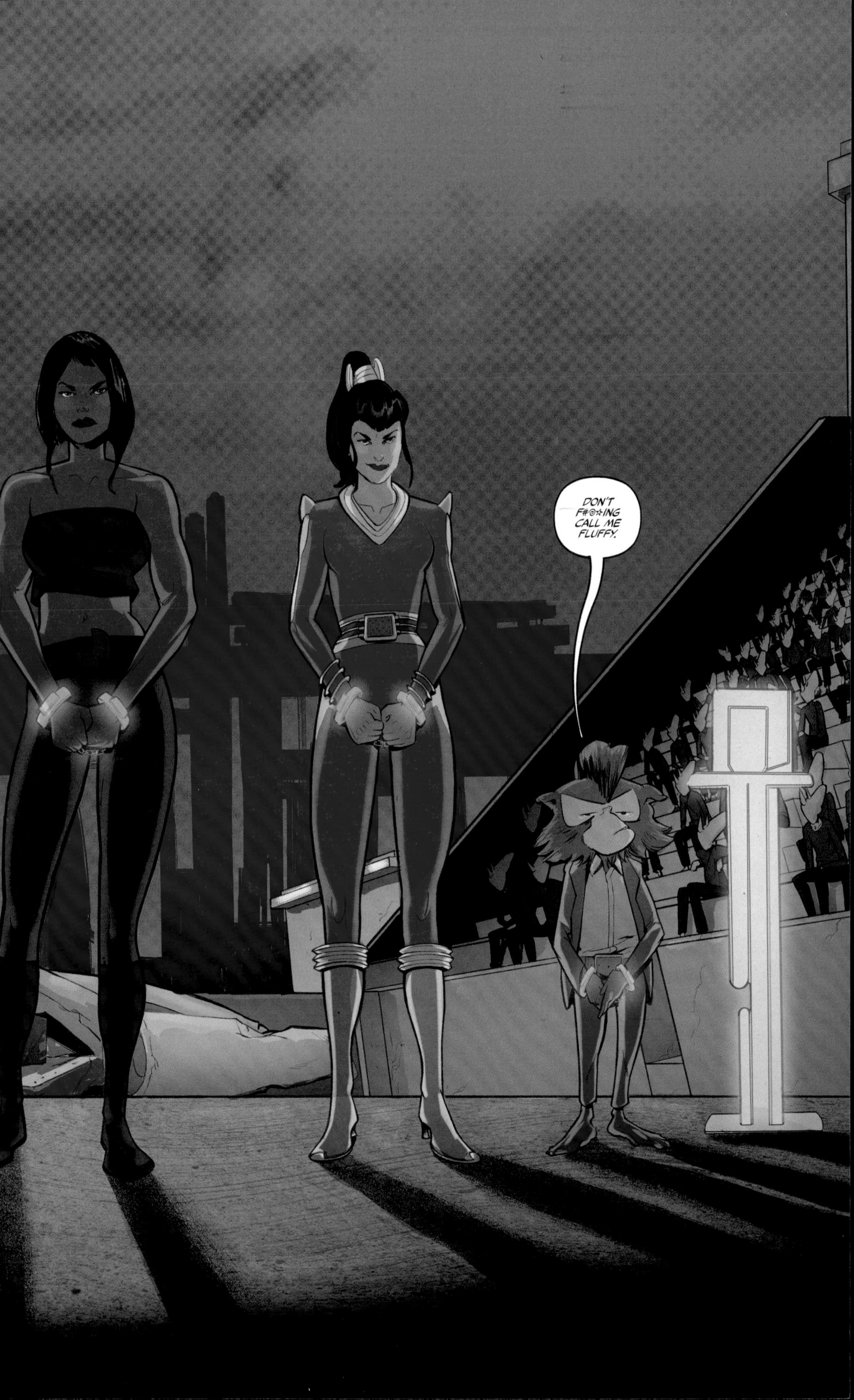
DON'T F#@☆ING CALL ME FLUFFY.

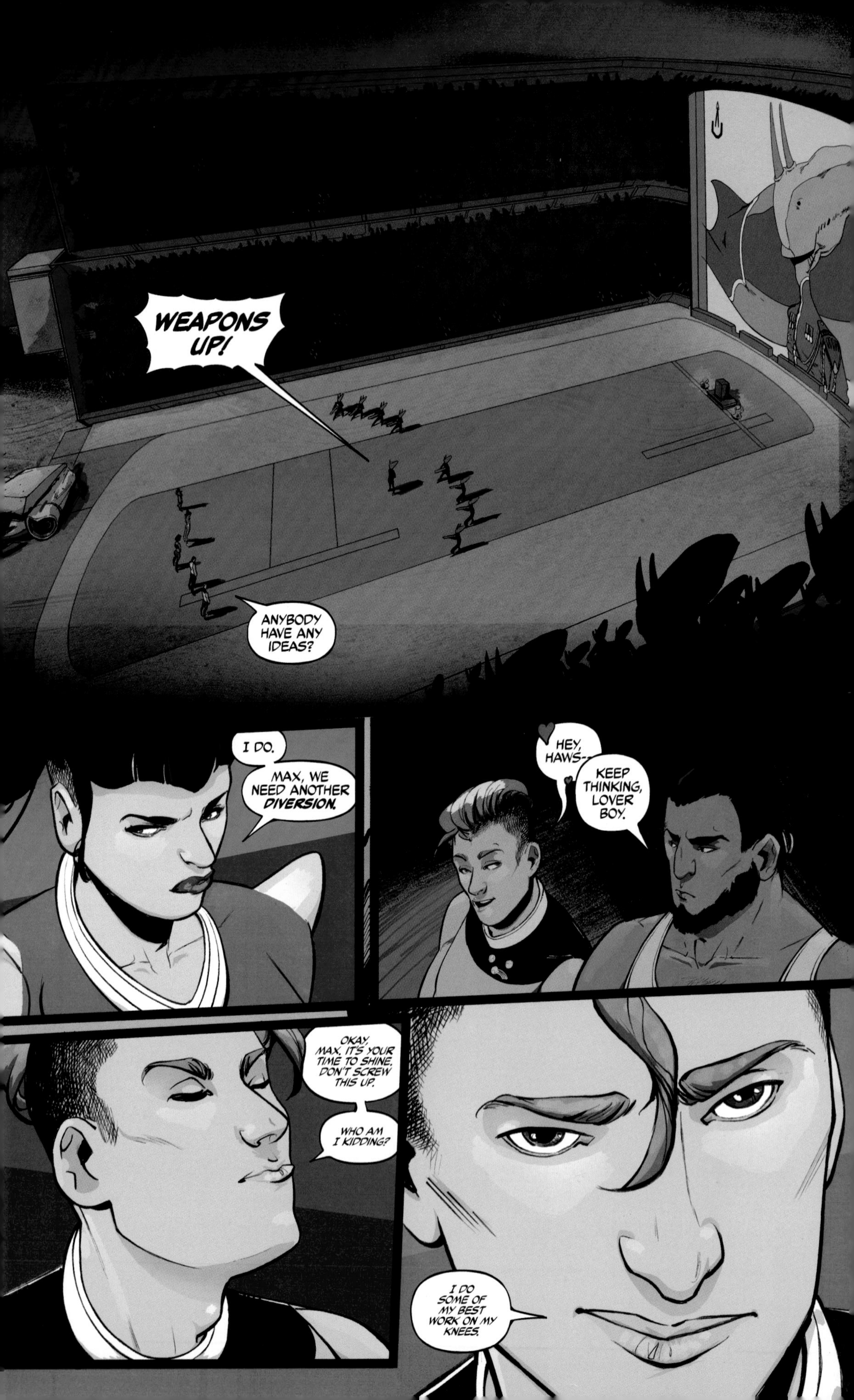
WEAPONS UP!
ANYBODY HAVE ANY IDEAS?
I DO.
MAX, WE NEED ANOTHER DIVERSION.
HEY, HAWS--
KEEP THINKING, LOVER BOY.
OKAY, MAX. IT'S YOUR TIME TO SHINE. DON'T SCREW THIS UP.
WHO AM I KIDDING?
I DO SOME OF MY BEST WORK ON MY KNEES.

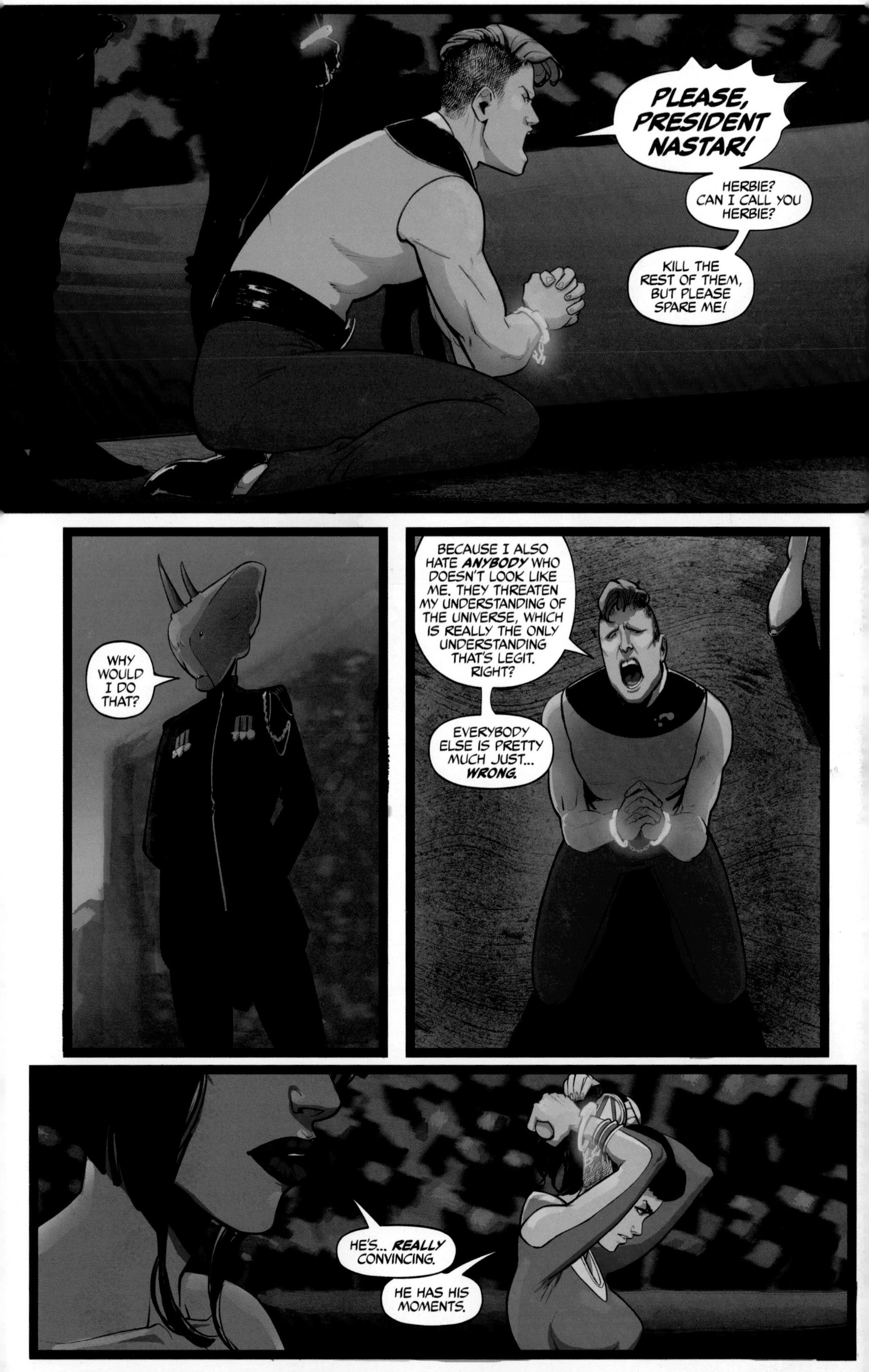
PLEASE, PRESIDENT NASTAR!
HERBIE? CAN I CALL YOU HERBIE?
KILL THE REST OF THEM, BUT PLEASE SPARE ME!
WHY WOULD I DO THAT?
BECAUSE I ALSO HATE ANYBODY WHO DOESN'T LOOK LIKE ME. THEY THREATEN MY UNDERSTANDING OF THE UNIVERSE, WHICH IS REALLY THE ONLY UNDERSTANDING THAT'S LEGIT. RIGHT?
EVERYBODY ELSE IS PRETTY MUCH JUST... WRONG.
HE'S... REALLY CONVINCING.
HE HAS HIS MOMENTS.

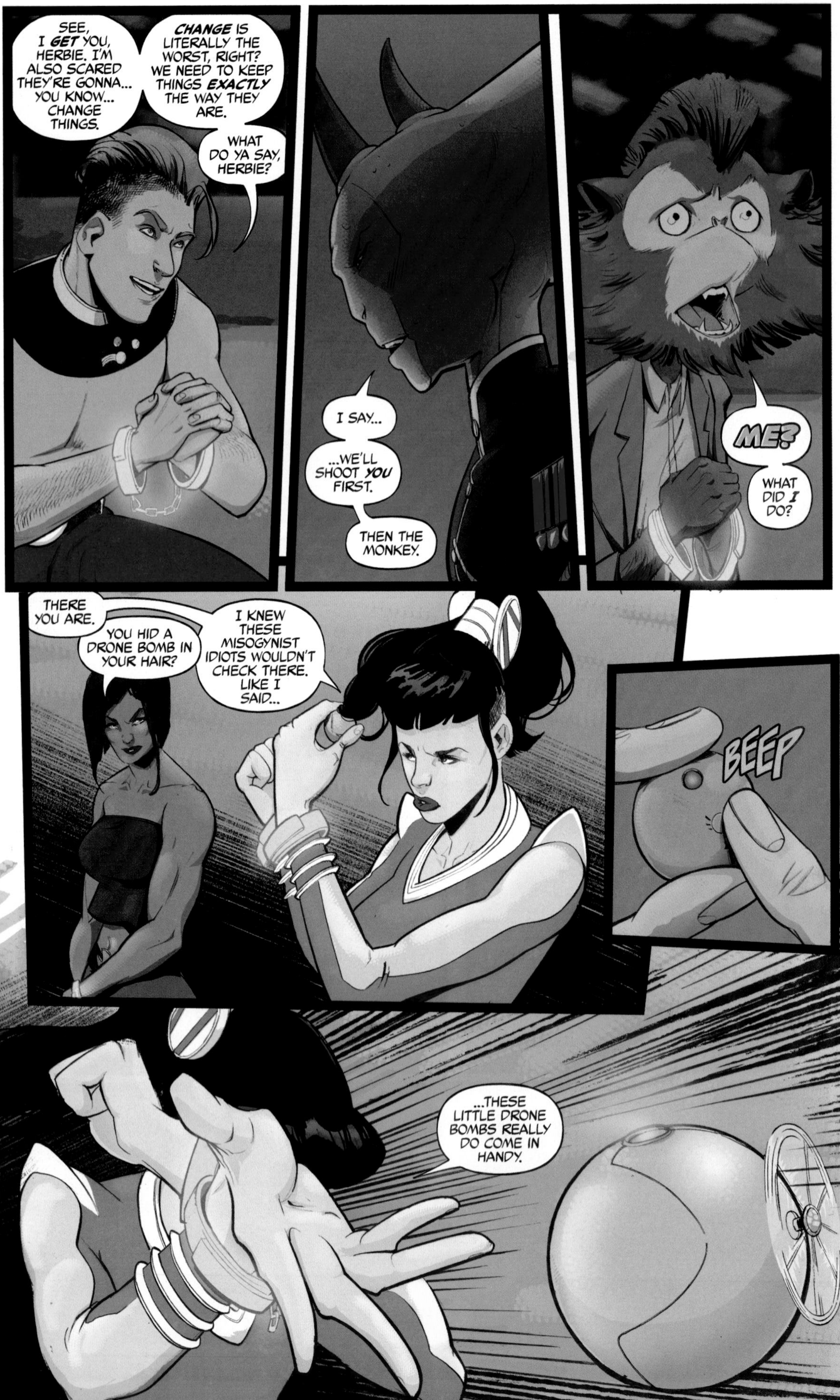
SEE, I GET YOU, HERBIE. I'M ALSO SCARED THEY'RE GONNA... YOU KNOW... CHANGE THINGS.
CHANGE IS LITERALLY THE WORST, RIGHT? WE NEED TO KEEP THINGS EXACTLY THE WAY THEY ARE.
WHAT DO YA SAY, HERBIE?
I SAY...
...WE'LL SHOOT YOU FIRST.
THEN THE MONKEY.
ME?
WHAT DID I DO?
THERE YOU ARE.
YOU HID A DRONE BOMB IN YOUR HAIR?
I KNEW THESE MISOGYNIST IDIOTS WOULDN'T CHECK THERE. LIKE I SAID...
BEEP
...THESE LITTLE DRONE BOMBS REALLY DO COME IN HANDY.

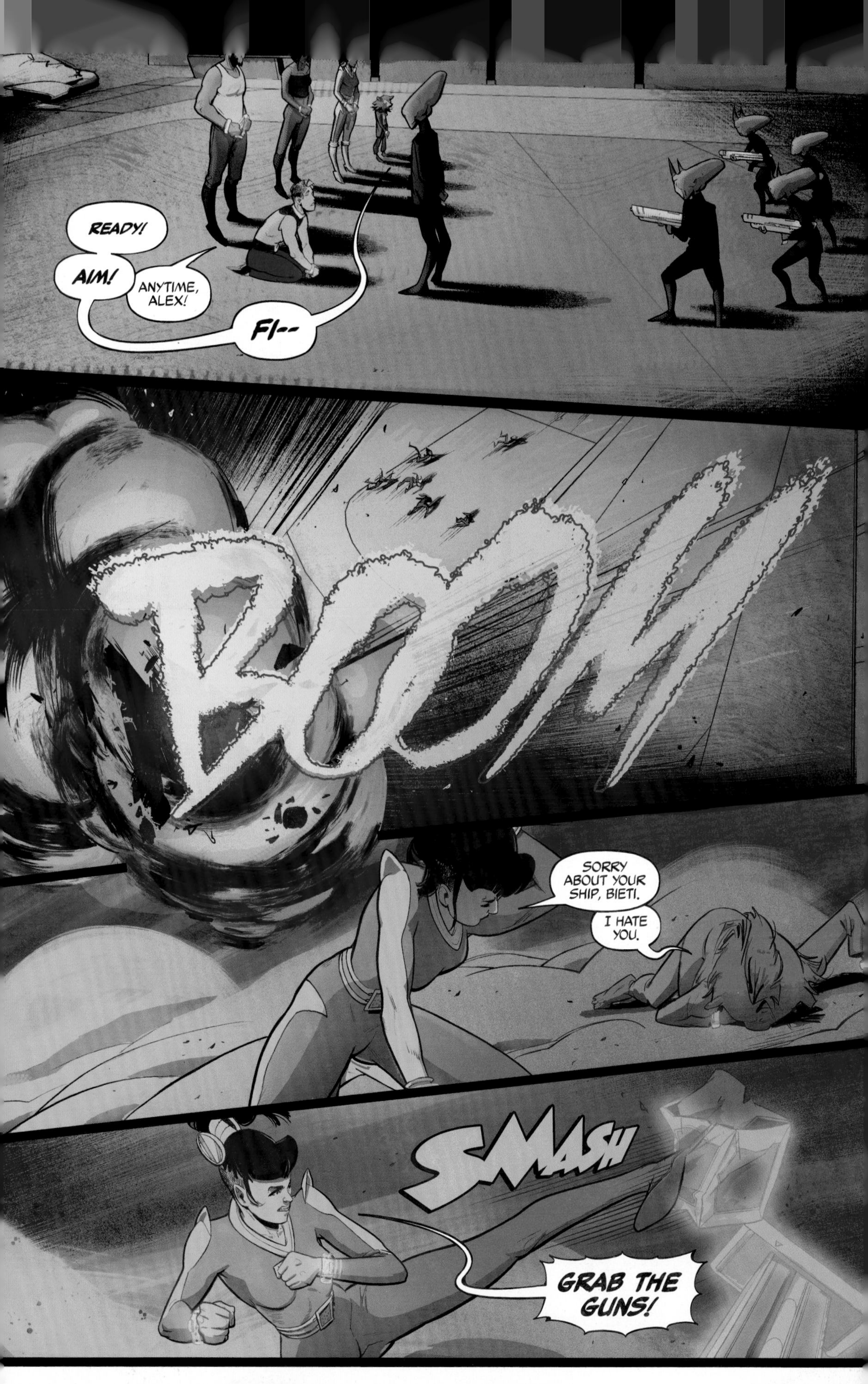
READY!
AIM!
ANYTIME, ALEX!
FI--
BOOM!
SORRY ABOUT YOUR SHIP, BIETI.
I HATE YOU.
SMASH
GRAB THE GUNS!

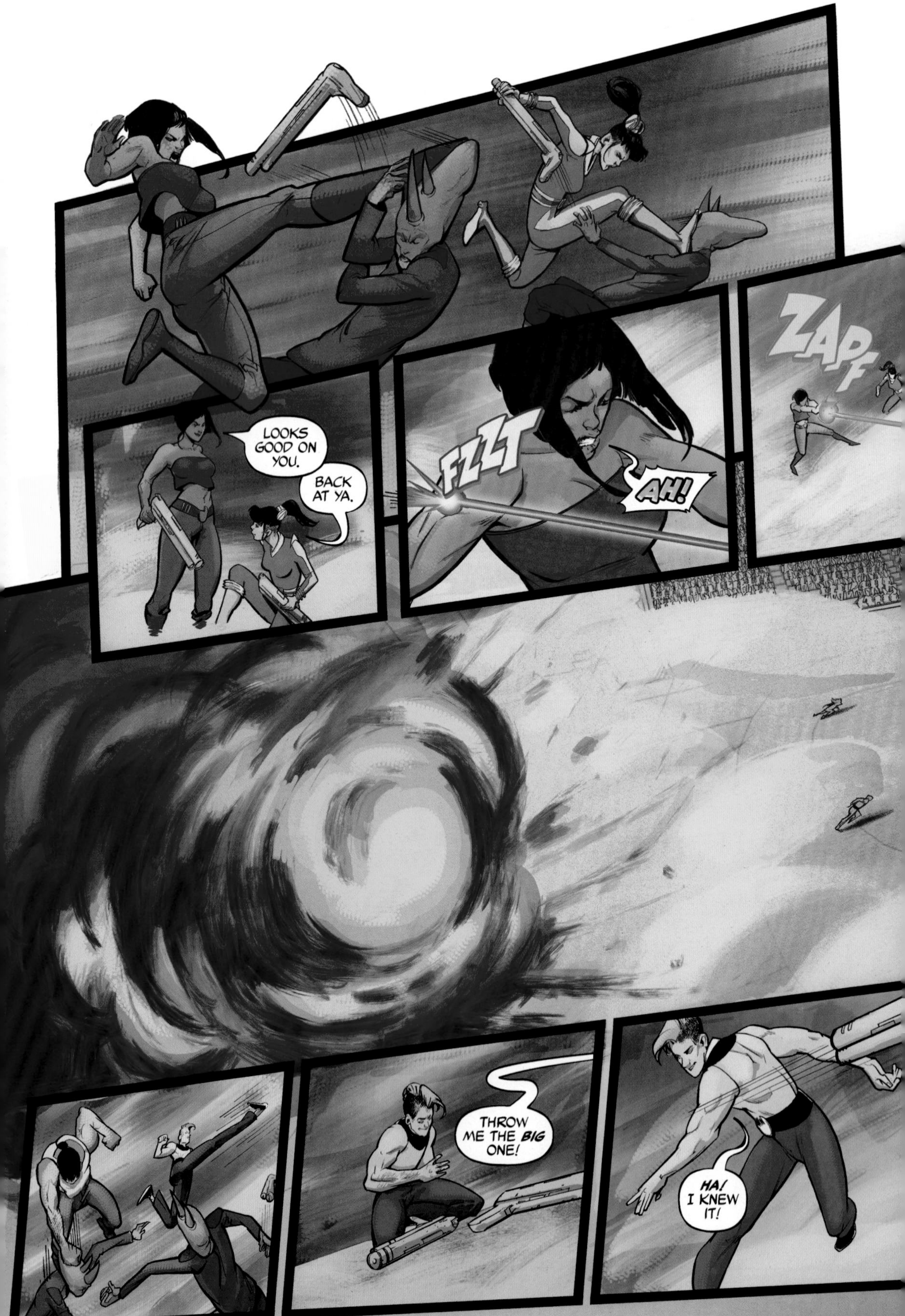
LOOKS GOOD ON YOU.
BACK AT YA.
FZZT
AH!
ZAPF
THROW ME THE BIG ONE!
HA! I KNEW IT!

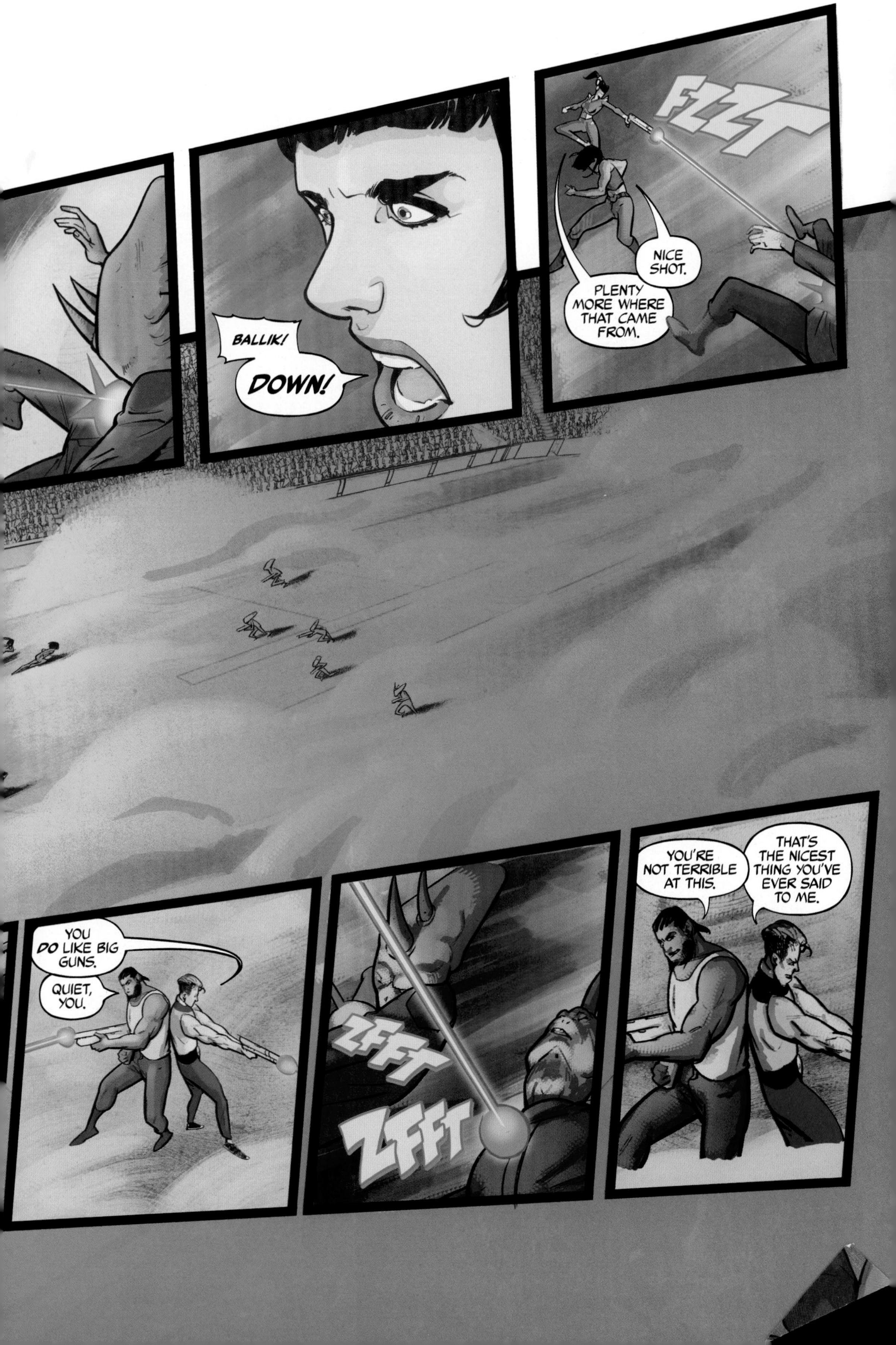

BALLIK!
DOWN!
FZZT
NICE SHOT.
PLENTY MORE WHERE THAT CAME FROM.
YOU DO LIKE BIG GUNS.
QUIET, YOU.
ZFFT
ZFFT
YOU'RE NOT TERRIBLE AT THIS.
THAT'S THE NICEST THING YOU'VE EVER SAID TO ME.

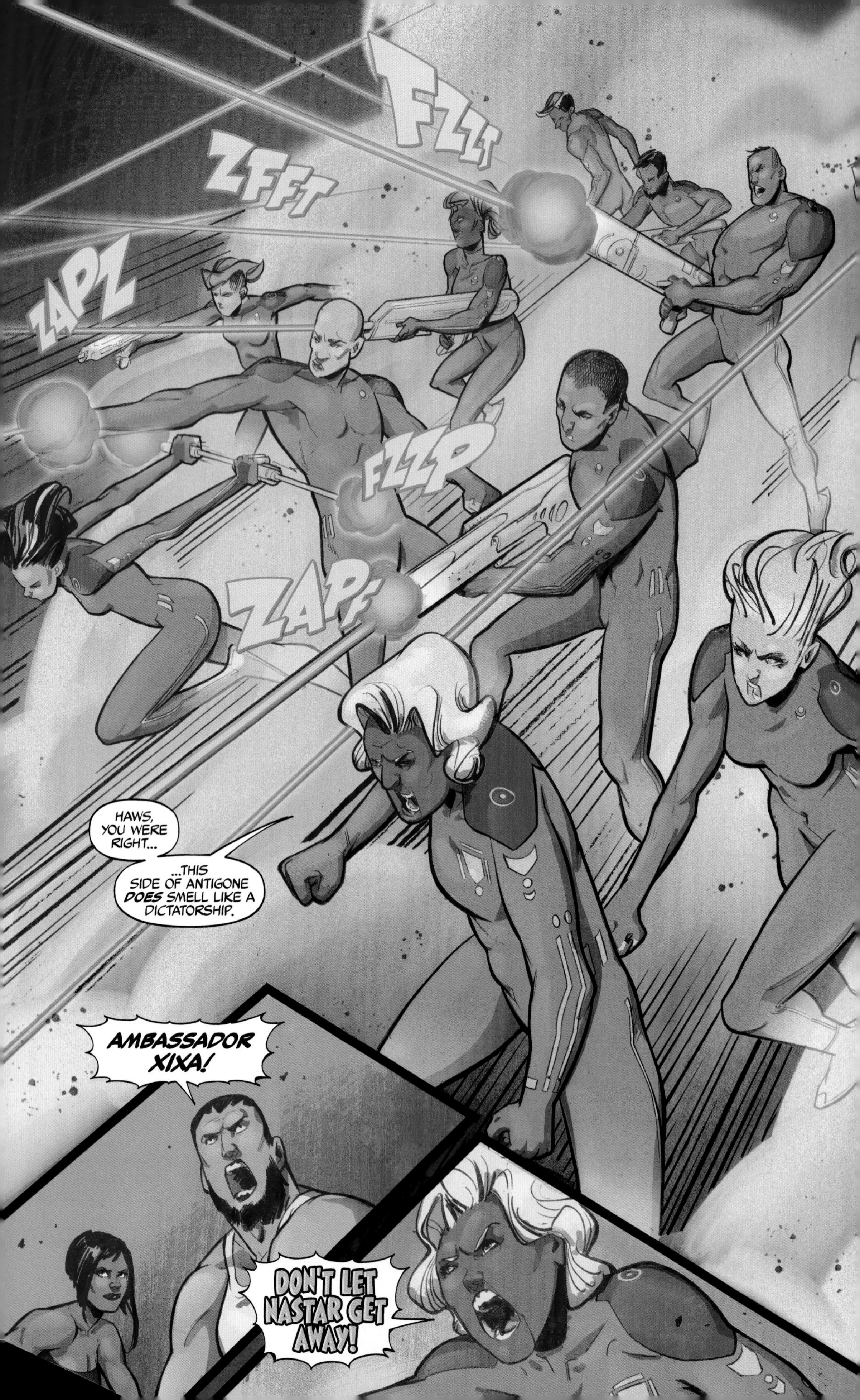
FZZT
ZFFT
ZAPZ
FZZP
ZAPF
HAWS, YOU WERE RIGHT...
...THIS SIDE OF ANTIGONE DOES SMELL LIKE A DICTATORSHIP.
AMBASSADOR XIXA!
DON'T LET NASTAR GET AWAY!

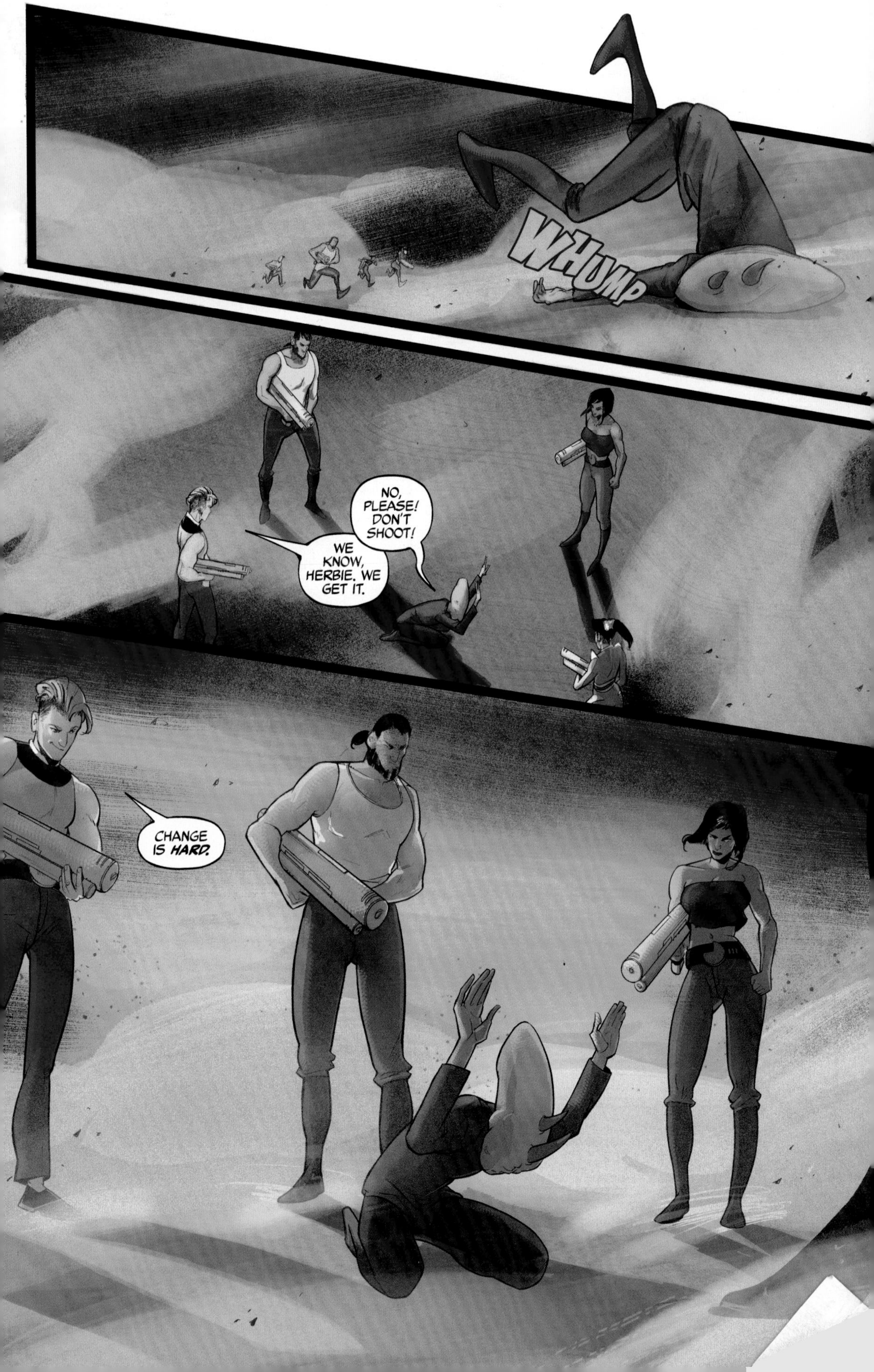
WHUMP
NO, PLEASE! DON'T SHOOT!
WE KNOW, HERBIE. WE GET IT.
CHANGE IS HARD.

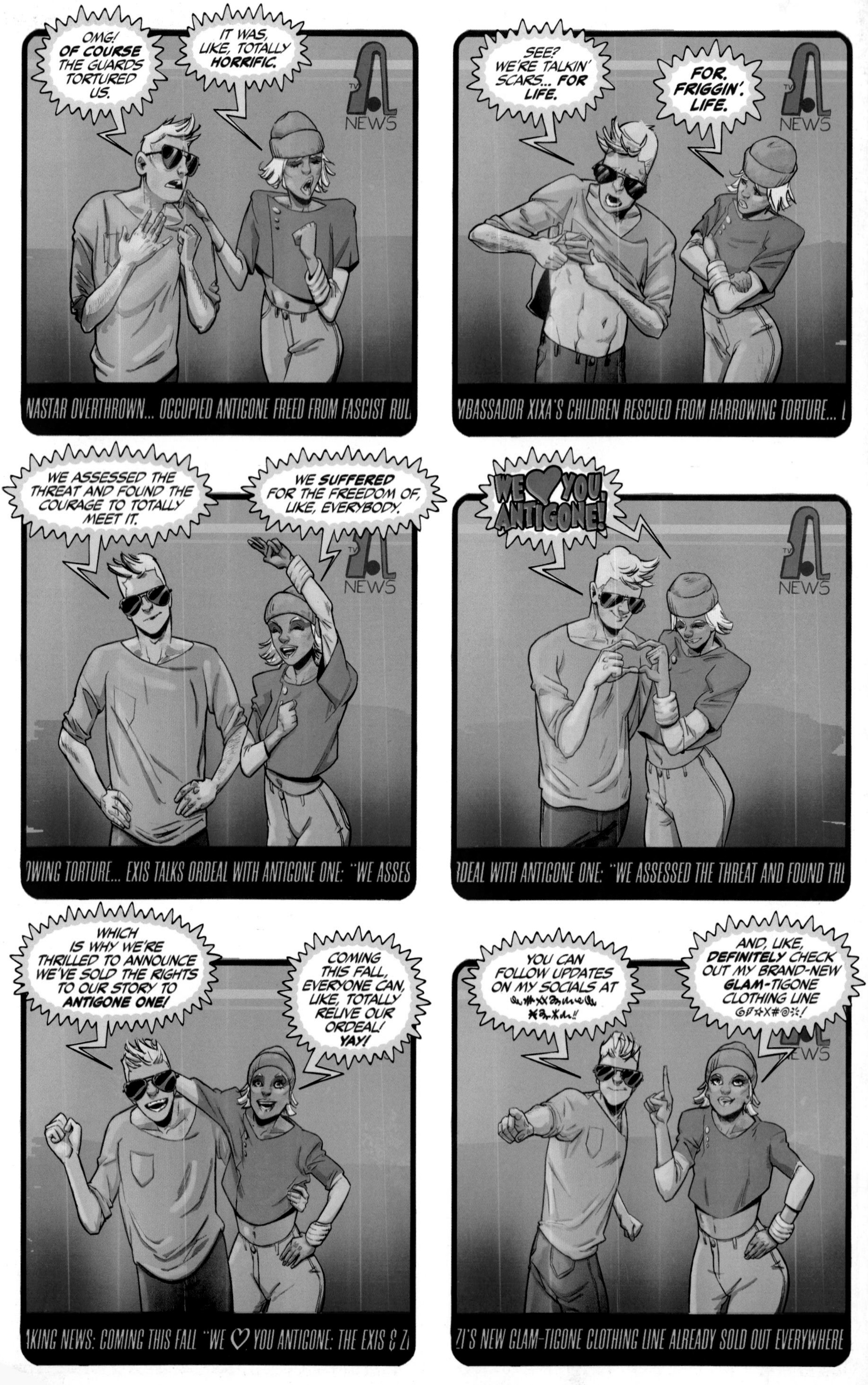

OMG! OF COURSE THE GUARDS TORTURED US.
IT WAS, LIKE, TOTALLY HORRIFIC.
TV NEWS
NASTAR OVERTHROWN... OCCUPIED ANTIGONE FREED FROM FASCIST RUL
SEE? WE'RE TALKIN' SCARS... FOR LIFE.
FOR. FRIGGIN'. LIFE.
TV NEWS
MBASSADOR XIXA'S CHILDREN RESCUED FROM HARROWING TORTURE...
WE ASSESSED THE THREAT AND FOUND THE COURAGE TO TOTALLY MEET IT.
WE SUFFERED FOR THE FREEDOM OF, LIKE, EVERYBODY.
TV NEWS
OWING TORTURE... EXIS TALKS ORDEAL WITH ANTIGONE ONE: "WE ASSES
WE ♥ YOU, ANTIGONE!
TV NEWS
RDEAL WITH ANTIGONE ONE: "WE ASSESSED THE THREAT AND FOUND TH
WHICH IS WHY WE'RE THRILLED TO ANNOUNCE WE'VE SOLD THE RIGHTS TO OUR STORY TO ANTIGONE ONE!
COMING THIS FALL, EVERYONE CAN, LIKE, TOTALLY RELIVE OUR ORDEAL! YAY!
AKING NEWS: COMING THIS FALL "WE ♥ YOU ANTIGONE: THE EXIS & Z
YOU CAN FOLLOW UPDATES ON MY SOCIALS AT
AND, LIKE, DEFINITELY CHECK OUT MY BRAND-NEW GLAM-TIGONE CLOTHING LINE
ZI'S NEW GLAM-TIGONE CLOTHING LINE ALREADY SOLD OUT EVERYWHERE

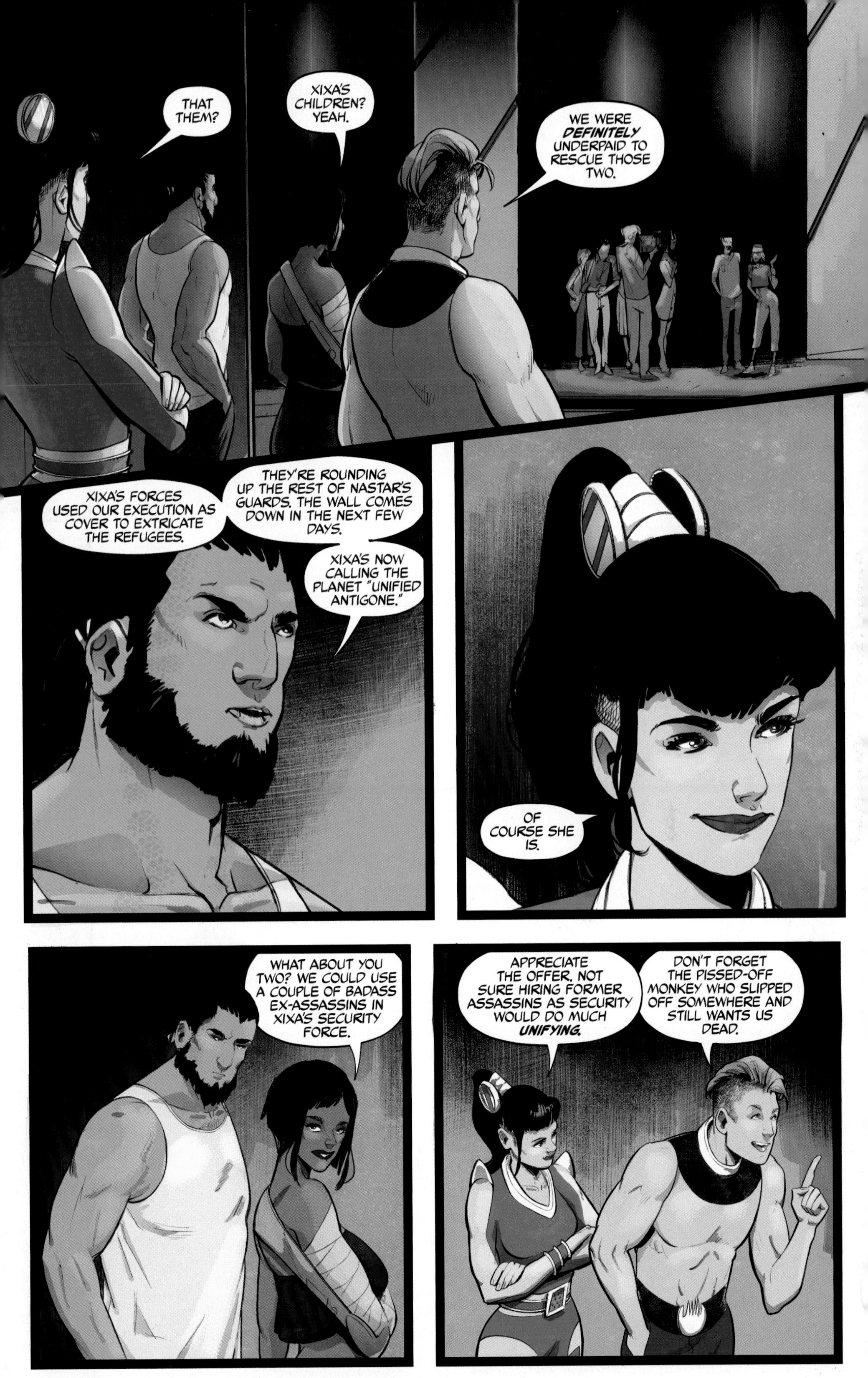
THAT THEM?
XIXA'S CHILDREN? YEAH.
WE WERE DEFINITELY UNDERPAID TO RESCUE THOSE TWO.
XIXA'S FORCES USED OUR EXECUTION AS COVER TO EXTRICATE THE REFUGEES.
THEY'RE ROUNDING UP THE REST OF NASTAR'S GUARDS. THE WALL COMES DOWN IN THE NEXT FEW DAYS.
XIXA'S NOW CALLING THE PLANET "UNIFIED ANTIGONE."
OF COURSE SHE IS.
WHAT ABOUT YOU TWO? WE COULD USE A COUPLE OF BADASS EX-ASSASSINS IN XIXA'S SECURITY FORCE.
APPRECIATE THE OFFER. NOT SURE HIRING FORMER ASSASSINS AS SECURITY WOULD DO MUCH UNIFYING.
DON'T FORGET THE PISSED-OFF MONKEY WHO SLIPPED OFF SOMEWHERE AND STILL WANTS US DEAD.

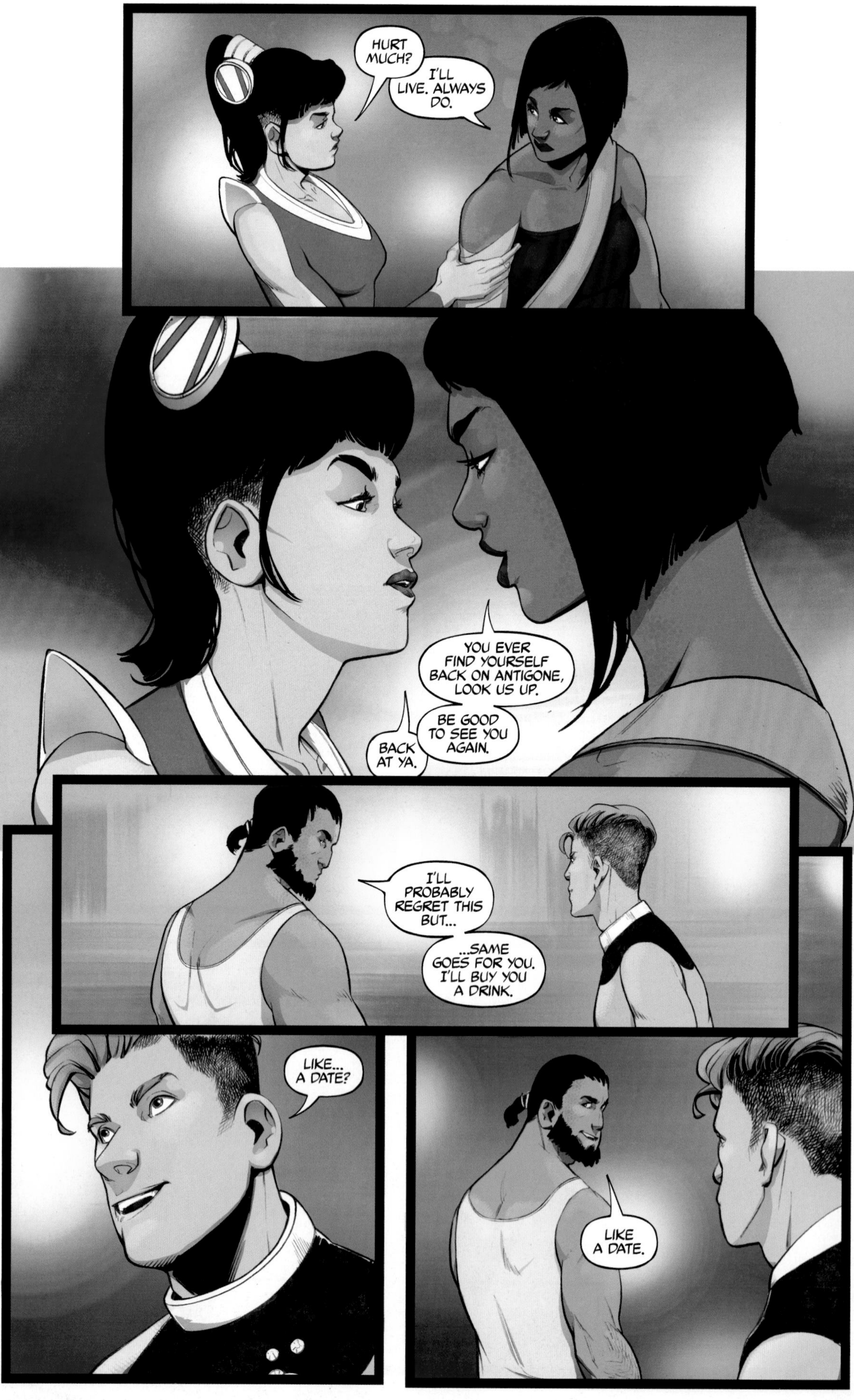
HURT MUCH?
I'LL LIVE. ALWAYS DO.
YOU EVER FIND YOURSELF BACK ON ANTIGONE, LOOK US UP.
BE GOOD TO SEE YOU AGAIN.
BACK AT YA.
I'LL PROBABLY REGRET THIS BUT...
...SAME GOES FOR YOU. I'LL BUY YOU A DRINK.
LIKE... A DATE?
LIKE A DATE.

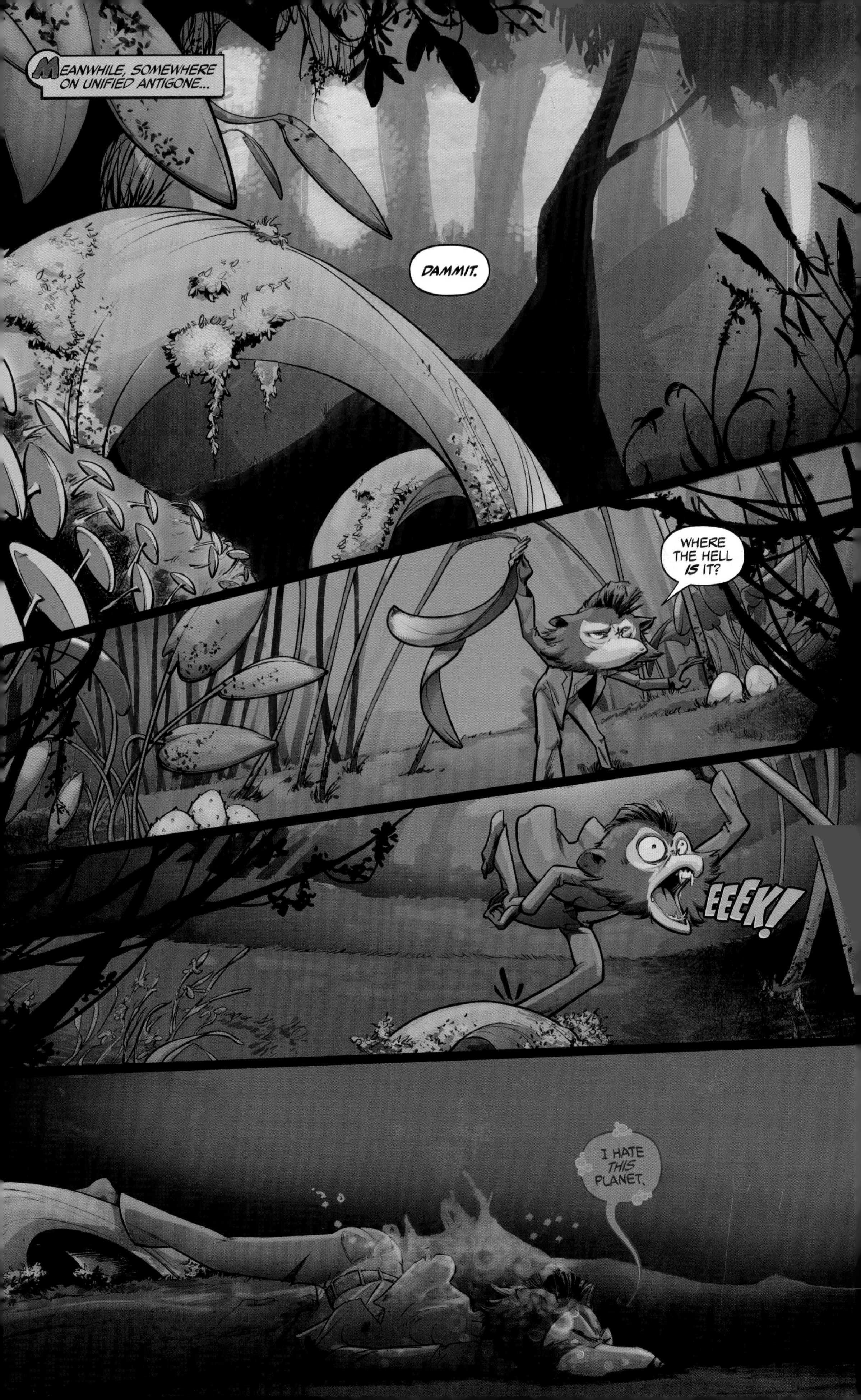
MEANWHILE, SOMEWHERE ON UNIFIED ANTIGONE...
DAMMIT.
WHERE THE HELL *IS* IT?
EEEK!
I HATE *THIS* PLANET.

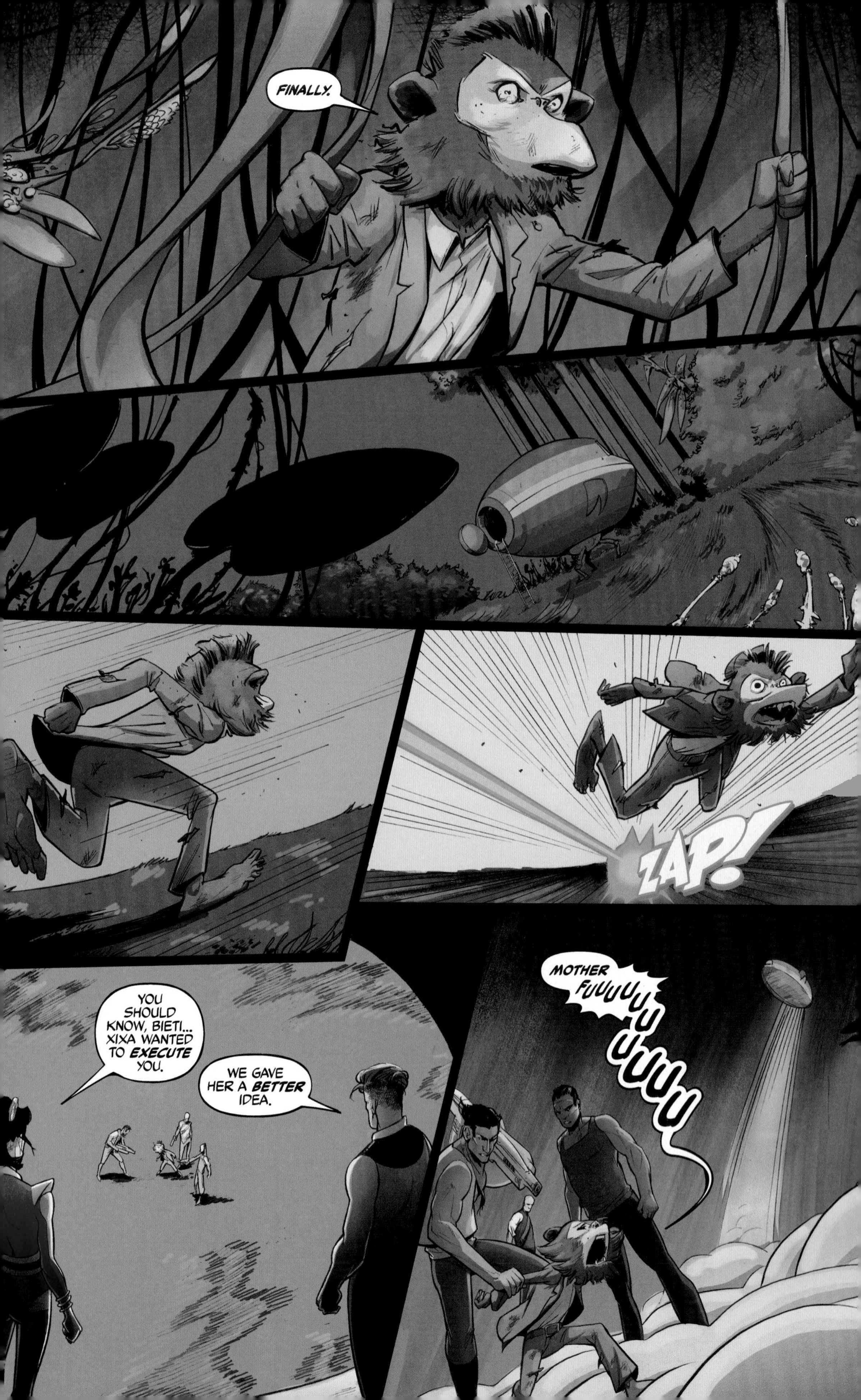
FINALLY.
ZAP!
YOU SHOULD KNOW, BIETI... XIXA WANTED TO EXECUTE YOU.
WE GAVE HER A BETTER IDEA.
MOTHER FUUUUUUUUUUUU

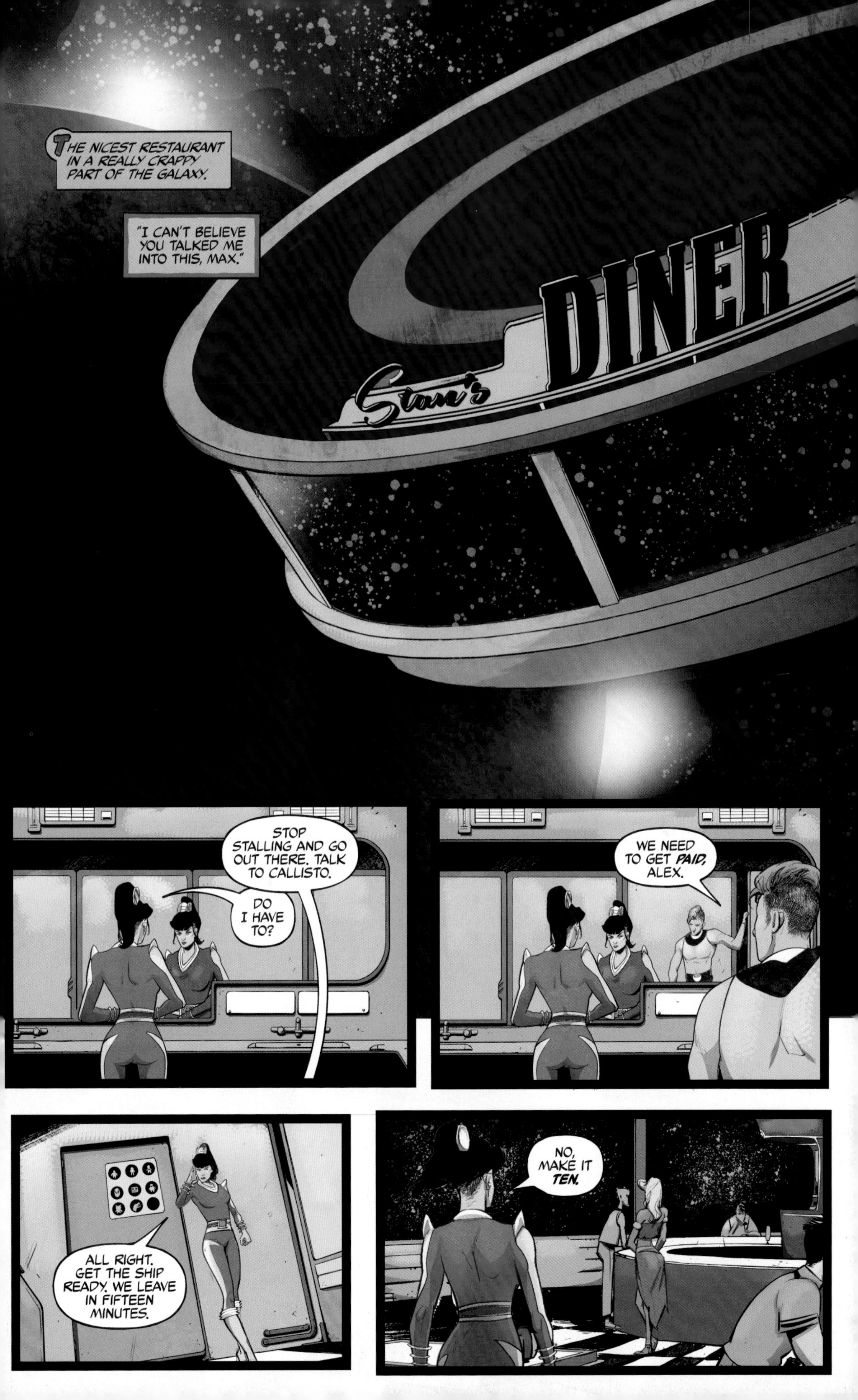
THE NICEST RESTAURANT IN A REALLY CRAPPY PART OF THE GALAXY.
"I CAN'T BELIEVE YOU TALKED ME INTO THIS, MAX."
Stan's
DINER
STOP STALLING AND GO OUT THERE. TALK TO CALLISTO.
DO I HAVE TO?
WE NEED TO GET *PAID,* ALEX.
ALL RIGHT. GET THE SHIP READY. WE LEAVE IN FIFTEEN MINUTES.
NO, MAKE IT *TEN.*

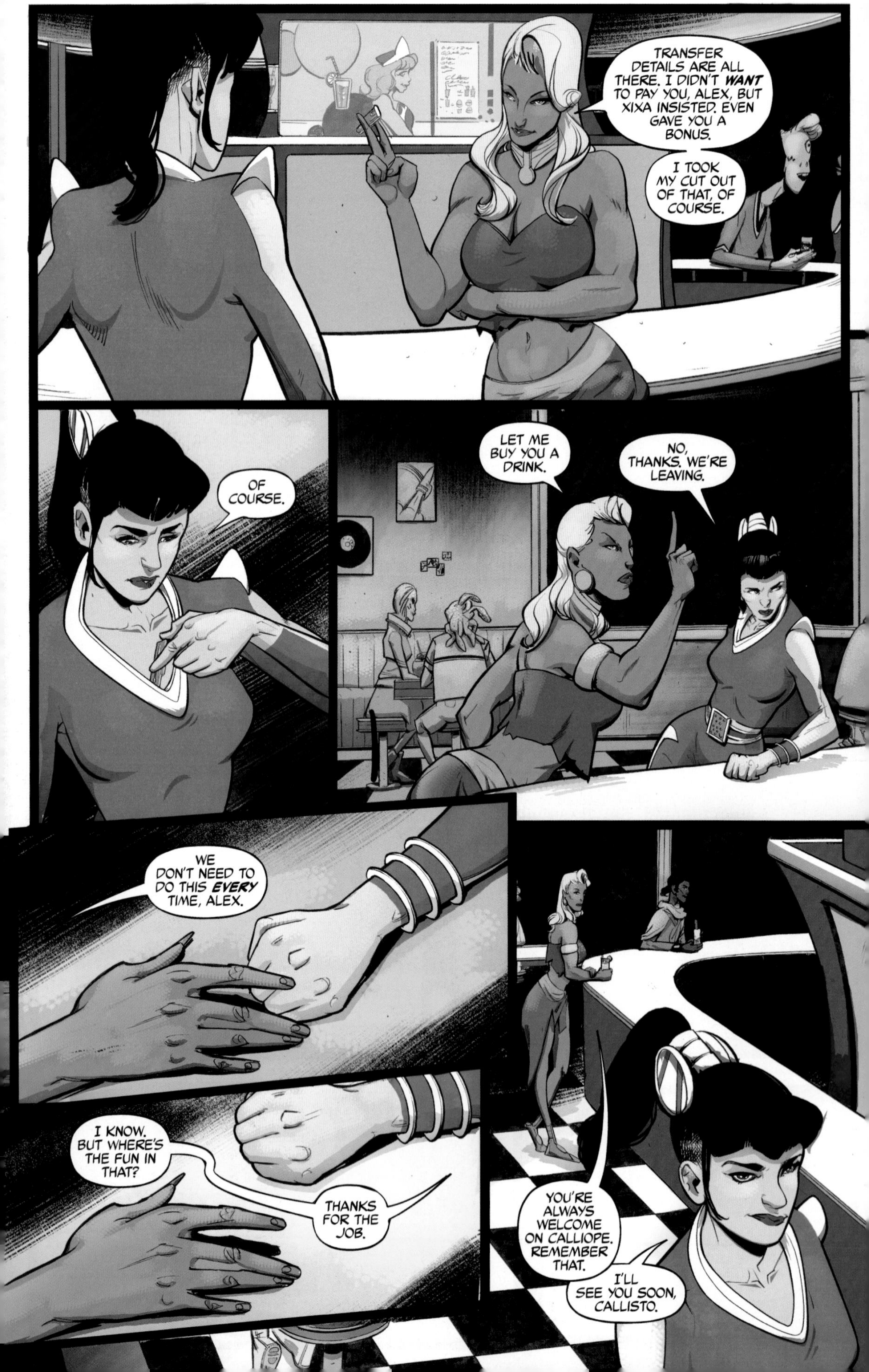
TRANSFER DETAILS ARE ALL THERE. I DIDN'T *WANT* TO PAY YOU, ALEX, BUT XIXA INSISTED. EVEN GAVE YOU A BONUS.
I TOOK MY CUT OUT OF THAT, OF COURSE.
OF COURSE.
LET ME BUY YOU A DRINK.
NO, THANKS. WE'RE LEAVING.
WE DON'T NEED TO DO THIS *EVERY* TIME, ALEX.
I KNOW. BUT WHERE'S THE FUN IN THAT?
THANKS FOR THE JOB.
YOU'RE ALWAYS WELCOME ON CALLIOPE. REMEMBER THAT.
I'LL SEE YOU SOON, CALLISTO.

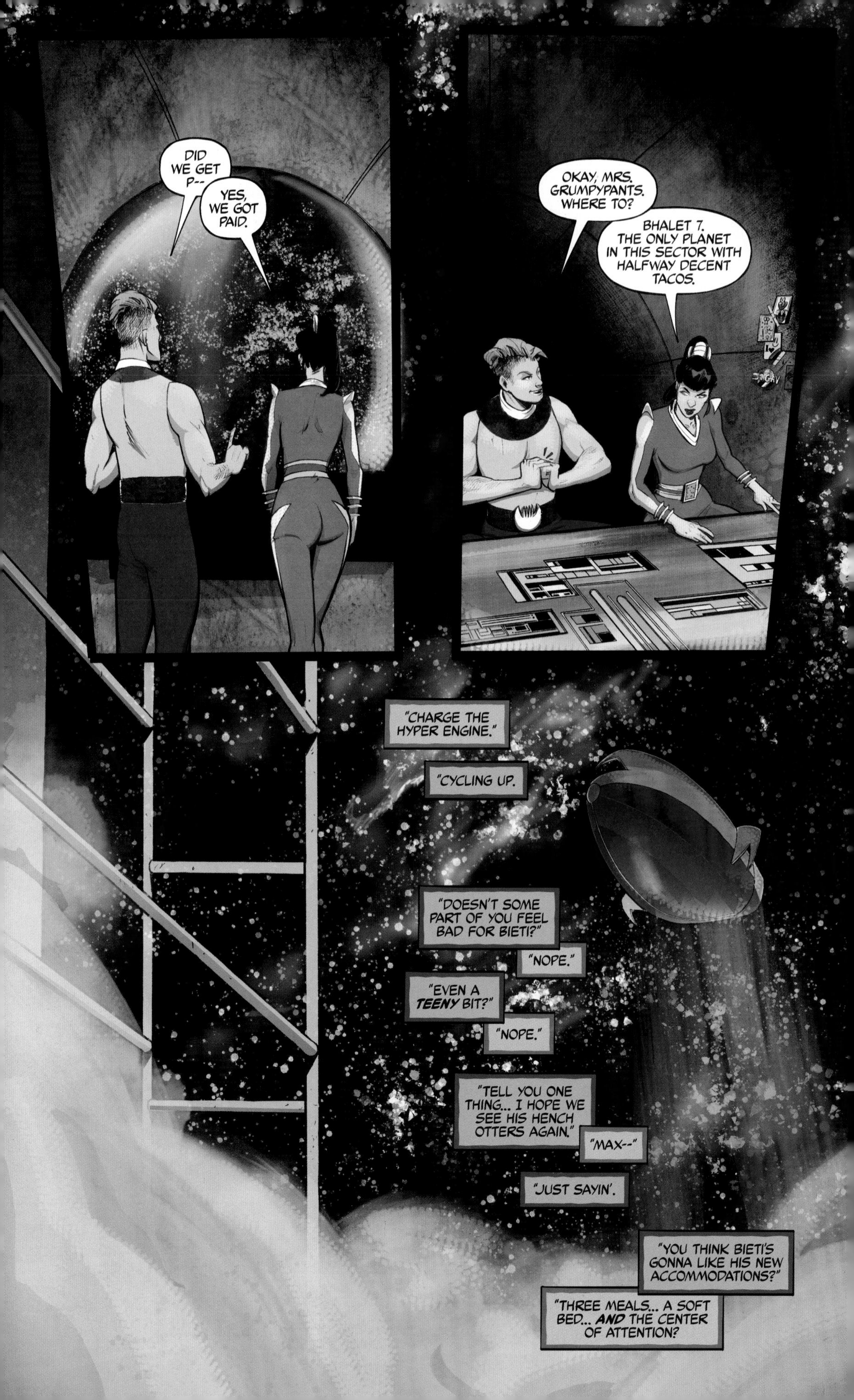
DID WE GET P--
YES, WE GOT PAID.
OKAY, MRS. GRUMPYPANTS. WHERE TO?
BHALET 7. THE ONLY PLANET IN THIS SECTOR WITH HALFWAY DECENT TACOS.
"CHARGE THE HYPER ENGINE."
"CYCLING UP.
"DOESN'T SOME PART OF YOU FEEL BAD FOR BIETI?"
"NOPE."
"EVEN A *TEENY* BIT?"
"NOPE."
"TELL YOU ONE THING... I HOPE WE SEE HIS HENCH OTTERS AGAIN."
"MAX--"
"JUST SAYIN'.
"YOU THINK BIETI'S GONNA LIKE HIS NEW ACCOMMODATIONS?"
"THREE MEALS... A SOFT BED... *AND* THE CENTER OF ATTENTION?

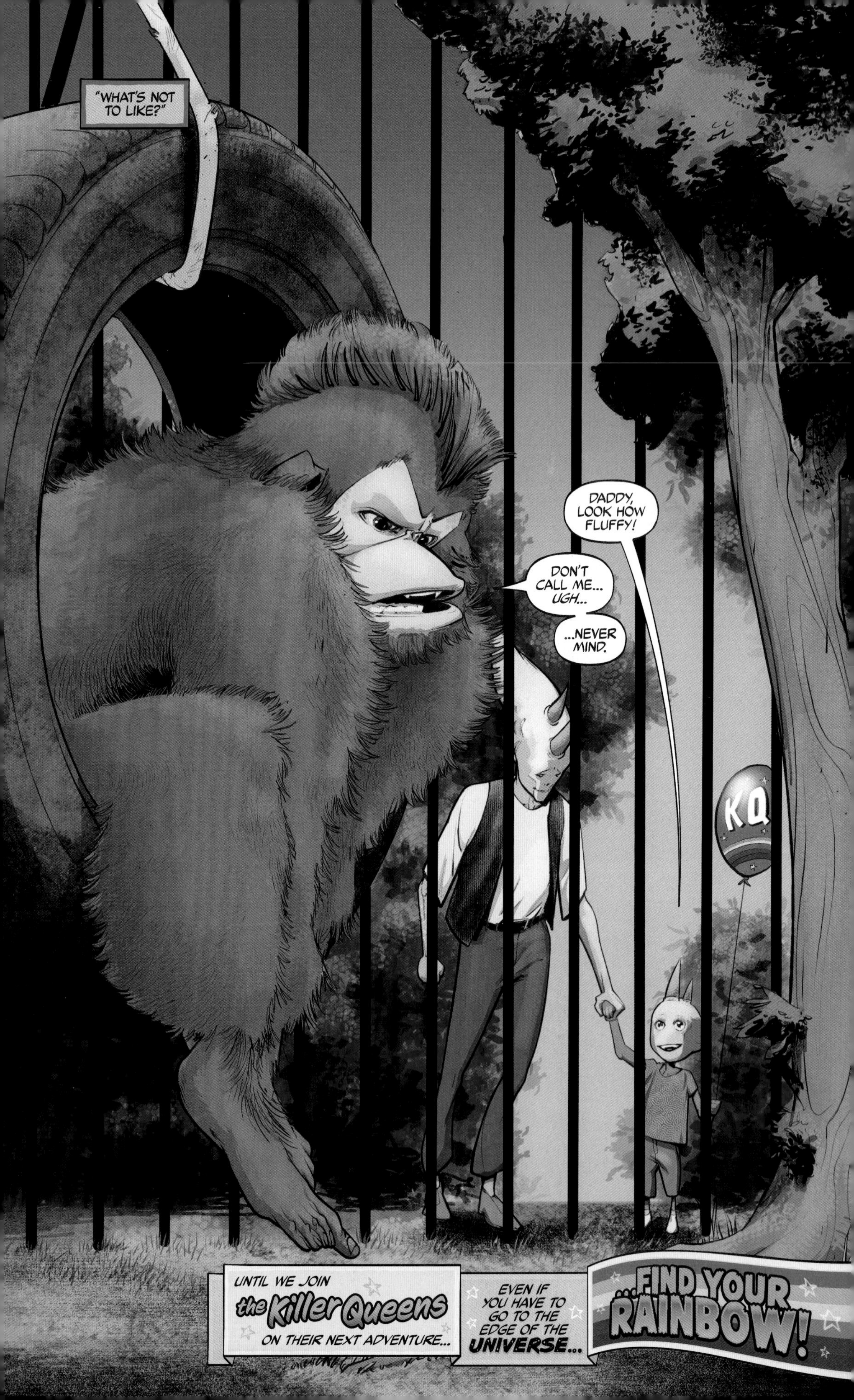
"WHAT'S NOT TO LIKE?"
DADDY, LOOK HOW FLUFFY!
DON'T CALL ME... UGH...
...NEVER MIND.
KQ
UNTIL WE JOIN the Killer Queens ON THEIR NEXT ADVENTURE...
EVEN IF YOU HAVE TO GO TO THE EDGE OF THE UNIVERSE...
...FIND YOUR RAINBOW!

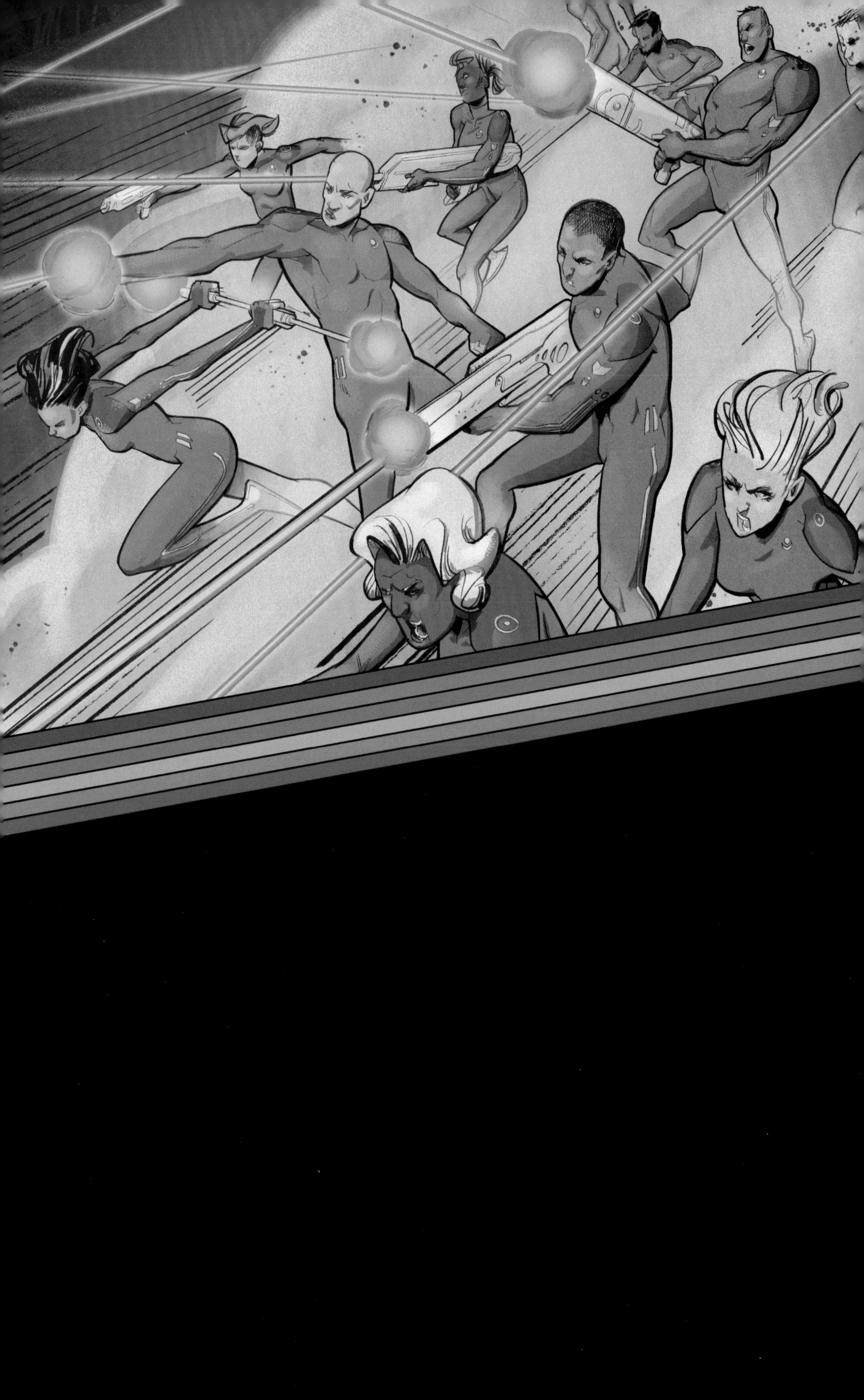

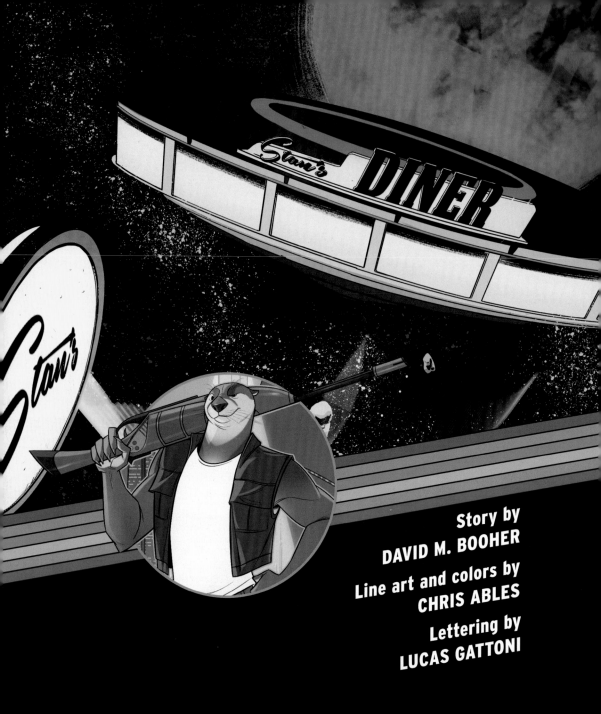

Story by
DAVID M. BOOHER

Line art and colors by
CHRIS ABLES

Lettering by
LUCAS GATTONI

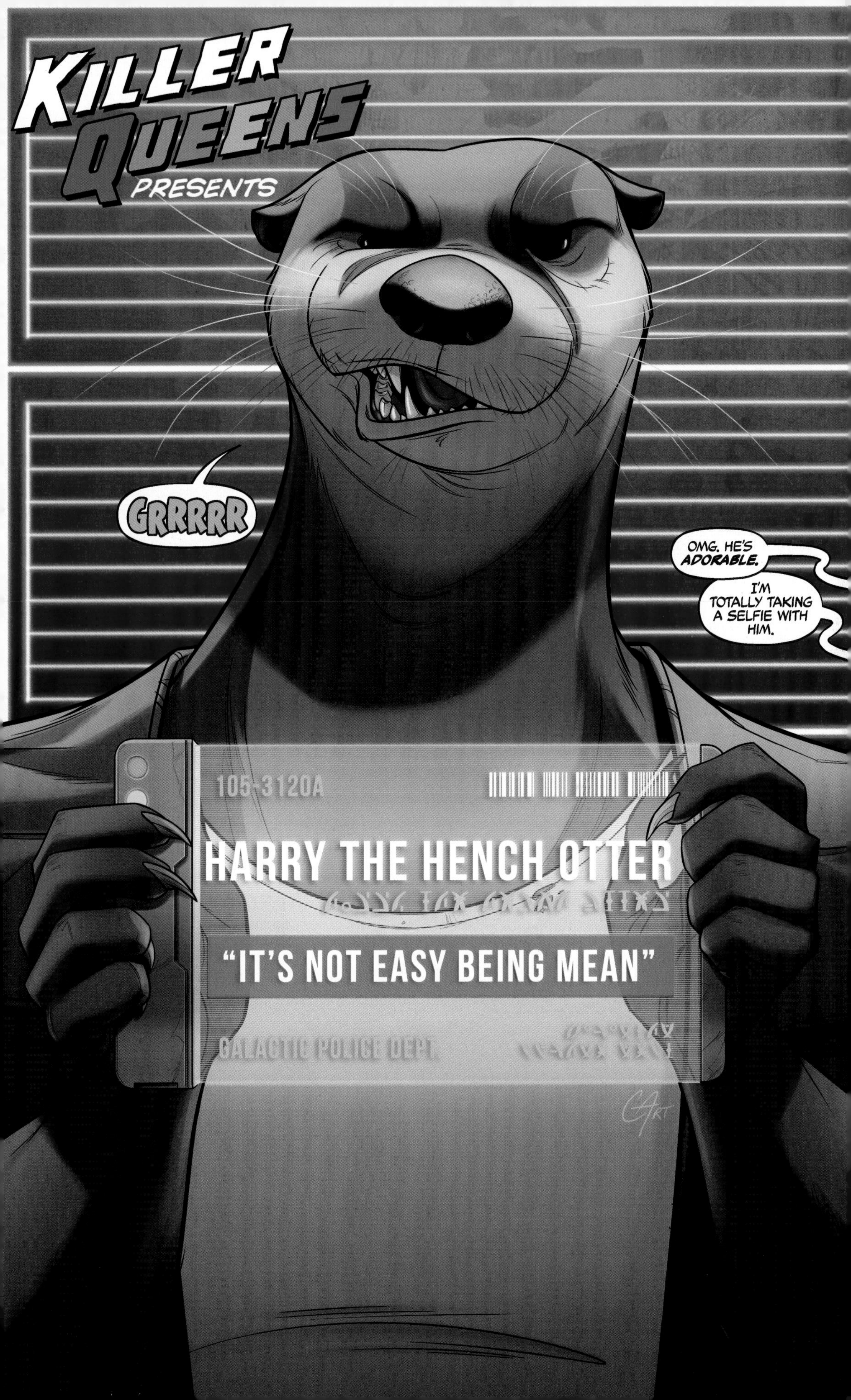
KILLER QUEENS
PRESENTS
GRRRRR
OMG. HE'S ADORABLE.
I'M TOTALLY TAKING A SELFIE WITH HIM.
105-3120A
HARRY THE HENCH OTTER
"IT'S NOT EASY BEING MEAN"
GALACTIC POLICE DEPT.

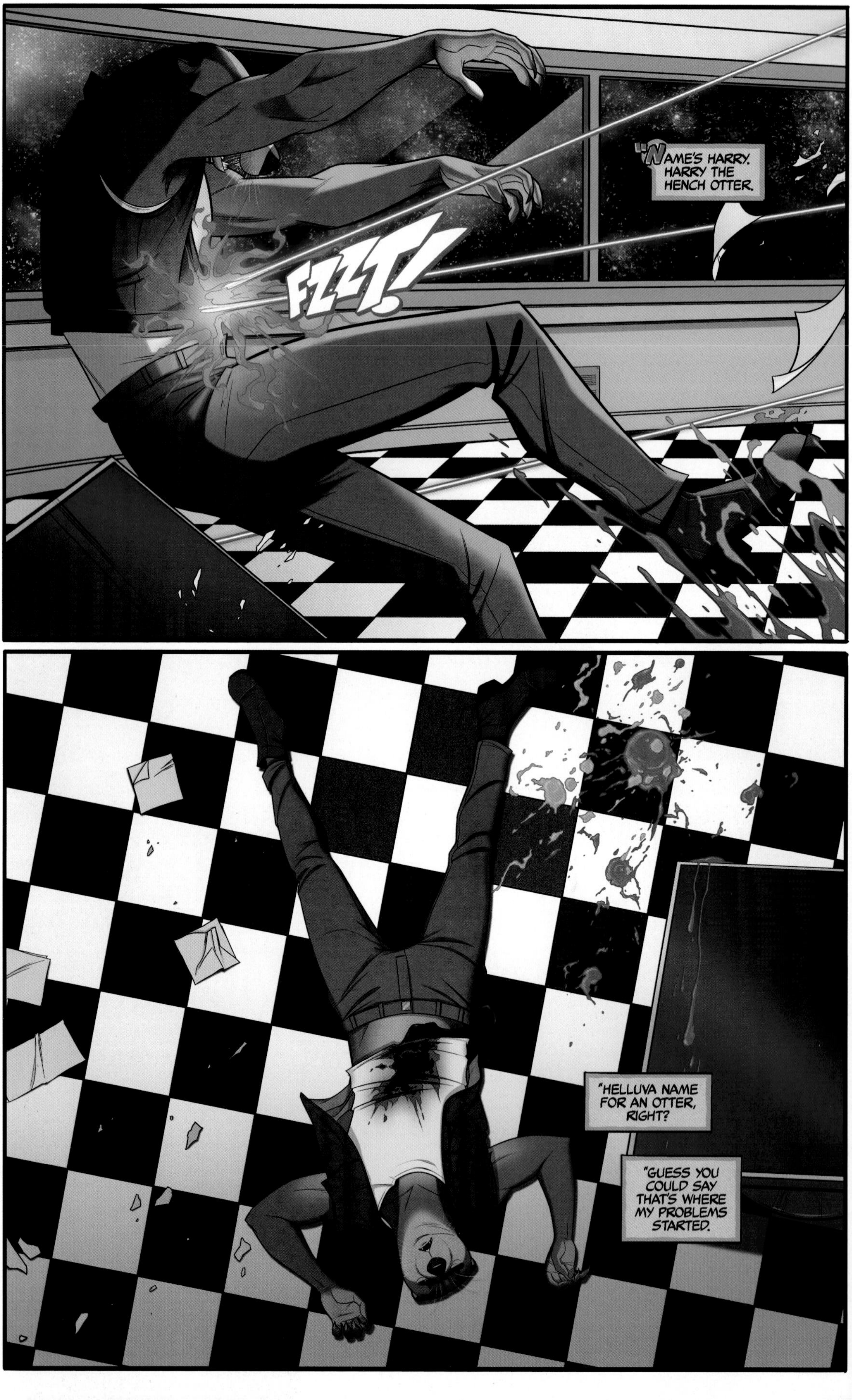
"NAME'S HARRY. HARRY THE HENCH OTTER.
FZZT!
"HELLUVA NAME FOR AN OTTER, RIGHT?
"GUESS YOU COULD SAY THAT'S WHERE MY PROBLEMS STARTED.

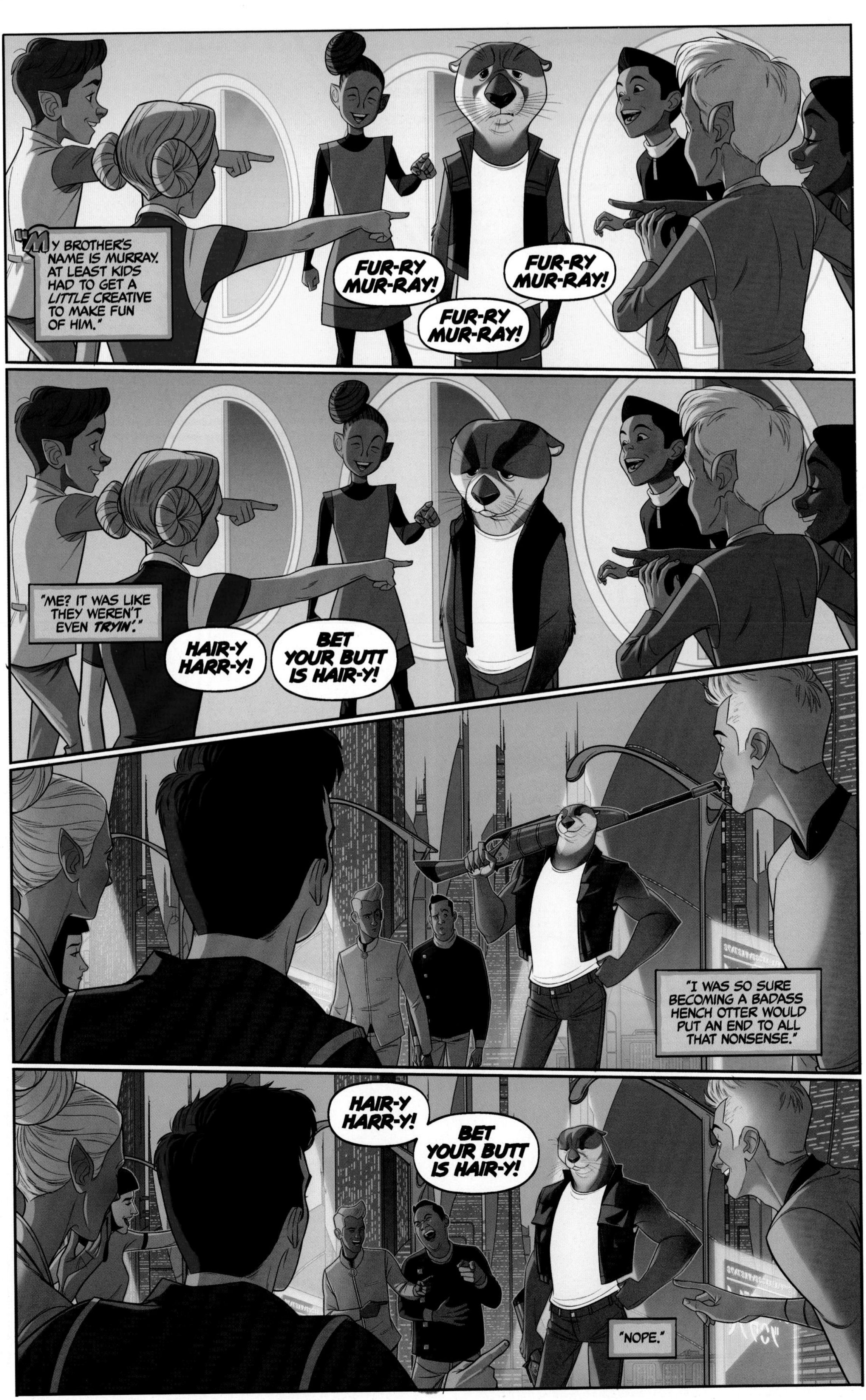
"MY BROTHER'S NAME IS MURRAY. AT LEAST KIDS HAD TO GET A *LITTLE* CREATIVE TO MAKE FUN OF HIM."
FUR-RY MUR-RAY!
FUR-RY MUR-RAY!
FUR-RY MUR-RAY!
"ME? IT WAS LIKE THEY WEREN'T EVEN *TRYIN'*."
HAIR-Y HARR-Y!
BET YOUR BUTT IS HAIR-Y!
"I WAS SO SURE BECOMING A BADASS HENCH OTTER WOULD PUT AN END TO ALL THAT NONSENSE."
HAIR-Y HARR-Y!
BET YOUR BUTT IS HAIR-Y!
"NOPE."

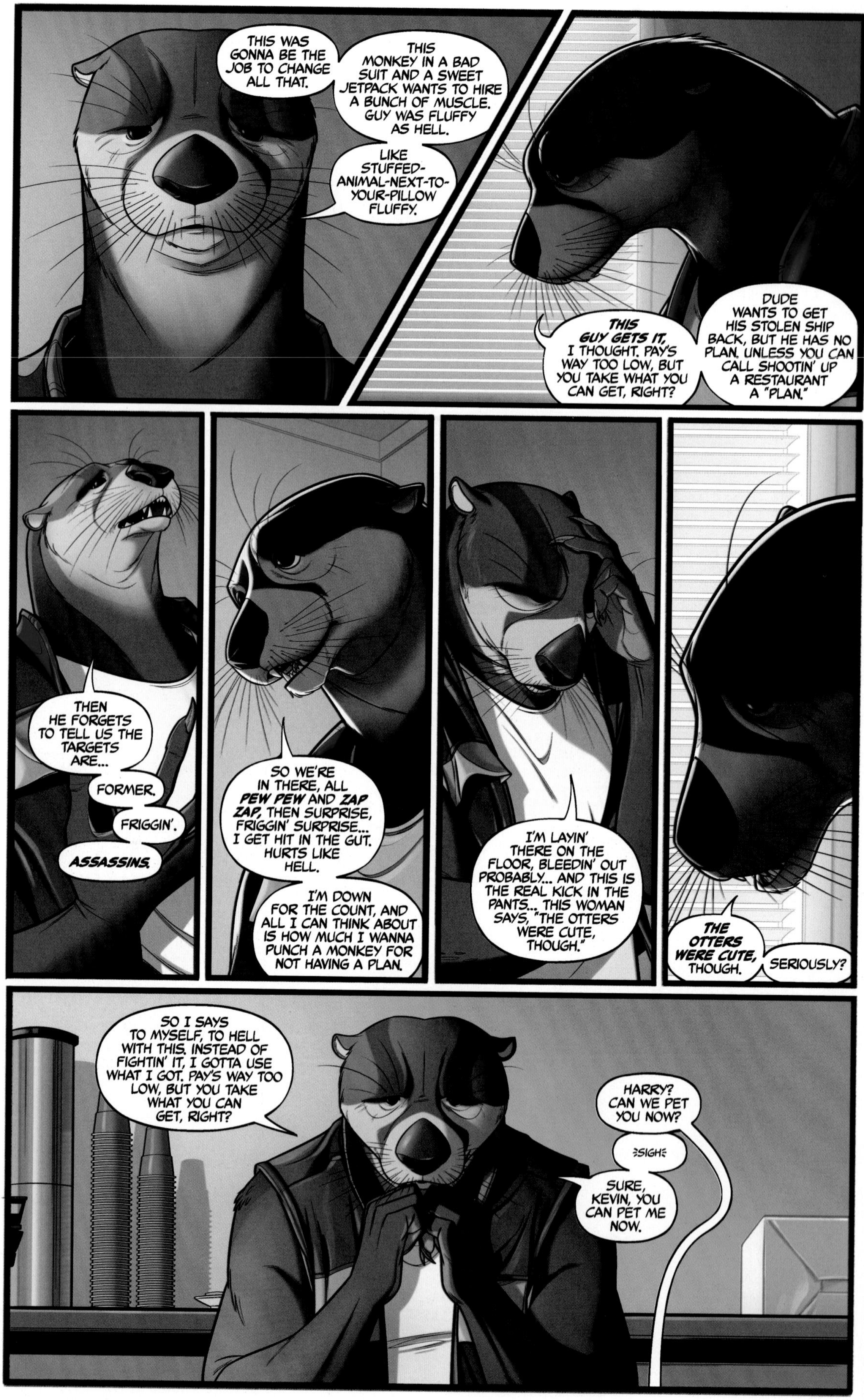
THIS WAS GONNA BE THE JOB TO CHANGE ALL THAT.
THIS MONKEY IN A BAD SUIT AND A SWEET JETPACK WANTS TO HIRE A BUNCH OF MUSCLE. GUY WAS FLUFFY AS HELL.
LIKE STUFFED-ANIMAL-NEXT-TO-YOUR-PILLOW FLUFFY.
THIS GUY GETS IT, I THOUGHT. PAY'S WAY TOO LOW, BUT YOU TAKE WHAT YOU CAN GET, RIGHT?
DUDE WANTS TO GET HIS STOLEN SHIP BACK, BUT HE HAS NO PLAN. UNLESS YOU CAN CALL SHOOTIN' UP A RESTAURANT A "PLAN."
THEN HE FORGETS TO TELL US THE TARGETS ARE...
FORMER.
FRIGGIN'.
ASSASSINS.
SO WE'RE IN THERE, ALL PEW PEW AND ZAP ZAP, THEN SURPRISE, FRIGGIN' SURPRISE... I GET HIT IN THE GUT. HURTS LIKE HELL.
I'M DOWN FOR THE COUNT, AND ALL I CAN THINK ABOUT IS HOW MUCH I WANNA PUNCH A MONKEY FOR NOT HAVING A PLAN.
I'M LAYIN' THERE ON THE FLOOR, BLEEDIN' OUT PROBABLY... AND THIS IS THE REAL KICK IN THE PANTS... THIS WOMAN SAYS, "THE OTTERS WERE CUTE, THOUGH."
THE OTTERS WERE CUTE, THOUGH.
SERIOUSLY?
SO I SAYS TO MYSELF, TO HELL WITH THIS. INSTEAD OF FIGHTIN' IT, I GOTTA USE WHAT I GOT. PAY'S WAY TOO LOW, BUT YOU TAKE WHAT YOU CAN GET, RIGHT?
HARRY? CAN WE PET YOU NOW?
SIGH
SURE, KEVIN, YOU CAN PET ME NOW.

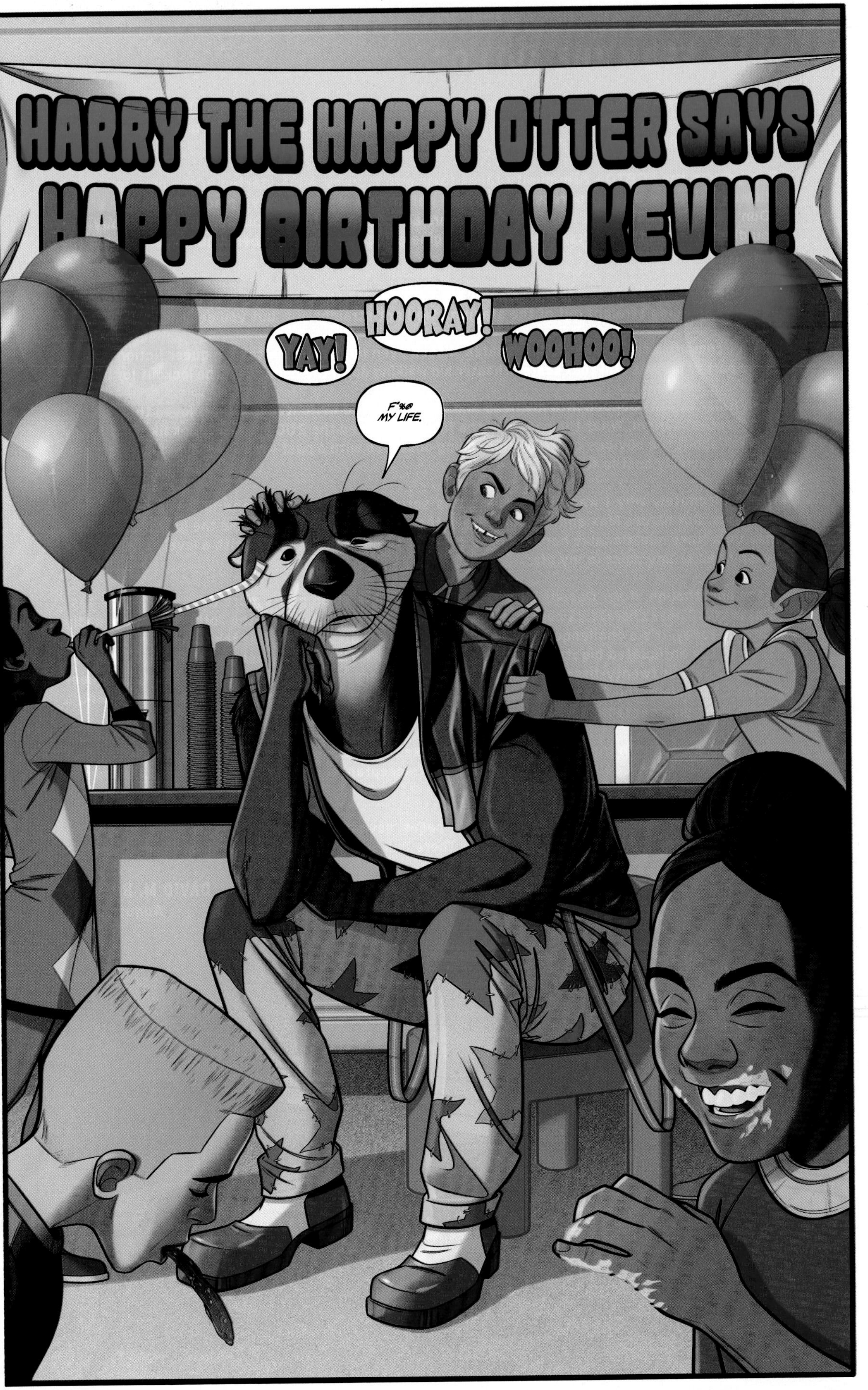
HARRY THE HAPPY OTTER SAYS
HAPPY BIRTHDAY KEVIN!
YAY!
HOORAY!
WOOHOO!
F*%@
MY LIFE.

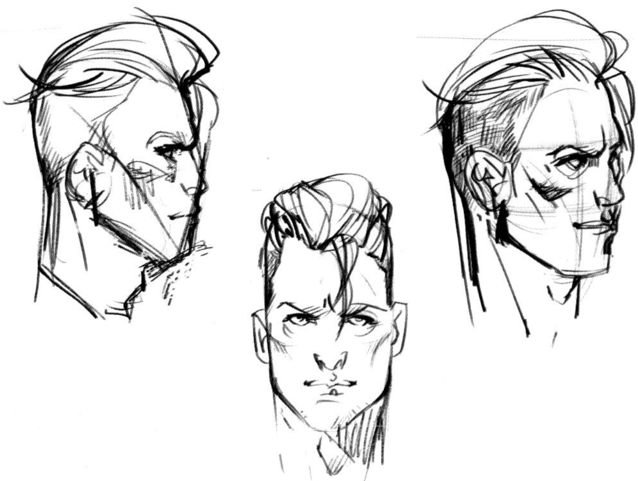
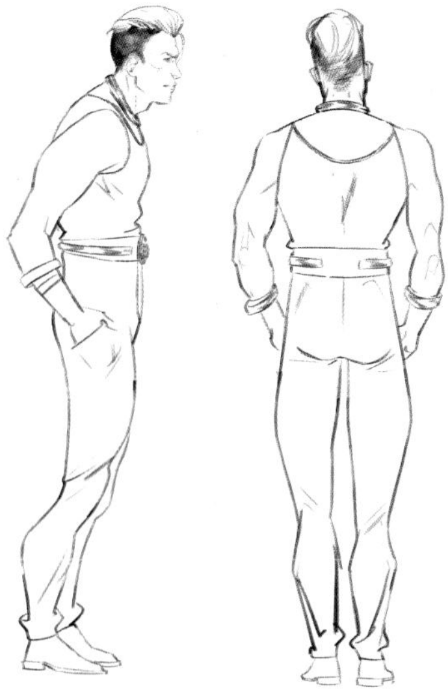
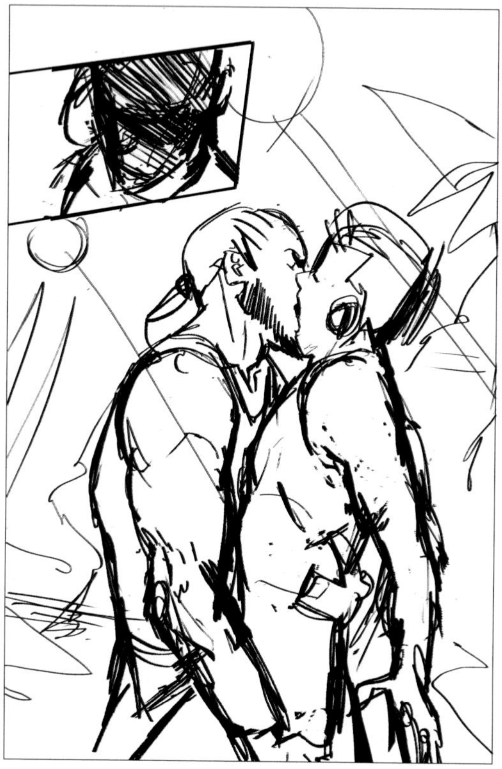
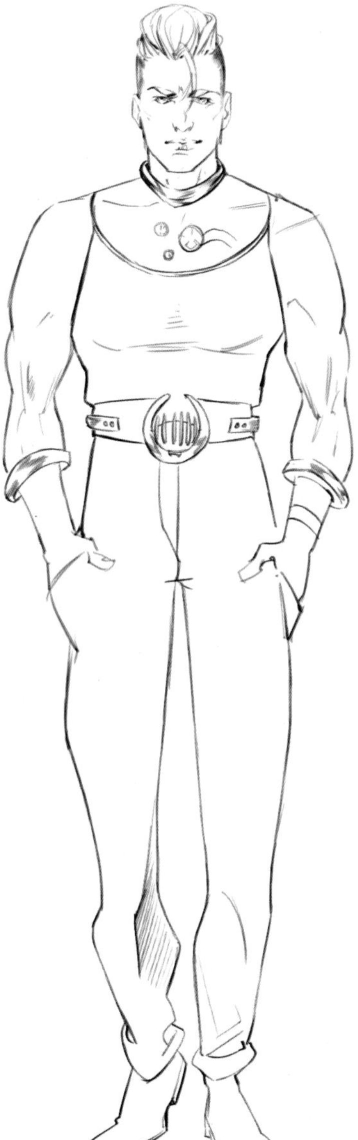
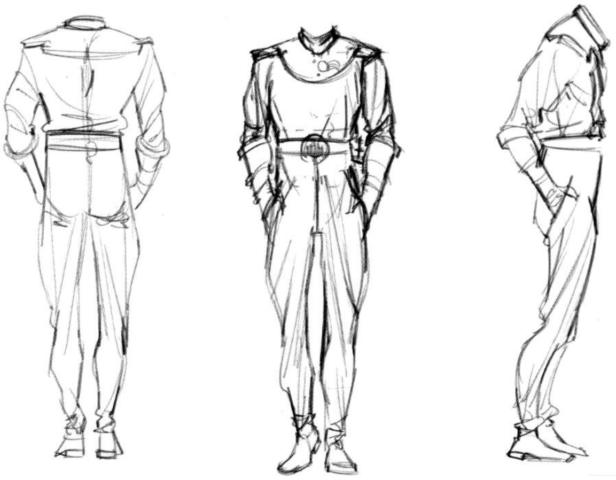

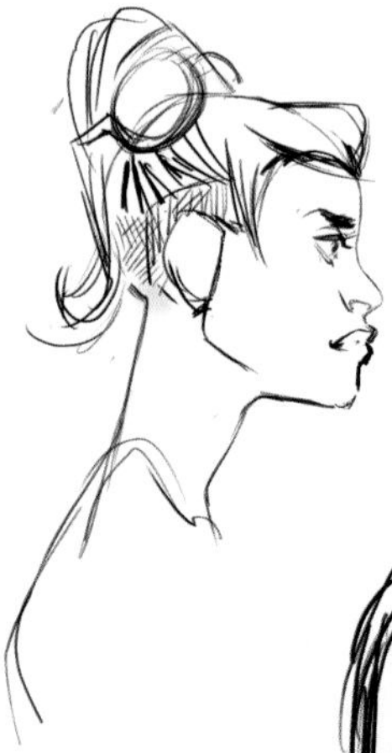
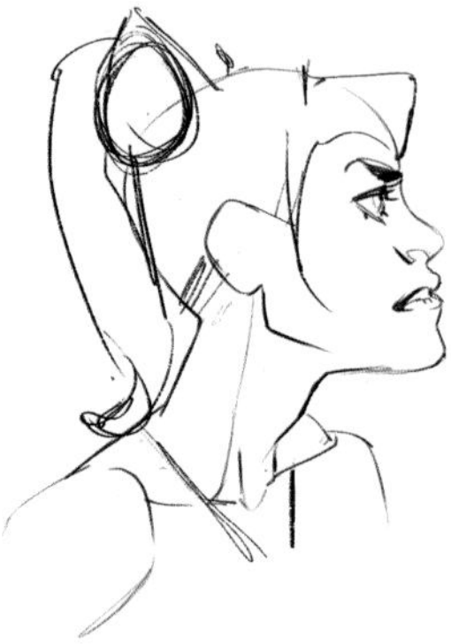
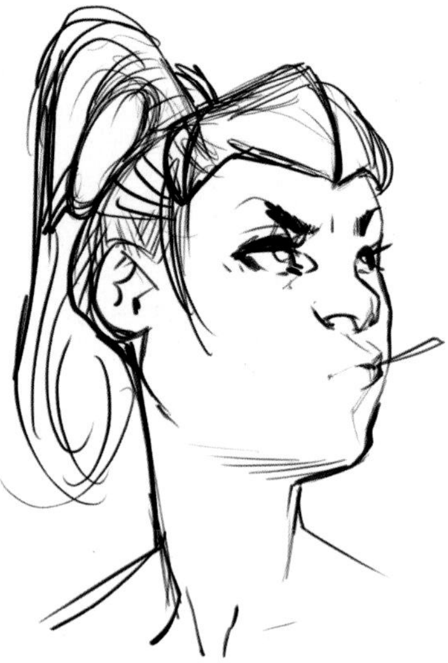
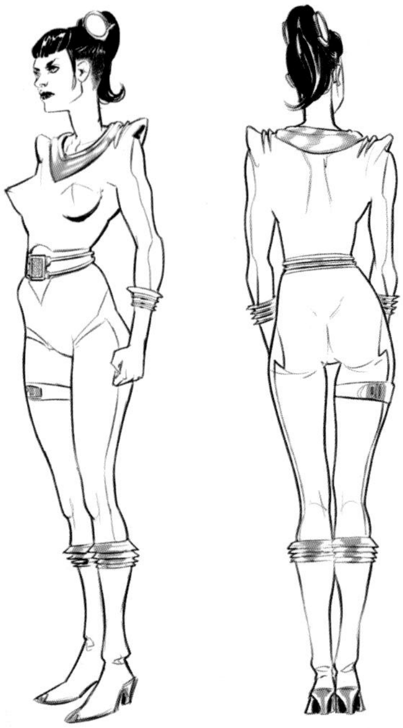
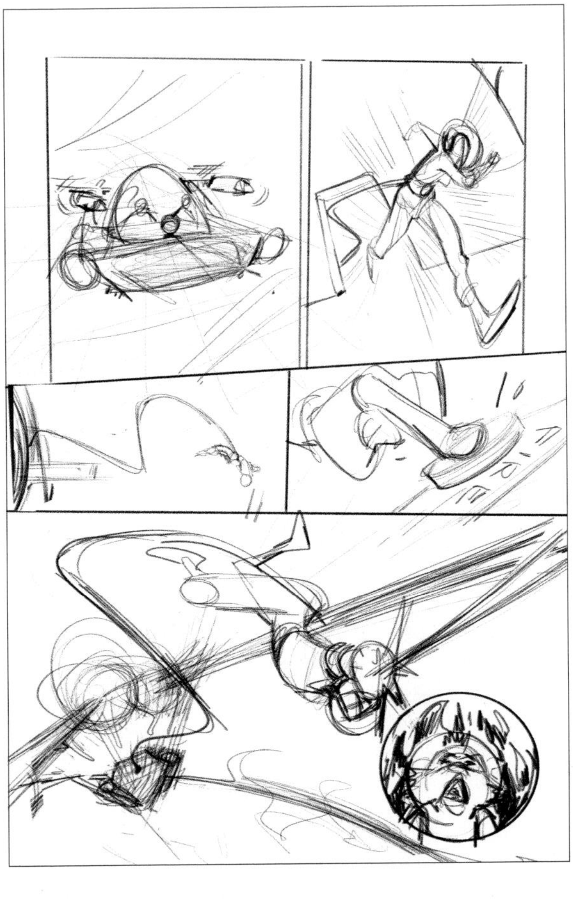
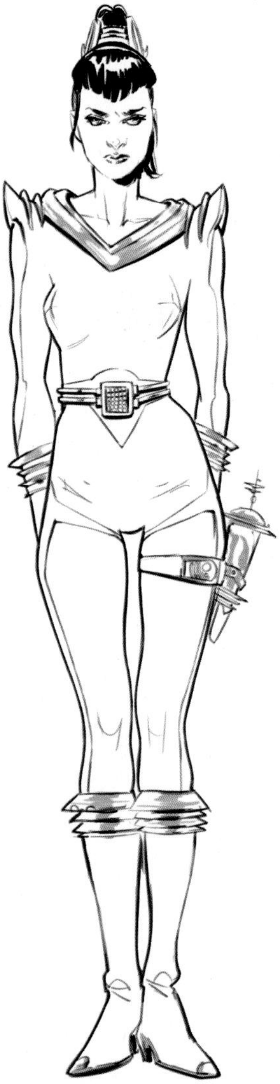

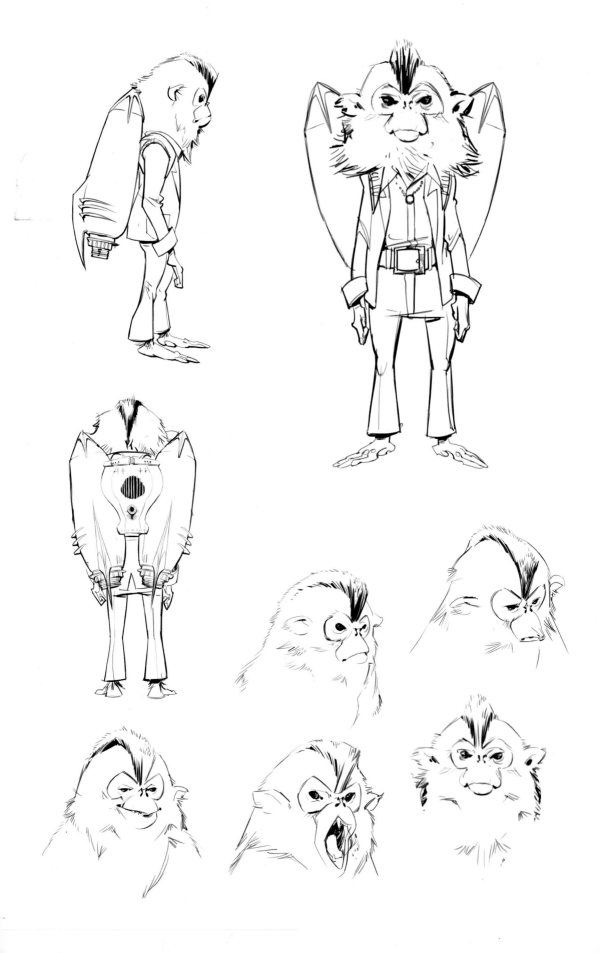

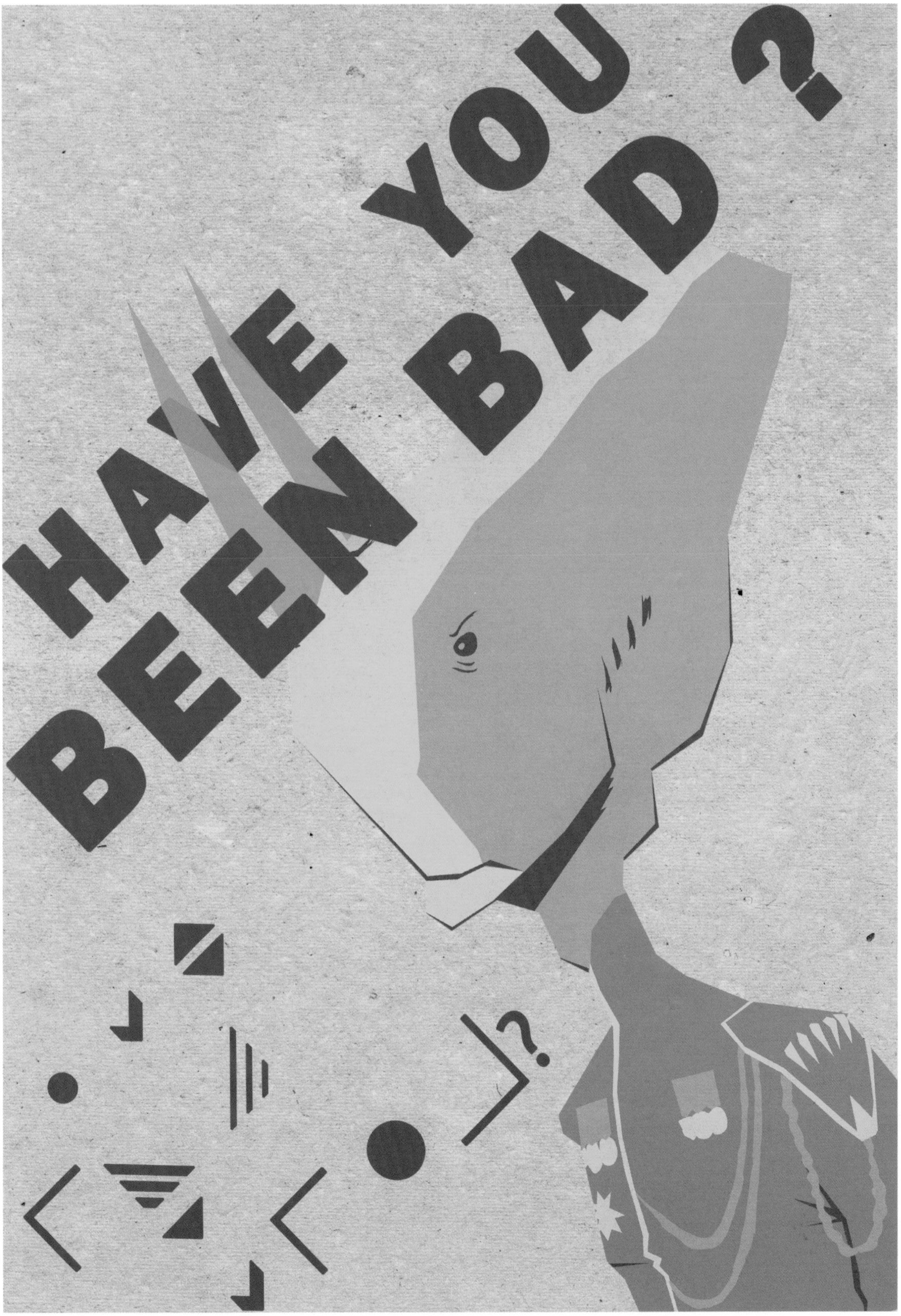
HAVE YOU
BEEN BAD ?

COVER ART BY JEN BARTEL

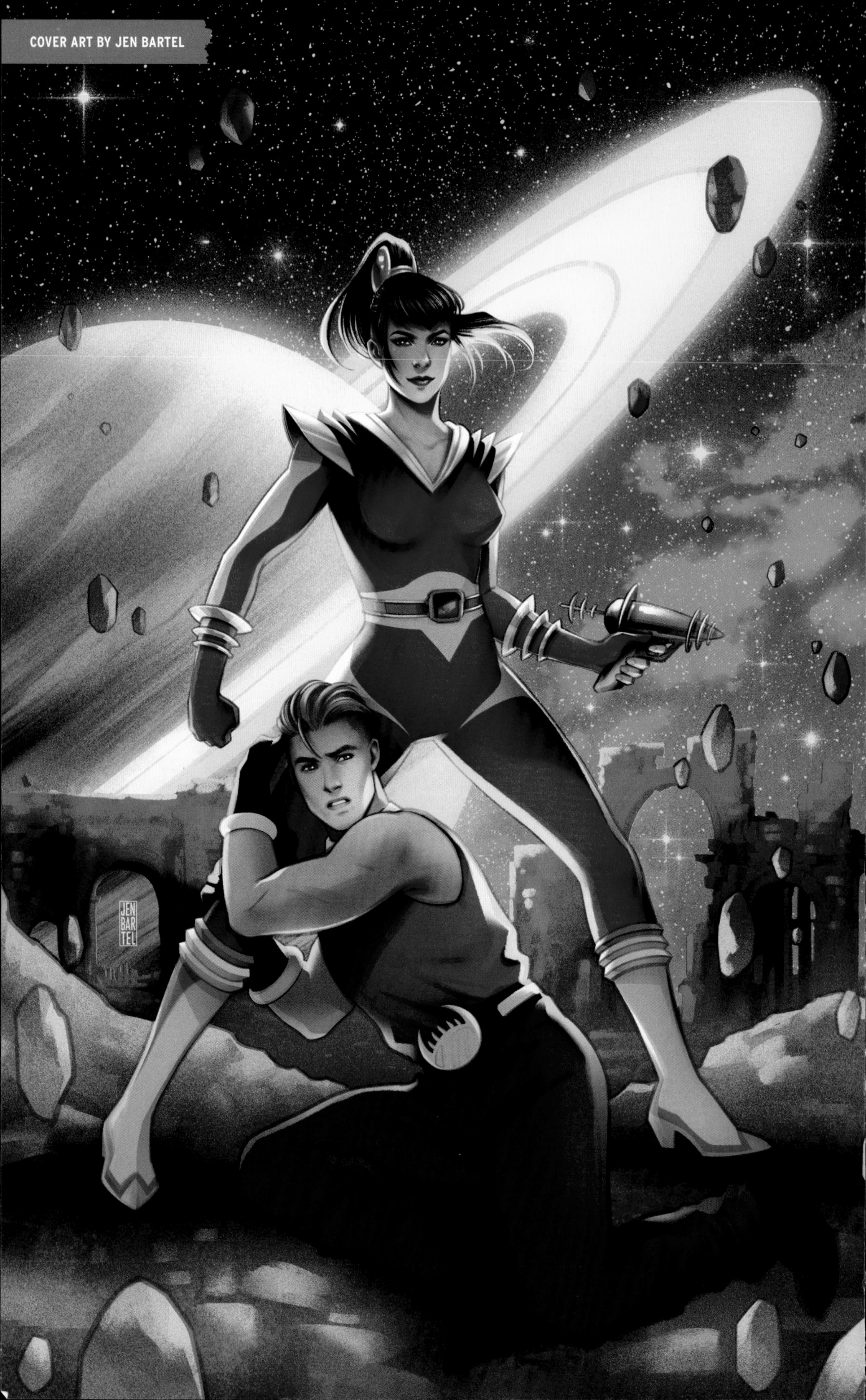
JEN
BAR
TEL

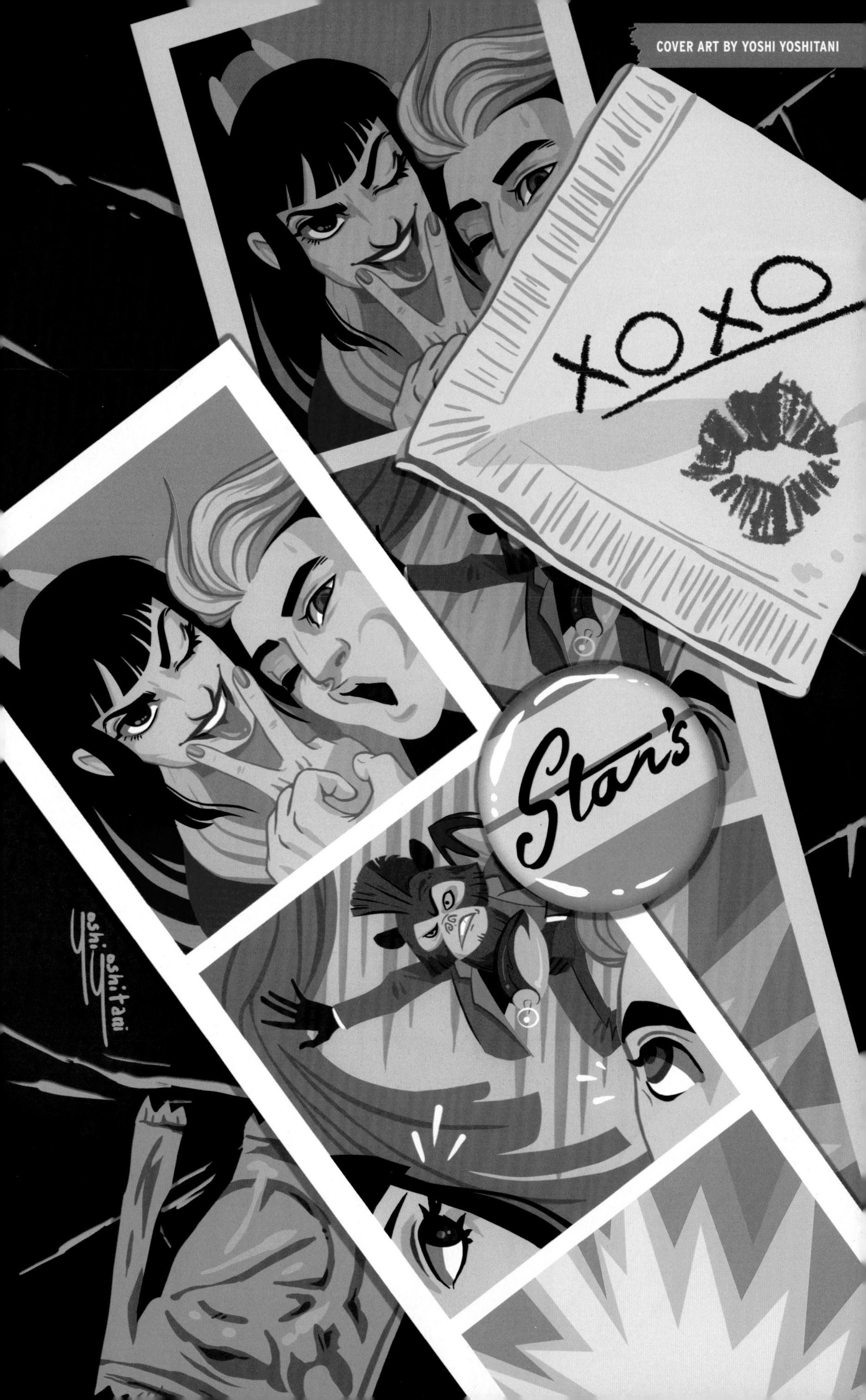
COVER ART BY YOSHI YOSHITANI
XOXO
Stan's
YoshiYoshitani

COVER ART BY CHRIS ABLES

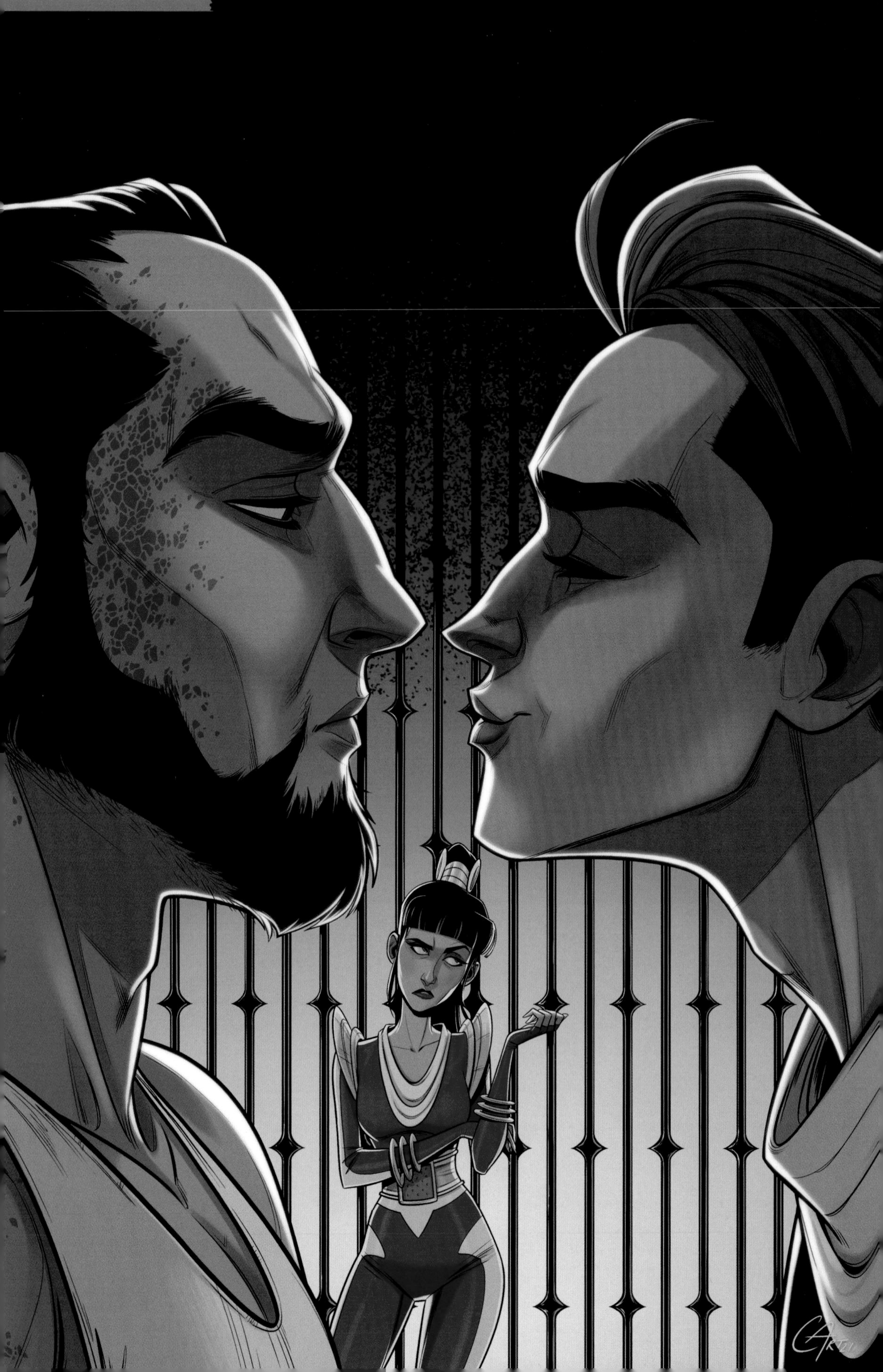

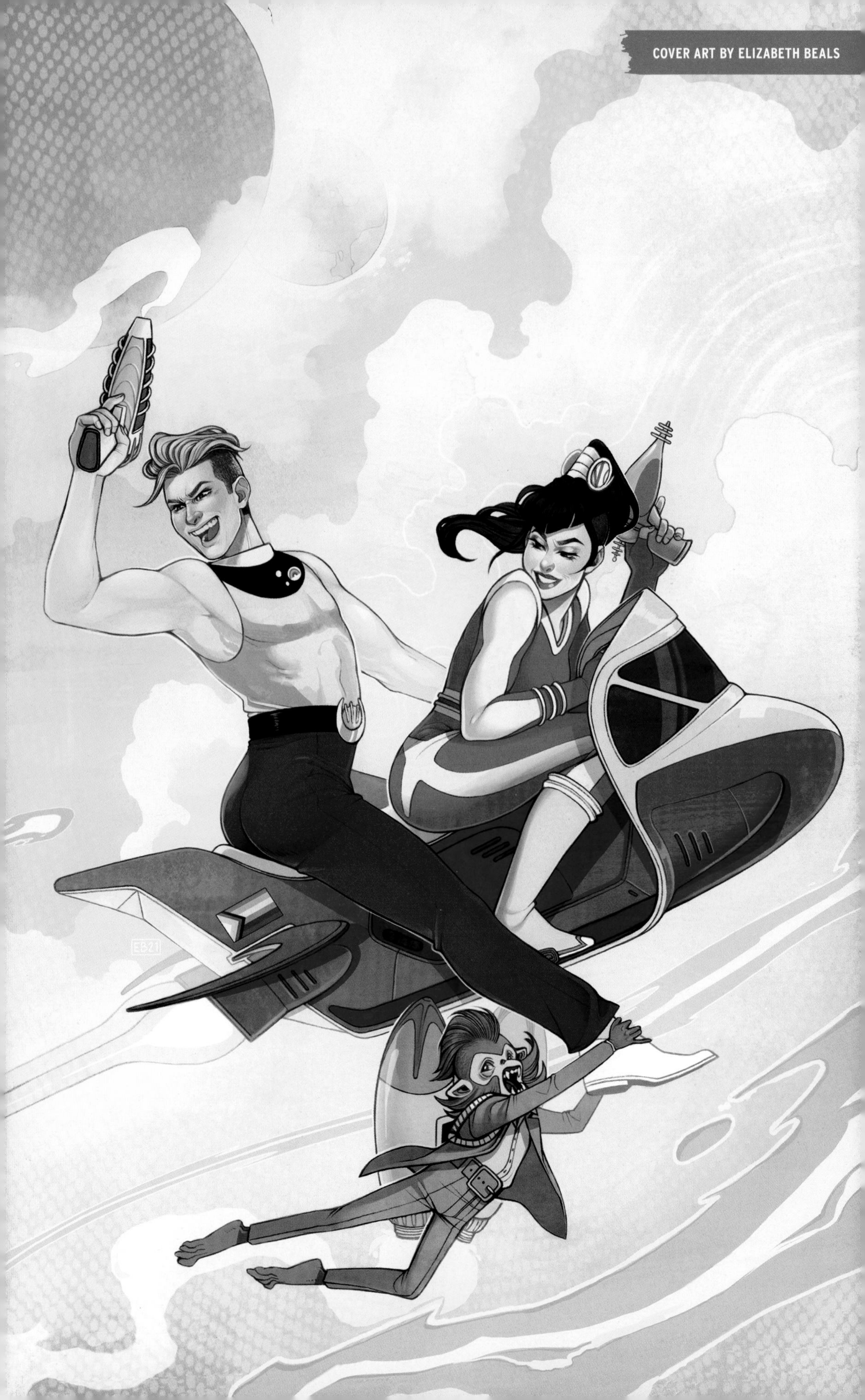
EB21

COVER ART BY ELIZABETH BEALS

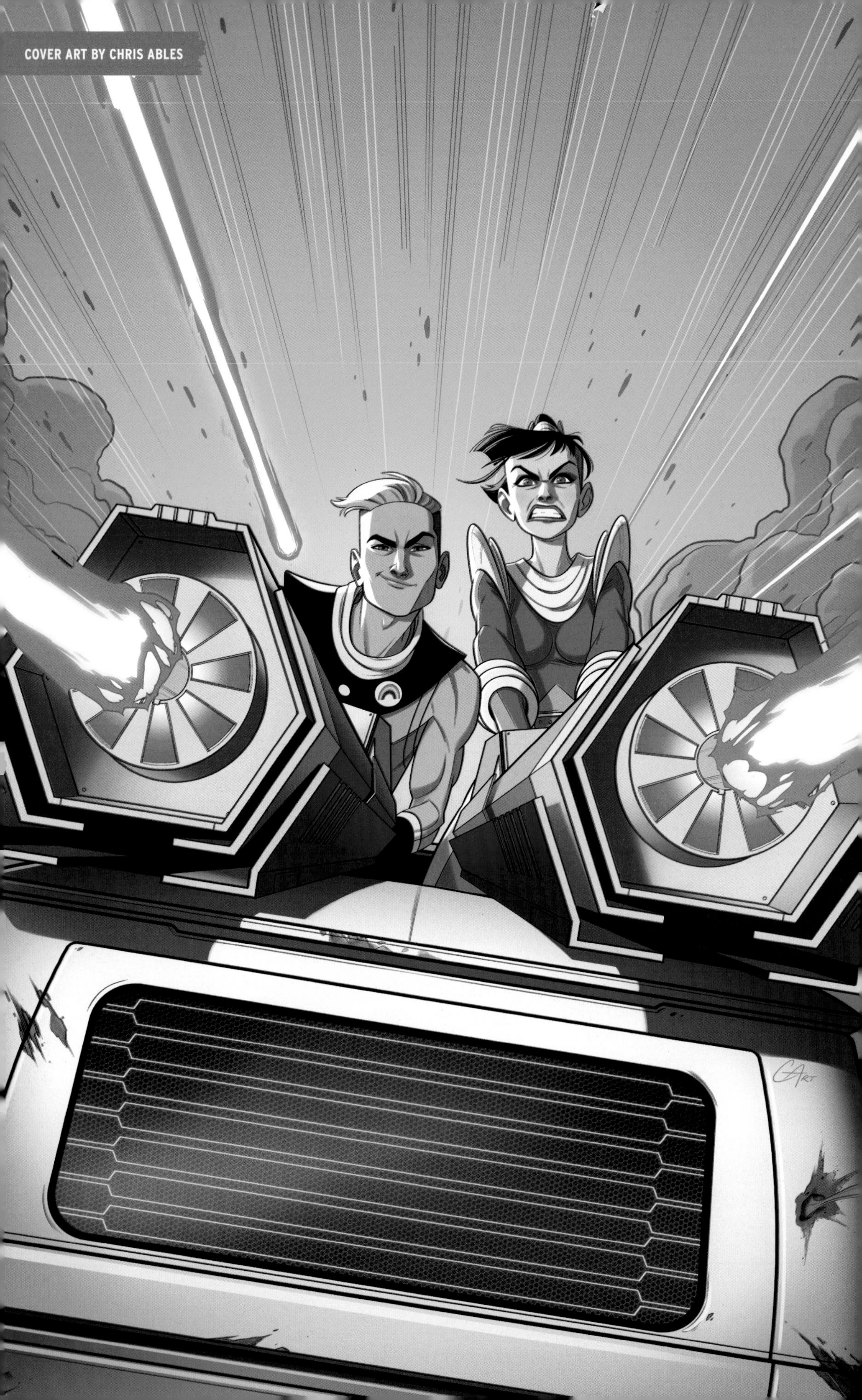

COVER ART BY CHRIS ABLES

COVER ART BY DAVID TALASKI

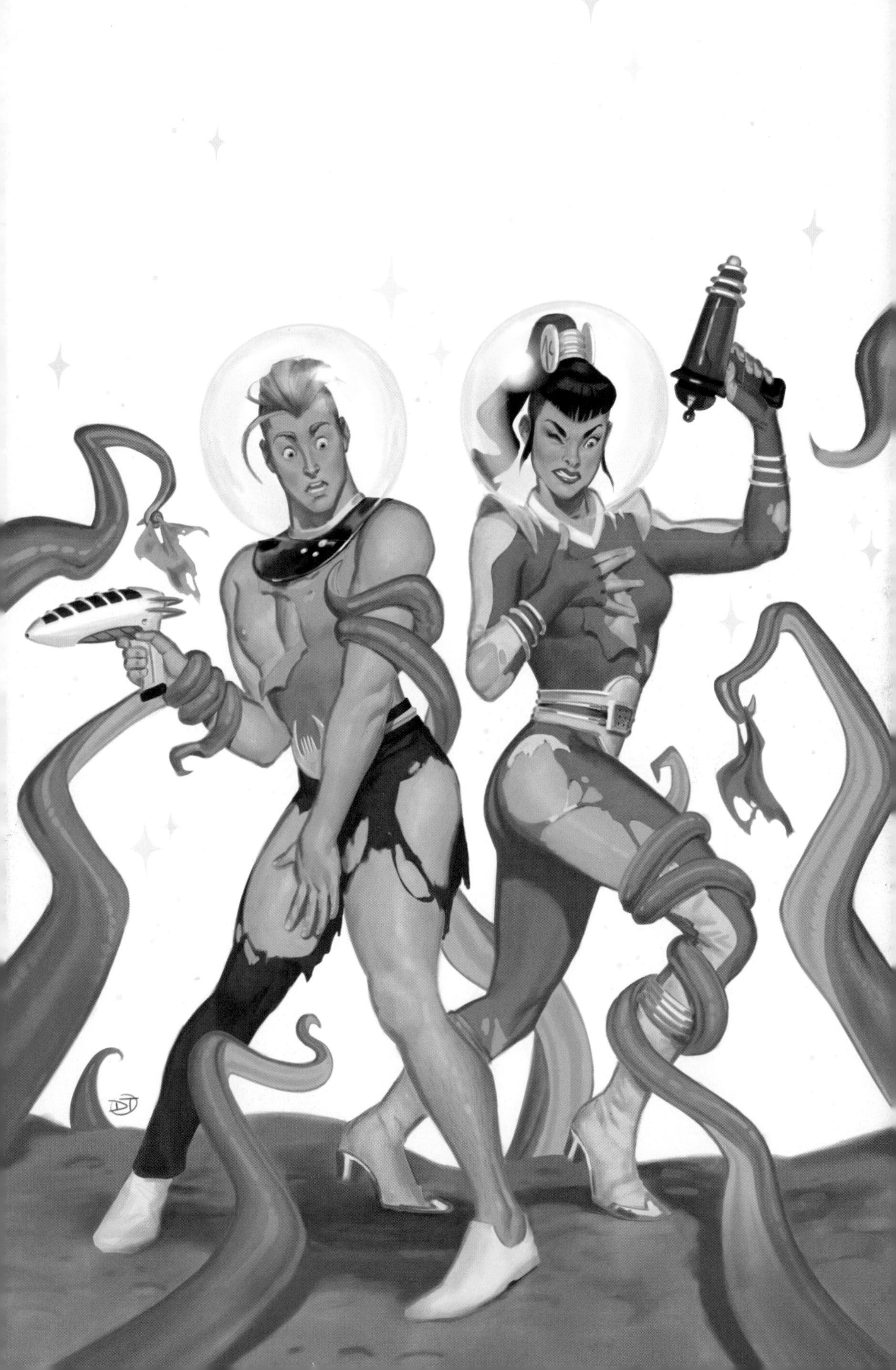

DST

COVER ART BY CHRIS ABLES

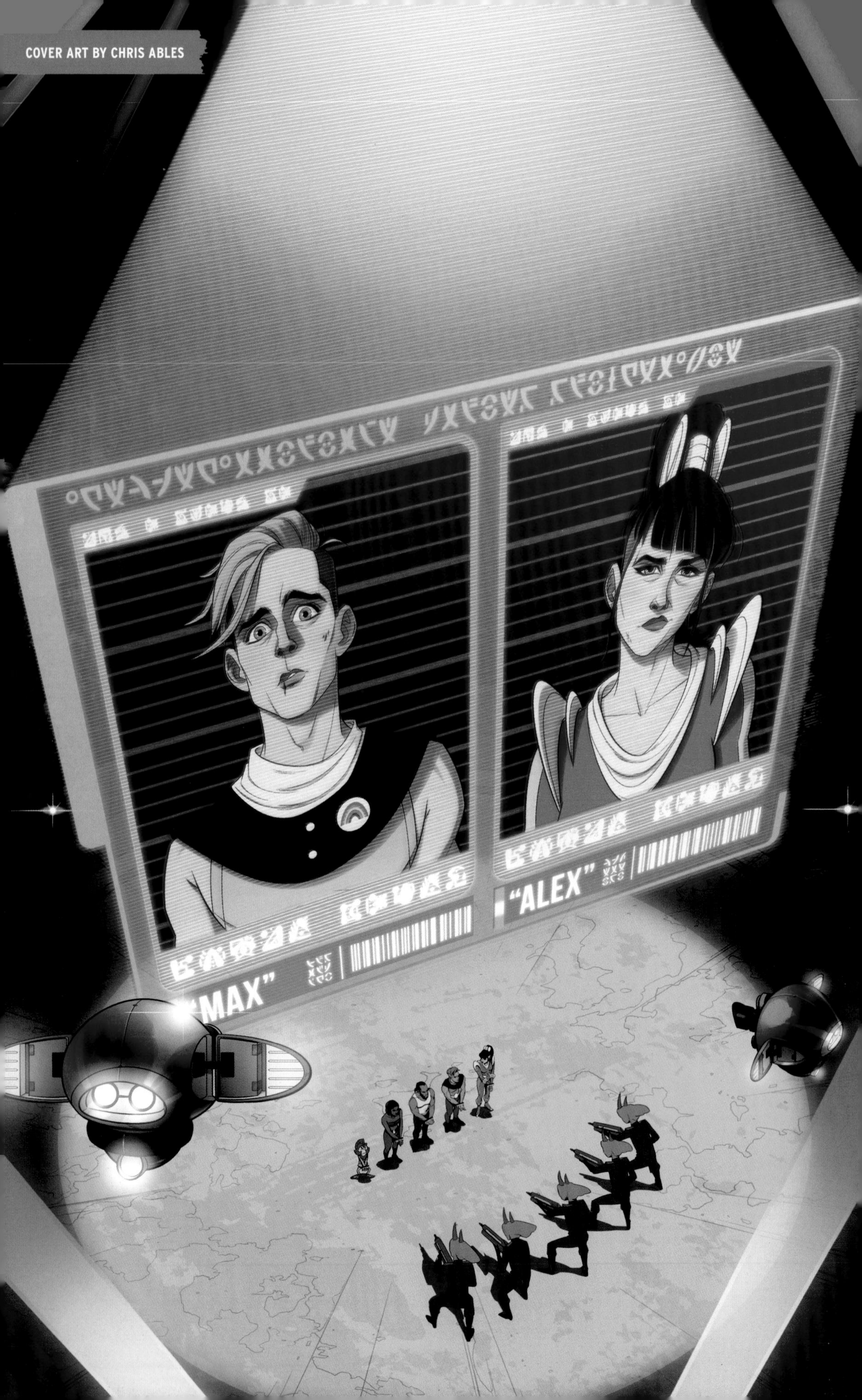

"MAX"
"ALEX"

COVER ART BY ALEX MOORE

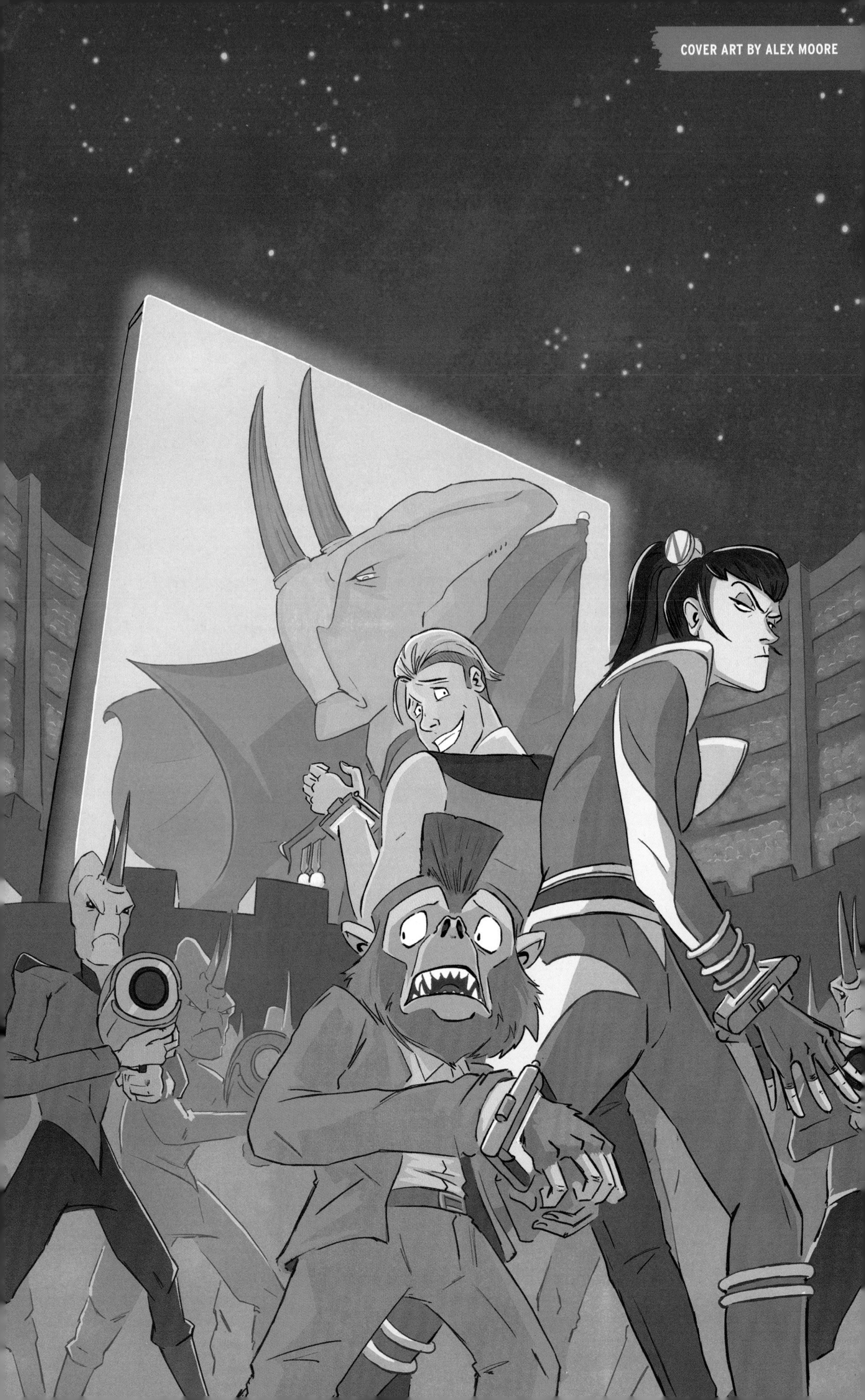

Channeling his 1980s sci-fi and fantasy upbringing, DAVID M. BOOHER has written comics for Dark Horse, Image, IDW, Boom! Studios, and Vault. His all-ages fantasy series *Canto* is now in development as a feature film with Westbrook Studios with David set to executive produce and write the screenplay. An attorney by training, he lives in Los Angeles with his husband and the true brains behind their operation—their adopted greyhounds.

CLAUDIA BALBONI is an Italian comic book artist. After working in animation studios as a storyboard artist and environment designer, she changed course to work on comics. Her work includes *True Blood: French Quarter*, *Star Trek*, *Robyn Hood*, *Grimm Tales of Terror*, and Susan Beneville's *L.I.S.: The Comic Book*. She's worked with many publishers, including Dark Horse, IDW, Image, Convict Comics, Take-Two Interactive, and Bugs Comics. Her other creator-owned books include *Black Jack Ketchum* and *Fairlady*, cocreated with Brian Schirmer.

HARRY SAXON is an illustrator and comics colorist from Greece. He is currently thirty-nine years old and irreversibly trans. You might know his work from titles such as Vault Comics' *Vagrant Queen* (and its successor, *Vagrant Queen: A Planet Called Doom*) and *Test*, and Black Mask's *Sex Death Revolution*. If you don't know his work, this is an excellent way of getting started: visit his webpage, HarrySaxon.art; follow him on Twitter, @Eru_Rouraito; and/or follow him on Instagram, @harrysaxonpm.

LUCAS GATTONI is a comic book letterer carrying over fifteen years as a graphic designer into a medium he's loved his whole life. He's lettered GLAAD Media Awards nominee *Liebestrasse* (ComiXology Originals), *Glitter Vipers* (Queer Comix), the Spanish versions of *Sonic* and *Locke & Key* (IDW), and lots of indie comics. He lives in Argentina with his husband and their six unnamed goldfish (yup, finally got new ones).

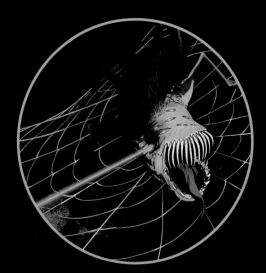